Pricing Decoded

Pricing is a key priority of every company globally, as both customers and businesses grapple with ever more challenging economic conditions. *Pricing Decoded* is an authoritative but easy-to-read guide to support the transition to robust pricing to drive profitability.

Renowned pricing experts Danilo Zatta and Maciej Kraus show organizations how to boost profitability and build a competitive advantage, transforming the way to set and manage prices. Case studies from the world's leading pricing practitioners in both B2C and B2B organizations, such as Alcatel-Lucent, Asashi, Google, BP-Castrol, Unilever, Microsoft, Borealis, Hilton, Nike, MediaWorld, Philips Healthcare, Schneider Electric, DHL, Zalando, Zuora, Workday, Assa Abbloy, and Coor, are presented throughout. This book makes smart and innovative pricing more accessible and understandable for all. It provides a strong foundation in the concepts as well as the application in business, empowering you to judge monetization opportunities in a more effective way and ultimately make better decisions.

The book is relevant to C-levels, managers, entrepreneurs, investors, as well as sales, marketing, and pricing managers, who want to learn more about topline potentials and monetization through pricing and achieve sustainable growth.

Danilo Zatta is one of the world's leading advisors and thought leaders in the field of pricing and topline excellence. As a management consultant for more than 20 years, he advises and coaches many of the world's best-known organizations. The *Financial Times* defined him as "one of the world's leading pricing minds".

Maciej Kraus is a leading figure in the pricing industry and is frequently mentioned on most influential pricing lists and interviewed in numerous business journals, for example, *Harvard Business Review* and *Forbes*. He is a guest lecturer at Stanford University's Graduate School of Business as well as a number of other top business schools. He has written three books on pricing.

"Pricing is a continuous journey, allowing you to discover the sweet spot where customers appreciate your value, and you achieve satisfying profitability. This sweet spot evolves constantly, often faster than traditional business practitioners think. The joint application of AI capabilities together with the creativity of your sales and marketing teams has the potential to unlock unprecedented value, at a speed never experienced before. Pricing Decoded will give you valuable insights how to consistently be delighting your customers with your value proposition while leaving your more traditional competitors scrambling."

—**Francesco Quaranta**, President and CEO, Hitachi Construction Machinery Europe

A must-read for the C-Level! Pricing Decoded provides a compelling insight into the world of pricing through real life use cases, underlining the significant value that empowered pricing organizations create every day.

—**Murli Mahalingam**, Group Pricing Director, Alliance Automotive Group

" 'Pricing Decoded' is an essential read for business leaders who want to grasp the significant impact of pricing on both their top and bottom lines. Dan Zatta and Maciej Kraus indeed provide actionable insights and real-world frameworks that can be immediately applied to drive sustainable growth and profitability. Dan Zatta and Maciej Kraus deliver actionable insights and practical frameworks that can be immediately implemented to conjugate growth with profitability. This comprehensive guide includes an in-depth exploration of modern recurring revenue models, often referred to as "total monetization." Insights from Zuora and Alcatel Lucent Enterprise in that specific section provide a practical roadmap for companies to implement recurring revenue models."

—**Simon Blunn**, SVP and General Manager EMEA, Zuora

Dan Zatta and Maciej Kraus's "Pricing Decoded" is an essential read for anyone serious about mastering the art and science of pricing. Through insightful case studies and expert analysis, the book reveals the strategies behind the success of top global companies. It's a comprehensive, accessible guide that transforms complex pricing concepts into practical applications, making it a must-have for business leaders aiming to boost profitability and gain a competitive edge.

—**Alberto Dall'Osso**, Global Pricing Excellence Leader, Bracco

Pricing

Decoded

How Leading Pricing Practitioners Manage Price to Boost Profits

Edited by
Danilo Zatta and Maciej Kraus

LONDON AND NEW YORK

Designed cover image: istock

First published 2025
by Routledge
4 Park Square, Milton Park, Abingdon, Oxon OX14 4RN

and by Routledge
605 Third Avenue, New York, NY 10158

Routledge is an imprint of the Taylor & Francis Group, an informa business

© 2025 selection and editorial matter, Danilo Zatta and Maciej Kraus; individual chapters, the contributors

British Library Cataloguing-in-Publication Data
A catalogue record for this book is available from the British Library

ISBN: 978-1-032-88195-9 (hbk)
ISBN: 978-1-032-86968-1 (pbk)
ISBN: 978-1-003-53596-6 (ebk)

DOI: 10.4324/9781003535966

Typeset in Minion Pro
by Apex CoVantage, LLC

To my parents Annemarie and Renzo, whom I miss every day.
To my wife, Babette, and to my children, Natalie, Sebastian, and Marilena,
who are my energy.

Danilo Zatta

To my family and my close friends, for their unwavering support and
encouragement throughout my life and for always being a source of strength.
You taught me the value of hard work and the importance of pricing one's
worth.

Maciej Kraus

Contents

Introduction to the sections

PART I: PRICE STRATEGY

The first part of the book contains contributions related to the topic of the price strategy. One aspect of a price strategy is the chosen pricing model. Innovative pricing models represent the new source of the competitive advantage as illustrated in the book *The Pricing Model Revolution*, where subscription models are described.

In this first part we find a deep dive into subscriptions with a number of examples from different industries that show the power of this pricing model.

Then the strategic shifts behind Philips Healthcare's success are revealed, offering valuable insights for companies in healthcare and beyond. Advanced digital pricing models for SaaS and beyond will be explained while deep diving the case of Google. Google will also be used to show how to navigate the digital ad space.

How to win with SaaS pricing will be illustrated by discussing the case of Workday.

PART II: PRICE SETTING

"Price setting" explores how businesses determine optimal pricing to maximize profitability through practical examples across different industries. This section begins with Media Markt, illustrating the use of dynamic pricing in retail to adjust to market demands. It moves to Assa Abloy, which adopts value-based pricing, aligning prices with customer perceptions to boost profitability. Zalando's use of AI in pricing demonstrates how technology can refine pricing strategies by analyzing extensive datasets for optimal pricing decisions. A comparison between Nike and Hilton further emphasizes the diverse strategies in retail versus hospitality.

PART III: PRICE REALIZATION

The third part of the book contains contributions related to the topic of the price realization.

One aspect of realizing prices is how to capture the value your company deserves to capture, and customer value management is a good example of how to do this. The case of Borealis shows how to succeed with it.

Another aspect of price realization is linked to managing price image for perceived value. The cases of Bonduelle and Unilever are great examples in this regard.

Two more cases provide deep dives into price realization, that is, proud pricing at Coor and terms and conditions excellence at DHL.

PART IV: PRICE ENABLEMENT

"Price enablement" covers the infrastructure and internal capabilities essential for sustaining effective pricing strategies. It starts with Asahi, discussing the need for adaptable pricing models across different consumer segments and regions. Schneider Electric's transformation journey underscores the importance of internal alignment and communication in adopting new pricing strategies. Lotte's development of a revenue management function exemplifies institutionalizing pricing excellence within a company. Lastly, the section highlights how economic indicators can guide pricing decisions, preparing companies to adjust to economic changes.

Disclaimer

The views and opinions expressed in this book are solely those of the authors and do not necessarily reflect the views, policies, or positions of any companies they are or have been associated with. The contributions within this book are made in the authors' personal capacities and are based on information that is publicly available. References to specific companies and their practices are intended solely for informational purposes and should not be interpreted as an endorsement or representation of the companies' official stance.

About the editors

 **DANILO ZATTA** is one of the world's leading advisors and thought leaders in the field of pricing and topline excellence. As a management consultant for more than 25 years, he advises and coaches many of the world's best-known organizations.

The *Financial Times* defined him as "one of the world's leading pricing minds".

Dan has also been recognized amongst the *Top 5 Pricing Thought Leaders* on LinkedIn, in the list of the most engaging and impactful pricing thought leaders globally. The leading Italian business newspaper defined him as "as one of the most recognized monetization authors in the world" (https://www.thinkers360.com/top-50-global-thought-leaders-and-influencers-on-sales-2024/).

He has led hundreds of projects both at national and global level for multinationals, small and medium-sized companies, as well as investment funds in numerous industries, generating substantial profit increases. His advisory work typically focuses on programs of excellence in pricing and sales, revenue growth, corporate strategies, topline transformations, and redesign of business and revenue models.

Dan has acted as CEO, partner, and managing director at some of the world's leading consulting firms, building up international subsidiaries, entire pricing and sales practices, and fostering growth.

Dan has also written 20 books, including *The 10 Rules of Highly Effective Pricing* (Wiley, 2023); the international bestseller *The Pricing Model Revolution* (Wiley, 2022), translated into ten languages; *At the Heart of Leadership* (Routledge, 2023), translated into three languages; and *Revenue Management in Manufacturing* (Springer, 2016). He has also published hundreds of articles in different languages and regularly acts as keynote speaker at conferences, events, associations, and at leading universities. He also supports as personal topline coach several CEOs of leading companies.

Dan graduated with honors in economics and commerce from Luiss in Rome and University College Dublin in Ireland. He got an MBA from INSEAD in Fontainebleau, France, and Singapore. Finally, he completed a PhD in revenue management and pricing at the Technical University of Munich in Germany.

Connect with Dan on LinkedIn at linkedin.com/in/danilo-zatta

MACIEJ KRAUS has dedicated over 20 years to mastering and innovating in the field of pricing. His career spans across corporate roles, consulting, academia, and entrepreneurship, with a focus on developing pricing strategies and technologies. His comprehensive expertise in pricing has established him as a leading figure in the industry frequently mentioned on most influential pricing lists and interviewed at numerous business journals (*HBR, Forbes*, etc.).

As a guest lecturer at Stanford University's Graduate School of Business since 2019, Maciej has also shared his knowledge at other prestigious institutions, including the London School of Economics, University of Hong Kong, and IESE Business School. James Perkins, director of Executive Programs at Stanford, commends Maciej for his exceptional teaching style and in-depth knowledge, noting the significant time he dedicates to engaging with participants beyond the classroom.

> Maciej has taught as a guest speaker in the Executive Program for Growing Companies for the Stanford Graduate School of Business since 2019. His sessions are a highlight of the program! His extensive knowledge of pricing, years of experience in multiple industries, and teaching style are just some of the reasons his class sessions are so well received. He creates bespoke sessions based on the demographics of the cohort and spends many hours after his classes to meet individually with program participants. I hope to work with Maciej for many years to come.
>
> (James Perkins)

Maciej has authored three books on pricing, including *The Naked Mind-Shortcuts to Sales: Neuromarketing Overview for Profitability and Business Success*, on the behavioral aspects of pricing, and *Future of Pricing. A Guide to the Next 10 Years of AI*, on AI applications in price optimization. His TedTalk on behavioral pricing has over 150k views, demonstrating his ability to engage a broad audience with complex subjects.

Maciej is an ICF certified business coach.

Maciej has received over 80 positive reviews on LinkedIn from clients and students, reflecting the high regard in which he is held within both academic and professional communities.

Maciej holds an MA degree in economics from the Warsaw School of Economics, a PhD from the University of Warsaw focusing on B2B multinational pricing, and postgraduate qualifications from Harvard Business School and Stanford Graduate School of Business.

Contributor bios

CH 1

Michael Mansard, principal director at Zuora, guides over 350 companies in subscription economy transformations. With 14 years at Deloitte, SAP, and mentoring start-ups, he chairs Zuora's Subscribed Institute and co-created INSEAD's Subscription Business Bootcamp.

Pierre-Yves Noel, with over 20 years at Alcatel-Lucent Enterprise, is an expert in enterprise communications, business model innovation, and strategic growth, sharing insights at global events like INSEAD's Bootcamp.

CH 2

Daniel Cho, head of Philips' strategic pricing CoE, excels in value monetization and pricing excellence, reporting to innovation and strategy. He's a top opinion leader and keynote speaker in pricing.

Philips, a 130-year-old health technology leader, specializes in diagnostic imaging, image-guided therapy, patient monitoring, health informatics, and consumer health. Globally, it is committed to sustainability and social responsibility.

CH 3

Mariusz Gasiewski, at Google since 2007, leads mobile gaming initiatives in CEE, supports Google for Startups in Warsaw, and founded GameCamp, a top mobile gaming community in Europe.

Google is a multinational technology company specializing in Internet-related services and products, including online advertising technologies, search engine, cloud computing, software, and hardware.

CH 4

Dawid Pawlak, senior digital value manager at Workday, supports investment decisions and benefits maximization in EMEA and North America. He has a master's in corporate finance management and a background in pricing and revenue management.

CH 5

Michał Wiczkowski, an expert in digital advertising, excels in optimizing campaigns with programmatic and data-driven strategies. He drives ROI through innovative ad technologies and is a recognized industry thought leader.

CH 6

Anna Sokólska-Krzemińska, head of pricing at MediaMarktSaturn in Warsaw, specializes in profit optimization, business strategy, and pricing. Previously at Simon-Kucher, she led over 30 projects across Europe.

MediaMarktSaturn, Europe's leading consumer electronics retailer, excites customers with a unique shopping experience, personal advice, and comprehensive services, simplifying life in the digital world.

CH 7

Karl Holm leads the pricing organization in Global Solutions at ASSA ABLOY. With a background in product management and engineering, he contributed to the book *Monetizing and Pricing Sustainability*.

ASSA ABLOY, the global leader in access solutions, offers access control, security doors, identification technology, and entrance automation. In 2023, it reported SEK 141 billion revenue with 61,000 employees worldwide.

CH 8

Vladimir Kuchkanov, senior product manager at Zalando, leads competitive pricing with 5+ years in AI-powered price optimization. He previously had a 10-year career in pricing analytics at top FMCG companies.

CH 9

Mohammed Ahmed, an expert pricing strategist, leads revenue management for Hilton in the Middle East, Africa, and Turkey. With cross-industry experience, he offers insights into diverse pricing strategies.

CH 10

Paolo De Angeli leads customer experience and value management at Borealis. With 15 years in pricing at Syngenta and Borealis, he founded the European Customer Value Management Think Tank in 2020.

Borealis, a global leader in sustainable polyolefin solutions, excels in polyolefins recycling and base chemicals production in Europe. Opinions in this book reflect the author's views, not Borealis's position.

CH 11

Anna Telakowiec, with 28 years of marketing experience, has led global brands at top multinationals. She holds an executive MBA and is a Chartered Institute of Marketing graduate.

CH 12

Jerker Johansson, an expert in pricing and change management since 2007, specializes in B2B industries. He has conducted over 300 workshops and 1500 coaching sessions. Jerker holds an MBA and served in the Royal Swedish Artillery.

Coor is the leading Nordic provider of integrated facility management (IFM) and facility management (FM) services, ensuring smooth and efficient operations for companies and public bodies.

CH 13

Jędrzej Rychlik, an expert in revenue management and business strategy, has driven margin growth and customer compliance in B2B and B2C markets. He specializes in optimizing trade terms across logistics and FMCG industries.

CH 14

Matthew Jipps, commercial and revenue management director at Asahi, has 25 years of experience driving profit through revenue growth. He excels in inclusive leadership, strategic execution, and cross-functional international team management.

Asahi Europe and International (AEI) is part of Asahi Group Holdings, managing 20 breweries globally and renowned beer brands like Asahi Super Dry, Pilsner Urquell, and Peroni. AEI operates in 90 markets with over 10,000 employees.

CH 15

Paola Andrea Valencia has ten years of experience in sales, marketing, and pricing. Trilingual in Spanish, English, and French, she specializes in pricing strategy and leadership, with expertise in ROI analysis.

CH 16

Jacek Wyrebkowski is the strategy and revenue manager at LOTTE Wedel, one of the largest confectionary company in Poland, subsidiary of LOTTE.

Wojciech Gorzen, head of Movens Advisory, offers pragmatic pricing and revenue management solutions. With 30 years of experience, he was formerly head of Warsaw's Simon-Kucher and global pricing lead at Syngenta.

CH 17

Thaynara DuBois is the global pricing lead at Charles River Development, with a decade of experience in pricing and business strategy. She holds a master of business intelligence, pursuing CPP, and has certificates from MIT, Harvard, and Babson.

Christien DuBois is a finance industry veteran passionate about blockchain and decentralized finance. He is experienced in business growth, regulatory navigation, and effective communication, and enjoys hiking and biking in New England.

Introduction

Pricing has become a key priority of every company globally. Inflation, raw material price volatility, new price models, and price as key lever to boost profits can be found daily in the news. Companies there need to understand how to transform their pricing to address all this.

While management consultants are creating entire pricing practices to serve the booming demand for pricing consulting and pricing software, corporations are establishing pricing functions and teams to address this key topic, which in the past was seldomly on the agenda of the top management.

However, readers cannot find an authoritative but easy-to-read book on that indicates which "ingredients" are needed on a corporate level to make pricing successful with concrete case studies.

This book closes this gap revealing the secrets of pricing practitioners at successful companies.

Most available books – both old and new – are either more academic or take a very in-depth look at single specific topics.

It is the first book whose ca. 20 authors have over 400 years of price management experience in some of the world's leading corporations across industries and geographies.

In *Pricing Decoded*, we show how to boost profitability and build a competitive advantage transforming the way companies set and manage prices through an insightful collection of case studies from the world's leading pricing practitioners.

For the first time ever, worldwide leading companies share and reveal their secrets around their pricing successes. The book investigates all key aspects of monetization with cases of both B2C and B2B companies like Alcatel-Lucent, Google, BP-Castrol, Unilever, Microsoft, Borealis, Hilton, Nike, MediaWolrd, Philips Healthcare, Schneider Electric, DHL, Coor, and more.

Concrete use cases from diverse industries and nations, facts and figures show how to transform the way companies price. Written in a simple way and with a lot of pragmatism, *Pricing Decoded* is a concrete guide to support the transition to a modern and robust pricing.

DOI: 10.4324/9781003535966-1

Pricing Decoded is also a lucid and passionate analysis of how pricing has become the most important source of profitability and competitive advantage. It a practical manual on one of the oldest forms of relationship in the world – price, a guide to everyday decisions in one of the most delicate economic periods humanity's history.

The book is divided into four sections: (1) price strategy, (2) price setting, (3) price realization, and (4) price enablement. Each sections contains cases and experiences from different companies across various industries that will shed light on these four key pricing topics.

We are curious to hear how you liked this book. Feel therefore free to reach out to us with feedbacks, comments, and thoughts and connect with us on LinkedIn.

Enjoy the reading!

Danilo Zatta
linkedin.com/in/danilo-zatta

Maciej Kraus
linkedin.com/in/maciej-kraus

Part I
Price strategy

1

Subscription pricing's success secrets at Alcatel-Lucent, Decathlon, Traton, and more

Michael Mansard and Pierre-Yves Noel

Disclaimer: The views expressed in this chapter are solely those of the authors and do not necessarily reflect the views or opinions of Zuora nor Alcatel-Lucent Enterprise. This contribution is made in the authors' personal capacities and is based solely on publicly available sources. Any references to Zuora or Alcatel-Lucent Enterprise are for informational purposes only and should not be construed as representing the official stance or endorsement of the companies.

0. CHAPTER'S FOREWORD

The forthcoming chapter delves into the subscription economy, a transformative business paradigm coined by Zuora CEO and Founder, Tien Tzuo. The subscription economy has revolutionized various industry sectors, impacting traditional business practices and operations profoundly. Our analysis begins with an examination of both historical and contemporary market trends, setting the stage for a deeper understanding of the subscription economy's rapid expansion. We then explore the strategic imperatives this model demands, the pivotal shift in portfolio strategies, and the organizational transformations necessary for success. Additionally, we outline a comprehensive road map for businesses to navigate this shift. The chapter concludes by deciphering ongoing developments in the subscription economy. Throughout, we enrich our discussion with engaging "spotlights", for instance on compelling subscription case studies or insightful explorations into the nuances of pricing and packaging strategies.

-----

1. SUBSCRIPTION: STATE OF THE UNION

The inception of subscription-based business models, although commonly traced to the digital revolution around 2007 with pioneers like Salesforce, Amazon, Netflix, and Box, finds its deeper historical roots in the nineteenth century's periodical publishing industry. This nascent form of subscription was a harbinger of the enduring appeal and practicality of such models, underscoring a fundamental shift in consumer-business relationships. From the first subscription offers in the English publishing industry in the seventeenth century,[1] through reading club book subscription with France Loisirs in the 1970s, to the first flat fee phone subscription "Déclic" by France

DOI: 10.4324/9781003535966-3

Table 1.1

Illustrative list of subscription services across industries || *note: in italic subscription offers that are featured in the chapter*

In the industry . . .	Y . . . ou can for example subscribe to	
Sports & Wellness	*Decathlon Kids Btwin – Access to children bike with ability to swap when needed*	Vail Resorts Epic Pass – Access to ski resorts and perks (discounts on lessons, lodging)
Food & Beverage	HelloFresh – Meal kit delivery service	Quench Water-as-a-Service – Filtered water service for offices
Education & Learning	Coursera – Online courses and degrees	MasterClass – Celebrity-led instructional videos
Fashion & Apparel	Nuuly – Personalized clothing subscription	Rent the Runway – Designer dress and accessory rentals
Gaming & Entertainment	Xbox Game Pass – Access to a catalog of games on console, PC, and cloud	Shadow Gaming – Access to a cloud-based high-performance gaming PC from any device
Automotive	GM OnStar – Connected services (emergency assistance, nav, remote access)	AMAG Clyde – Comprehensive all-electric car mobility subscription and mobility services
Public Transportation	SNCF TGV Max – Unlimited access to high-speed trains for a monthly fee	EasyJet Plus – Subscription to benefits (free seat selection, priority counter, speedy boarding)
Travel & Leisure	Inspirato – Access to book luxury travel and lifestyle at members-only nightly rates	eDreams Prime – Subscription to discounts on flights, hotels, car rentals, and more
Office Equipment	Nornorm – Flexible and sustainable workspace furnishing service	Recygo – Recycling services, incl. sorting equipment, employee support, collection, and data
Home Equipment	iRobot Select – Access to a robot cleaner and services (parts, protection plan)	Haier WashPass – Professional washing experience with IoT, AI, dedicated detergents, services
Consumer Packaged Goods	*Synsam – Eyewear subscription and services (eye exam, lens swaps)*	HP Instant Ink – Automatic ink replenishment service with pay-per-page model
Retail	*Amazon Prime – Access to a range of benefits (free delivery, deals, streaming)*	*Costco Membership – Right to access wholesale club's products and perks (rewards, deals, etc.)*

(Continued)

Table 1.1 **(Continued)**

Illustrative list of subscription services across industries || *note: in italic subscription offers that are featured in the chapter*

In the industry . . .	Y . . . ou can for example subscribe to	
Heavy Machinery	*Traton Rio – Digital services for the entire transport and logistics ecosystem*	CAT Connect – Insights on equipment and operator behaviors to improve safety and productivity
Discrete Manufacturing	Assa Abloy Vostio – Guest access management services for the hospitality industry	Schneider Electric SmartConnect – UPS remote smart power monitoring, diagnostics, upgrades
Healthcare	Siemens Healthineers Advance Plans - multi-tiered digitally powered service plans	*Philips Enterprise-Monitoring-as-a-Service – Access to a extensive patient monitoring solution*
High Tech	*ALE Rainbow – Enterprise communications in and out the office as a monthly fee*	NCR – All-in-one Point-of-Sale, inventory mgmt and digital commerce suite for SMB

Telecom in 1996,[2] some famous avant-garde examples have paved the way for various industries.

In sectors like software or media, where change is rapid and ongoing innovation a necessity, the subscription economy has become the dominant paradigm from a revenue model perspective in less than two decades. In fact, digital attackers and "subscription-natives", such as Spotify or Zoom, have pushed established players such as New York Times or Microsoft to embrace the models. For example, New York Times successfully transitioned from heavy reliance on challenged advertising revenue streams to a more digitally oriented subscription model, reaching 67% of revenue contribution by 2022 with more than 9 million subscribers.

Today, the subscription model has permeated diverse industries, ranging from software and media to healthcare, consumer services. The adoption isn't confined to digital products; it includes physical products such as bikes, or IoT-enabled services from connected products that provide added-value services, such as asset tracking or predictive maintenance. Here is a purely illustrative list of subscriptions across industries, demonstrating variety and coverage.

The subscription economy has witnessed remarkable growth, escalating from an estimated $650 billion in 2020 to a forecasted $1.5 trillion by 2025, as per UBS projections. This growth trajectory aligns with the 17% compound annual growth rate observed for companies indexed in Zuora's Subscription Economy Index (SEI) between 2012 and 2022, significantly outpacing the 4.6% growth of the S&P 500 during the same timeframe. Concurrently, the transition from traditional product-centric models to subscription services highlights a shift towards customer-centricity and ongoing engagement. This change transforms product delivery and marketing from one-off transactions to long-lasting relationships. In an era of economic instability, subscription models offer predictable and stable revenue, with their flexibility enabling quick adaptation to market and technology shifts. The logic behind the shift from transactional to subscription models in enterprises is multidimensional and grounded in practicality.

The subscription model's profound impact is also seen in the shift from ownership to usership. This paradigm shift reflects a deeper alignment with customer needs and the dynamics of long-term relationships. In fact, this transition is not merely a market trend but a strategic realignment of business models, also resonating with the principles of the circular economy. It represents a move towards sustainability, not just in environmental terms, but also in terms of building economically sustainable, long-term customer relationships.

Subscription spotlight: Synsam[3]

Synsam, a leading Nordic lifestyle company in optical retail, launched Synsam Lifestyle in 2016. It is an eyewear-as-a-service subscription offer that promises "Always the Right Sight", by bundling amongst other regular eye exams, eyewear with adapted lenses as eyesight changes, ability to regularly swap frames, and insurance for peace of mind. By addressing key customer pain points and functions, Synsam has reached close to 600,000 subscribers to Synsam Lifestyle. By 2023, the subscription service not only remained the largest contributor to growth, experiencing double-digit growth, it also accounted for over 50% of total revenue. Profitability has also been on the rise with EBITDA margins surpassing 25% in Q3 2023, higher than its peers' average and similar to leading providers, despite much smaller scale. In fact, Synsam's eyewear-as-a-service approach led to such marked success it has inspired business model transformation across the optics retail industry, with many other optic retailers following suit across the globe.

Subscription spotlight: Philips

As healthcare faces cash flow and capex constraints, which can prevent investment in new digital technologies, MedTech leader Philips launched in 2022 an enterprise monitoring as a service (EMaaS) model to provide health organizations with patient monitoring support aligned to their goals. EMaaS subscription allows the monetization of the actual usage of the monitoring per patient, per acuity, per day for a predictable spend connected to the hospital's varying patient volume. This results in a virtuous loop where Philips can align the hospital's daily needs and long-term goals based on patient volume. In fact, the EMaaS model is designed to provide ongoing support, clinical transformation, and continuous improvement of system use over the long term, enabling organizations to realize the promised benefits of modern monitoring systems. EMaaS's flexible cost model ultimately aligns better with the hospital revenue model to optimize cash flow management and redirect capital to other revenue generating areas. In terms of results, Philips and customer internal teams in the high-acuity units in one Florida hospital have estimated that "13,331 staff hours will be saved annually from workflow improvement and automation of manual tasks", thanks to using a standardized monitoring solution.

2. WHY DID IT BECOME SO BIG AND WHY IS IT ACCELERATING NOW?

The substantial growth and accelerating adoption of the subscription economy can be attributed to several key components reshaping the landscape of consumer behavior and corporate strategies. In the next paragraphs, we will go through each factor that has catalyzed this trend, ranging from shifting consumer preferences, technological advancements, pandemic influence, and the economic resilience of subscription models, as well as their impact on enterprise valuation and revenue predictability.

First, the cornerstone of the subscription model's ascendance is a significant shift in consumer behavior. People are generally becoming more digitally savvy and less inclined towards ownership. In fact, 68% of adults across the globe believe that a person's status is no longer defined by what they own.[4] So instead of owning products, customers want flexible access to services that adapt to their ever-evolving needs. Subscribing and using services instead of owning products sets people free from hassles, maintenance costs, and constant upgrades. Digital services, for instance, are natively subscription-based nowadays. Let's take ChatGPT as an illustration. For the vast majority, it would be unthinkable to buy your own technical infrastructure, train your own large language model, or install a bot on a home server – and all these efforts for questionable results. OpenAI provides a directly leverageable solution, with different levels of subscription, aligned to users' needs, including a free entry level. Beyond digital services, the previously featured Synsam "spotlight" also shows that rapid shifts can occur in the world of physical products. This paradigm shift is not just a fleeting trend but a fundamental change in the consumer psyche, valuing experiences and convenience over the traditional pride of ownership.

Then, this shift towards subscription models has been greatly facilitated by technological advancements. The explosion of the Internet of Things (IoT) and the advent of faster network technologies like 5G have created a fertile ground for these models to thrive. These technologies enable businesses to interact with consumers at an unprecedented scale, gathering valuable insights that drive efficiency in both delivery and management of services. The resulting data is the lifeblood of subscription services, allowing for tailored experiences, predictive analytics, and improved customer engagement – as the TRATON RIO "spotlight" featured at the end of this section illustrates.

Another catalyst that fuels the acceleration of subscription-based models is the outbreak of crises, such global economic turmoil or recent pandemic, or high inflation that started in 2021. As a matter of fact, the 2001 "Dot Com Bubble" and the 2007 "Financial Crisis" surprisingly match with inflexion points in the subscription economy, respectively SaaS and media.[5] Subscription models are relevant models in times of uncertainty – as customers are often more constrained in terms of investments and ability to commit. A minimal threshold for entry, coupled with a lower level of commitment and the ability to easily change subscriptions – including upgrading, downgrading, suspending, or resuming services – becomes crucial for consumers. Meanwhile, subscription businesses gain from enhanced resiliency compared to their transactional counterparts during crises. Notably, according to Zuora,[6] four out of five subscription businesses experienced growth during the COVID-19 pandemic.

And indeed, from an enterprise perspective, subscription models do offer predictability in revenue, which is a highly valued trait in financial planning and valuation. A striking illustration: 70% to 80% of subscription business revenues come from their existing subscribers according to the Subscribed Institute.[7] Steady, predictable revenue streams facilitate better resource allocation, risk management, and strategic planning and ultimately driving predictable earnings too!

Driven by customer demand, technological advancements, and the shifting landscape of consumer preferences, the subscription model has moved from a niche strategy to a central pillar of modern business practice. Its continuous growth, projected expansion, and adaptability across various industries highlight its enduring appeal and effectiveness. All these factors combined together paint a picture of a robust and growing subscription economy, reshaping industries and redefining how businesses operate.

Now, let us summarize the key traits of the modern subscription economy in light of the elements we have articulated so far, as compared to the "old" subscription model. It is a customer-centric, recurring business model, focused on the subscriber relationship, source of mutually valuable data, enabling continuously improving service and experience value, powering personalized offers, that can adapt flexibility to the customer need across its lifetime, while ideally supporting a more sustainable model (cf. Decathlon spotlight hereinafter as a relevant illustration). But as Tien Tzuo, Zuora CEO and Founder put it, "if the Subscription Economy is about anything, it's about a fundamental return to customer relationships". In short, it is about the subscriber, not so much about subscription.

Subscription spotlight: Decathlon

Decathlon, the world's largest sports retailer, has been trialing and accelerating with multiple subscription initiatives across the globe. One of the most compelling services is called "Btwin Kids", a subscription service for children's bikes, designed to address the problem of quickly outgrown bikes and reduce environmental impact. Indeed, many parents often keep well-functioning kids' bikes idle, even after they've become too small or outdated for their children. This offering, starting at €3 to €8 per month, encompasses not only the use of children's bikes but also incorporates comprehensive services like maintenance and insurance. Importantly, it offers the flexibility to swap bikes, ensuring children always have access to appropriately sized bikes as they grow, enhancing the convenience and practicality of the subscription. The success of this pilot has led Decathlon to expand the subscription service across geographies, but also across more product ranges and use cases.

Subscription spotlight: Traton

With its brands Scania, MAN, or Volkswagen Truck & Bus, TRATON is one of the world's leading commercial vehicle manufacturers. In the logistics space, there is a larger number of small fleet operators. Small fleets often lack digitization, while operating mixed brands fleets, generating areas of inefficiencies. The TRATON RIO platform is a cloud-based solution that consolidates services for fleet managers, freight forwarders, and vehicle rental companies. It offers digital services and solutions for trucks, vans, and buses, independent from the specific vehicle brand. The RIO platform helps collect data from telematic/IoT devices and other external sources to provide real-time information such as vehicle position, current status, tachograph status, speed, engine temperature, or fuel consumption. Some specific examples of the services monetized by the RIO platform are GPS tracking of freight, geofencing, maintenance management, monitoring driving times, or route and order management. Those can be accessed in a self-service manner via RIO's marketplace platform, with a transparent price per day and per vehicle. As a matter of fact, the RIO platform collaborates with Volkswagen Group Logistics as their cloud-based telematics operating system, managing about 18,000 truck moves a day across Europe.

3. SUBSCRIPTION IS NOT A STRATEGY

In the landscape of contemporary business strategies, it is imperative to recognize that subscription models, while increasingly popular, are not strategies in themselves. They are tactical elements within a broader strategic framework. This understanding is critical for businesses contemplating the adoption or enhancement of a subscription model.

Subscription models are fundamentally customer-centric, recurring business models. They require an "outside-in" approach[8]: beginning with an understanding of the customer's needs, quantifying customer's pains, followed by the development of a valuable solution. Initiating a subscription service without this foundational understanding may lead to "subscription-washing", where the model is adopted without clear alignment with customer needs or strategic intent.

Aligning subsequently a subscription model with specific inside-out strategic objectives is crucial. Objectives may include capturing new market segments, increasing share of wallet, achieving sustainable business growth, differentiating from competitors through services, escaping price wars, increasing gross profit margins, forging direct customer relationships, and driving new customer habits. The choice and hierarchization of these objectives significantly influences the subscription model's design and execution. The exemplary cases of Costco and Amazon Prime serve as illuminating illustrations, underscoring the necessity of a customer-centric approach and strategic alignment.

Costco, a multinational retailer operating a chain of membership big-box warehouse club retail stores across eight countries in 2023, stands as the third largest retailer globally. At the heart of its business model since 1976 is Costco's compulsory subscription membership, grounded in a value proposition that transcends mere low pricing. This value proposition, characterized by "Costco's absolute pricing authority", encompasses not just competitive pricing but a commitment to exceptional value through a blend of quality, price, and a curated product selection. It's a virtuous cycle: the more customers shop at Costco, the more they realize the value of their membership, which in turn reinforces their loyalty to the brand and justifies the renewal of their subscription. This strategic focus on delivering continuous value has culminated in an impressive >90% renewal rate among its 127.9 million members. While membership fees account for just a modest segment of Costco's overall revenue, their impact on the company's financial health is disproportionately significant, especially in terms of profitability. As of fiscal year 2023, Costco's membership fees generated around $4.6bn out of $237.7bn, while driving approximately 72% of Costco's operating margins, illustrating the efficacy of this strategic approach.

Amazon Prime, launched in 2005, adopts a strategic approach inspired, but distinct from Costco's model. Priced at $139 per year, or $14.99 per month, it offers a comprehensive array of benefits, including expedited shipping and access to entertainment options like music and video streaming. This multifaceted strategy is not just about providing transactional benefits; it is central to Amazon's goal of increasing customer spend and enhancing its overall value proposition. The substantial value offered by Amazon Prime makes it a compelling choice for consumers, often described as a "no-brainer", driving over 200 million subscribers. This perception is bolstered by the quantification of Prime benefits, which, according to a JPMorgan analyst, are estimated to be worth around $1,000. The main impact of Amazon Prime is to promote much higher spending on the platform: according to a Bank of America analysis, Prime members spend on average $1,968 annually on Amazon, which is about four times the expenditure of non-Prime shoppers. It underscores the indirect nature of revenue and margin contribution of Amazon Prime leveraging bundled and subsidized benefits. The continuous enhancement and expansion of these benefits are key to Prime's success, aligning with Amazon's strategic objectives of increasing customer spending and differentiating from competitors. While specific margin contributions of Prime are not publicly detailed, the model demonstrates how a subscription service can effectively contribute to a company's financial objectives not just through direct subscription fees, but through the broader, value-added impact on customer purchasing behavior.

In summary, while both Amazon Prime and Costco memberships operate on subscription-based models, their strategic foundations and executions are distinct. Costco's model focuses on leveraging subscriptions for margin enhancement and customer loyalty, whereas Amazon Prime uses its diverse offerings to increase customer spend and enhance its value proposition. This highlights that a subscription model is not a standalone strategy but a component of a larger strategic plan, requiring a thoughtfully defined, customer-centric approach and alignment with specific business objectives.

4. STRATEGIC PLAYS TO TRANSITION A PORTFOLIO: A PRACTICAL ILLUSTRATION WITH ALCATEL-LUCENT ENTERPRISE

In this section, we will explore how companies can strategically map how to transition their portfolio from transactional business models to subscription models, drawing upon the experiences of the authors at ALE International (ALE) operating under the brand Alcatel-Lucent Enterprise. These "plays" represent a conceptual framework based on tactics generally observed in the market. In fact, the three plays served as a high-level framework to guide the transformation of ALE's portfolio, with multiple pilots conducted to enhance the likelihood of success and accelerate the process. While they are insightful examples of how businesses can evolve, it is important to recognize that these are not the sole pathways to transformation. Each play will be examined in detail, using ALE's practical experiences as illustrations.

Alcatel-Lucent Enterprise at a glance: high-level elements to better understand the three plays

ALE has been a strong player in enterprise communications and networks for decades, with 1 million+ B2B customers and 3,400+ partners are across the globe and continents. Quality of the technology and a strong network of partners are some of the top explaining factors of a strong position. Traditionally, ALE's business model has been transactional, with a focus on hardware sales, supplemented by software licenses and services. More specifically, ALE's revenue for the past decades has been driven by hardware sales and solutions, such as private branch exchange (PBX), interactive voice response (IVR), endpoints (phones), network routers, Wi-Fi solutions, etc. Those products are for the vast majority sold indirectly through a partner ecosystem of distributors and system integrators.

However, like many sectors, the software and digital portion has progressively taken a bigger share, directly impacting the business model. In fact, the late 2010s marks the acceleration of cloud-based enterprise communications and the rise of digital-native companies such as Microsoft Teams or Zoom offering collaborative solutions in the form of subscriptions. Embracing these deep transformations, ALE proactively began its transition towards subscription-based models through three strategic "plays".[9]

PLAY 1: CONNECTED SERVICES

This play is relevant for companies having an existing installed base producing data that can be collected. Innovative digital services can be proposed as a complement to existing customer investments.

Given ALE's very significant existing customer base and partner network, launching cloud-based subscription services that offer incremental value to existing users as an overlay can be seen as a "path of least resistance". It increases the value of existing customer investments, thanks to digital services that enhance capabilities provided by products purchased sometimes years before.

Also, this approach empowers ALE's partner ecosystem with new avenues for revenue through the monetization of new cloud services. More importantly, it builds up and secures a recurring relationship with their end-customers. Finally, it serves as a foundation for the adoption of cutting-edge services and technologies, smoothly transitioning both customers and channel ecosystem to new subscription-based business models and technological landscapes.

A prime example of this play was the introduction of Rainbow by Alcatel-Lucent Enterprise[10] platform in 2018. Rainbow is a cloud collaboration and communications platform, whose distinctive advantage is to blend with the existing physical communication infrastructures on customers premises – that is, PBXs, end points, etc. – in order to extend it with modern communication and collaboration services. During the pandemic, Rainbow was, for example, instrumental to open up previously closed enterprise communication infrastructures, to rapidly enable remote work with colleagues and third parties. Deployed in only a few hours into an existing infrastructure, it does not require long-range training for the partner's service workforce, making it simple for the partners to position those services to end-customers. Rainbow is charged on an end-user basis.

Going one step further and leveraging the openness of Rainbow, ALE launched an enterprise communications business continuity offering that can function in any environment. "Rainbow Guardian" is a ready-to-use communications collaboration environment that can be activated on-demand in the event of a crisis. A concrete use case would be a cyber attack that has paralyzed an entire company. Rainbow Guardian allows business continuity teams to communicate effectively during the crisis, and employees to continue operations from any location while the threat is tempered with. "Rainbow Guardian" customers pay for the environment that is constantly fully synchronized and ready to use at any time, providing peace of mind. This innovation in the cloud collaboration solutions space is made possible by both the flexibility of the technology and subscription nature of the pricing model.

PLAY 2: REPACKAGE TO RECURRING

This second play is compelling to enterprises with existing transaction offers that they want to migrate to subscription-based offerings, for instance, as a way to differentiate or to address a growing customer demand for a specific segment.

The second play of our portfolio transformation is to transition typical one-off "CAPEX" offers to subscription offerings. Those can be proposed to new customers, but also as an evolution to existing customers. This profound transformation is often made possible thanks to connectivity, which enables us to collect customer usage data – in order to track the asset, invoice properly, learn from behaviors to adapt offers, etc.

In the enterprise communications and networking sector, customers traditionally invest in their hardware, such as PBXs and routers, leading to these assets being recorded on their financial statements. Proposing them as "As-a-Service offers" brings additional flexibility to customers, beyond mere "flat leasing".[10] The value proposition for the customer is to pay for the infrastructure over time and based on how much it is utilized, not fully when bought or installed. For network infrastructure, Network-As-A-Service[11] is offered as a price per active "networking port" per month, while for communication, Purple-On-Demand[12] is offered as a price per active user per month.

It is important to note that while distinct, products in transactional sales, hardware, and software are typically merged in those subscription offers. One major impact is the change of risk balance between the customer and the vendor (now turned into a solution provider). But it also offers many upsides. Typically, infrastructure investments are made for seven to nine years: proposing subscription offers embedding hardware and software can also incentivize customers to "refresh" their services more often, or to upgrade to high service tiers.

Another opportunity in this play is that when customers are adopting recurring subscription models, they will progressively transition from on-premise hardware-based offers to new generation digital cloud-based offers. In that spirit, ALE's "Move to Cloud" program enables a wealth of deployment and pricing models to better support its customer transitions based on their individual specificities.

PLAY 3: VERTICAL SERVICES OFFERS

This last play will resonate for offers meant to deliver value-added services to specific segments, combining technology innovation with business model innovation. Subscription model is a great vector to align monetization of segment specific services to the key performance indicators of customers – that is, value-based and outcome-based models. The offers in this category are designed as a service from the "get-go" and are "subscription-native". Customers have no preconception of a pricing structure or reference value: their perceived value becomes the reference.

As the go-to-market and ecosystem get experienced on subscription models, it becomes possible to create offers that address specific verticals or use cases. But proposing a solution to a problem is not enough: it has to be brought with a relevant monetization model so that the value created can be shared between service providers and customers.

Business models tailored to performance metrics relevant to specific segments can effectively address underserved or niche markets. A compelling example is found in the transportation sector, where ALE's Rainbow platform caters to the unique needs of the cruise ship industry. Known as "Rainbow Edge," this solution is implemented within the cruise ship's private data center, ensuring secure, comprehensive collaboration services for employees, even under limited satellite connectivity. The range of services includes messaging, voice calls, conferencing, alerting, and business process workflows, all designed to meet the distinctive requirements of maritime operations. In this case, the most relevant pricing model that was identified with the customers is based on a "per employee" basis, allowing the cruise carrier to align the value of the platform with one of their important metrics.

Another example of a disruptive monetization model lies in the healthcare ecosystem: the Rainbow platform can orchestrate the care pathways of patients in a given territory. The overarching objective is to allow for the best treatments to be provided in due time to patients, while optimizing the time for caregivers. This can be delivered by collecting and organizing patient data securely from multiple sources, by leveraging artificial intelligence to detect where optimizations can be made, and ultimately by orchestrating real-time communications between caregivers and patients in the territory. In this example, services to caregivers and patients are monetized on a "per caregiver" per month basis, charged to the healthcare agencies.

WHAT CAN WE LEARN FROM ALE'S THREE PLAYS

The experimentations that led to those three plays at Alcatel-Lucent Enterprise underscores a critical insight: innovation in highly competitive markets extends beyond technology. The design of offers and innovative monetization strategies now play pivotal roles in driving innovation, crucial for companies seeking to stand out in the subscription economy. By blending technological innovation with creative monetization approaches, companies can forge business models that more closely align with customer needs and preferences.

5. TRANSFORMING THE ORGANIZATION: A 360° CHANGE

Transitioning to a subscription model involves a paradigm shift from a product-centric, one-time transaction focus to a customer-centric, ongoing relationship approach. This model emphasizes customer lifetime value and consistent engagement, requiring a holistic reconfiguration of business strategies and operations. In short, every single function needs to operate differently. The previous illustration and the Alcatel-Lucent Enterprise (ALE) plays to shed light on what it means. Let's now focus on how an organization transforms in order to embrace the subscription economy, that ALE is also transitioning through.

First, let's remind an important data point that will help understand why such holistic transformation is important and deep: 70% to 80% of subscription business revenues come from their existing subscribers, according to the Subscribed Institute.[11] On the other hand, it costs 4× to 8× times[12] more money to acquire than retain or expand an existing client. This leads to payback periods, a crucial metric that indicates the time it takes to recoup the cost of acquiring a new customer, often ranging from 1 to 6 months for B2C businesses, 6 to 12 months for SMB businesses, or 12 to 18 months for B2B Enterprise businesses.[13] Also, we have been witnessing a sharper increase in customer cost of acquisition these past three years, making it an imperative to center your model around your subscribers. In fact, the best run subscription businesses are those not only very good at acquiring but have mastered the art of retaining and expanding their existing subscriber base.

Our objective here is to provide a short summary of some of the key transformations to operate per function, regardless of the industry. We will then purposely follow with a dedicated spotlight on pricing and monetization transformations.

1. Strategy

- Customer-Centricity: Unlike traditional models that focus on single transactions, subscription models prioritize long-term customer relationships. Strategies are developed to maximize customer lifetime value, requiring ongoing engagement and retention efforts.

- Flexible Strategic Planning: The dynamic nature of subscription models necessitates agile and adaptable strategies. Companies must be prepared to rapidly respond to market changes, customer preferences, and feedback.

- Data Utilization: Leveraging customer data becomes a cornerstone of strategic planning. Insights gained from customer interactions and usage patterns guide product development, customer service improvements, and personalized marketing efforts.

2. Engineering/product development

- Iterative Product Development: Shifts from a "launch and leave" approach to a model of continuous iterations and improvement, integrating agile methodologies for rapid iteration based on customer feedback, firsthand data and market changes. When physical products are included, they should be designed for service "from the get go" – both from an experience perspective and from an operational management perspective.

- Customer-Centric Product Design: Prioritizes user experience, ensuring ease of use and long-term customer satisfaction. Emphasizes the development of features that allow personalization and customization to cater to diverse customer needs. Responsive design changes based on an effective feedback loop – for example, direct customer feedback, usage data, and customer support interactions.

- Security and Compliance: Enhances security measures continuously, given the ongoing data collection and storage that is central in subscription models. Stays compliant with relevant regulations, particularly in data protection and privacy.

3. Marketing

- Customer (Re)-Segmentation: The transition from product-based to service-oriented offerings in subscription models necessitates a more nuanced approach to customer segmentation. As a matter of fact, new pain points or new buyer persona are most likely being addressed, requiring a deeper analysis of customer behavior and expectations. Effective segmentation in this context is critical for tailoring marketing efforts and service enhancements, ensuring that they resonate more profoundly with the specific needs and experiences of diverse customer groups.

- Value Proposition: Articulating the ongoing value and benefits of the subscription is essential, differentiating it from one-time purchase models. It also requires building new narratives that aligns with the brand's mission, values, and the unique advantages of the subscription model.

- Pricing, Packaging, and Monetization strategies: needs to be completely revamped when moving to subscription – cf. dedicated "spotlight" in this section.

- Data-Driven Marketing: Continuously utilizing data analytics to understand and respond to customer behaviors, preferences, and life cycle stages is crucial. This approach enables targeted marketing efforts at various customer journey points.

- Subscriber Journey Design: The entire (new) subscriber journey, from discovery to renewal, has to be designed and mapped. Every single touch-point is of strategic importance given the continuous relationship building process at the core of the subscription business model.

- Life Cycle Marketing: Traditional marketing often emphasizes customer acquisition, while subscription models require a focus on the entire customer life cycle. This includes strategies for acquisition, retention, upselling, and loyalty building.

- Personalization at Scale: Advanced data analytics also enables highly personalized marketing campaigns, tailored to individual customer needs and preferences, a sharp contrast to the one-size-fits-all approach in traditional models.

- Content and Educational Marketing: Continuous customer education and engagement through content marketing are critical in nurturing long-term relationships.

4. Go-to-market strategies and sales

- Efficient Go-to-Market Strategies: The GTM strategy in a subscription model focuses on cost-effective ways to acquire and retain customers. Cost of acquisition has indeed to be balanced as compared to customer lifetime value, which may involve having more efficient sales campaigns – for example, leveraging digital channels or inbound marketing tactics. The GTM approach is designed to be scalable and adaptable, allowing businesses to quickly adjust to market changes and customer feedback without incurring excessive costs. This is absolutely critical especially in the first stages of the subscription offer.

- Long-Term Customer Engagement: Moving away from the traditional focus on one-time transactions, sales teams in a subscription model prioritize building and maintaining long-term customer relationships. This approach involves understanding customer needs over time and providing ongoing value. Sales teams will typically need to adopt a more consultative role, guiding customers through the value and benefits of a subscription over the long term, rather than focusing on immediate sales closure or features and function – for instance through a land-and-expand approach.

- Subscription Dynamics Fluency: Sales teams require specialized training to understand the intricacies of subscription selling, including the emphasis on recurring revenue and customer retention. Training includes techniques for handling common objections to subscriptions and strategies for ensuring successful renewals and upsells.

- Redesigned compensation models: Sales and channel compensation models are realigned to reflect subscription objectives, such as annual contract value retention and customer lifetime value, rather than just initial sales. New performance metrics are thus introduced, reflecting customer retention rates, subscription renewals, and the expansion of customer accounts over time.

- Incentivization to Boost Adoption: Temporary incentives can be employed to further influence go-to-market team members behaviors. For example, a bonus multiplier for subscription offers.

5. Finance

- Subscription-Specific Metrics and KPIs: Setting up dedicated, fit-for-purpose subscription metrics is essential to be able to steer the business. Key metrics such as annual contract value, churn rate, net retention rate, or customer lifetime value (CLV) are essential for evaluating customer retention and long-term profitability.

- Recurring Revenue Financial Models: Moving to recurring services revenue streams require companies to adopt specific accounting practices – typically aligning with IFRS 15 or ASC606 standards. This means significant changes in the revenue recognition process.

- Profitability Analysis: Specific profitability analysis to address the desynchronization between revenue flows and cost flows is needed, a common characteristic in subscription businesses. This involves closely monitoring the cost of customer acquisition (CAC) and comparing it against the long-term revenue generated by each customer cohort. Time-cohort analyses for instance become crucial in this context, as they help in understanding the value of customers acquired at different times, enabling more informed strategic decisions about marketing spend, resource allocation, and overall business sustainability in the subscription model.

- Cash Flow Management: Finance teams will need to accommodate the unique cash flow characteristics, especially due to the initial lag in revenue realization relative to costs. This involves securing adequate financing planning and funding to cover upfront customer acquisition costs and cost to serve until the recurring revenue streams reach a stable and sustainable level. This is especially important for subscription offerings that include physical products at their core.

6. Customer support and service

- Effective Onboarding and Activation Processes: robust onboarding processes is key to ensure a smooth introduction of new customers to the subscription service and its value. This step is crucial for initial customer engagement and understanding of the service's value, preventing early stage churn. Onboarding serves as the foundation for customer satisfaction and long-term relationship building, setting the stage for subsequent customer success interactions.

- Leveraging Customer Feedback for Improvement: Ongoing Support and Satisfaction Models: more than ever, customer service strategies need to focus on continuous support and engagement, aiming to enhance overall customer satisfaction and foster long-term relationships. This also means actively use customer feedback as an important source to inform and drive iterative improvements in products or services. This is critical to prevent churn and identify expansion opportunities

- Role of Customer Success Managers: Customer success, a recent function especially visible in the software as a service world, transcends traditional customer service by proactively guiding customers to achieve their desired outcomes with a product or service, thereby ensuring not just satisfaction but also the realization of value from their subscription.

7. Digital operations and IT

- Enhanced Digital Customer Experience: Optimizing digital touchpoints, including websites, mobile apps, and customer portals, is crucial for providing an engaging and intuitive subscriber experience. This enhancement aids in retaining subscribers by ensuring easy access to services and information.

- Robust Subscription Management: Implementing a comprehensive digital infrastructure is essential for efficiently managing the inherent flexibility and complexity of subscription businesses – especially in terms of order-to-revenue process. This infrastructure supports the seamless operation across the subscription life cycle, typically including offer definition, sign-up, up/cross-down-sells, renewal, ensuring accuracy and convenience. The infrastructure also need to tackle the resulting, more volumetric, and complex back-office operations: recurring invoices (e.g. usage tracking and rating, prorations over subscription changes, etc.), digital recurring payments and collections, specific revenue recognition rules, dedicated subscription metrics, provisioning/deprovisioning of services, etc.

- Rigorous Cybersecurity and Data Privacy: In a subscription's digital-first environment, prioritizing cybersecurity and strengthening data privacy measures is imperative. Protecting customer data not only fosters trust but also aligns with regulatory compliance, safeguarding the business and its customers from potential digital threats.

As a summary, the transformation to a subscription-based business model represents a comprehensive shift across all functional areas, requiring meticulous planning and execution. Crucially, such an extensive organizational change necessitates robust support from Human Resources and effective change management practices. HR plays a pivotal role in facilitating this transition, aligning the workforce with new objectives, organizing training across functions to acquire new skills, hire new external skills, or fostering a culture adaptable to the subscription economy. Effective change management ensures that these functional transformations are smoothly integrated into the organization, minimizing disruption and maximizing the potential for success. This integrated approach, combining functional transformation with strong HR and change management support, is essential for businesses to thrive and maintain a competitive edge in the dynamic landscape of subscription-based models. This is also why such transition rarely happens overnight or as a big bang, as we will discuss in the next section.

Pricing/packaging/monetization spotlight: three data-driven insights

Previously, we noted that the subscription economy revolutionizes the approaches to pricing, packaging, and monetization. In this spotlight, we present a curated selection of three data-driven insights that reveal the uniqueness of best practices[14] – which are crucial ingredients for success. Many of these recommendations may feel familiar based on your user experience with subscription leaders such as Netflix, Box, Zoom, or Hubspot. Remember, in the subscription economy, you will charge your customer on a recurring basis – hence, any mistake is a recurring mistake. As a result, every minute spent on the matter is a minute well spent, regardless of your use case or industry.

1) **Packaging, first, price point, second**: in transactional product pricing, there is one price point for a given product – or "SKU". In the world of subscription, there is an infinite number of ways to "package" offers by combining your offer features together. For example, you can package your offer based on personas such as LinkedIn, based on depth or maturity using good/better/best such as Zoom or Netflix, or build-your-own approach for Amazon Web Services. You can also define add-ons or options to complement your core package. In short, packaging becomes a vital step to be nailed and aligned with your customer (re)-segment, way before even thinking of price points. In fact, experiences across B2C and B2B have shown that successful subscription offer repackaging often leads to double digit impacts on revenue!

2) **Pricing metrics almost always beats "flat" pricing**: once you've designed your package, it is not yet the time to define your price point. In fact, in the world of subscription, it is often highly recommended to define pricing metrics. A pricing metric can be declarative, such as a "number of users"/"number of contacts" or metered such as a "number of miles driven"/"number of AI responses". Defining a price metric is crucial to support monetization by correlating price with customer value perception and delivery. Essentially, a well-chosen price metric enhances customer satisfaction and business growth by making the cost-value equation clear and equitable. In fact, B2B companies with predominantly metric-based recurring pricing tend to grow 30% faster than companies that predominantly use flat recurring pricing.

3) **Putting subscribers in the drivers' seat rhymes with growth**: it has become a common practice to provide subscribers with an easy way to adjust their subscriptions, to upgrade, downgrade, suspend, or cancel with clear conditions to opt out. Such customer-centric flexibility allows them to find the right fit, places them in control, directly impact satisfaction and loyalty. Such "rightselling" mindset not only accommodates changing needs but also strategically enhances customer lifetime value by offering alternatives to outright cancellation. As a matter fact, the Subscribed Institute data, for example, shows that suspension allows to retain one subscriber out of six. What's more, the number of changes per subscription directly correlates with growth: the Subscribed Institute noted that companies that let their customers make changes to their subscriptions after the initial sign-up grow up to three times faster than peers that don't. It means that pricing/packaging in the realm of subscription becomes dynamic and relationship-centered, taking into account the monetization potential across the entire subscriber lifetime value, as compared to a static "point-in-time" product pricing.

6.   ROAD MAP TO TRANSFORM: ZUORA'S JOURNEY TO USERSHIP

Moving towards subscriptions requires a big transformation, which as mentioned earlier, does not happen overnight. Zuora's "Journey to Usership" is a simple yet powerful road map guiding businesses through the transition to a subscription model. It encompasses four key stages – Launch, Iterate, Scale, and Lead – each characterized by specific focus areas and objectives. The framework also emphasizes five critical business skills or focus areas that span across these stages, ensuring a holistic approach to subscription management. The five business skills – offering design, subscriber experience, operational execution, financial management, and technology infrastructure – play a pivotal role by ensuring a balanced approach catering to both customer needs and business sustainability. Here is a very high level summary of each stage and these cross-cutting skills:

1.   **Launch**: This stage is about introducing the subscription offering to the market. It's a time of exploration and establishing the initial customer base.

     Key activities include defining the value proposition, setting up basic operational and financial structures, and acquiring the first customers.

     Focus is on "Offering Design" to ensure the product or service meets market needs and "Subscriber Acquisition" to start building the customer base.

     The framework provides best practices for market analysis and initial customer engagement and cautions against overextending resources.

2.   **Iterate**: The Iterate stage involves refining the offering based on customer feedback and performance data. Emphasis is placed on enhancing "Subscriber Experience" and continuously improving "Operational Execution". This stage is crucial for increasing customer satisfaction, retention, and optimizing internal processes. It is important also during that stage to be responsive to customer feedback and to avoid stagnation in service offerings.

3.   **Scale**: In the Scale stage, the focus shifts, broadening the service portfolio, expanding the customer base through cross and up-sells, and entering new markets. "Financial Management" becomes critical as businesses need to handle increased revenue streams, investments, and increase its reporting scrutiny. Scaling up "Technology Infrastructure" to support growth is also a key aspect. It is advised during that stage to build for sustainable growth while warning against unchecked expansion that could strain resources and dilute customer experience.

4.   **Lead**: The final stage, Lead, is about establishing market leadership and influencing industry trends. Here, "Innovation" is paramount to stay ahead in the market, along with maintaining strong "Subscriber Relationships" for sustained growth. Businesses focus on setting industry standards and exploring new business opportunities. It creates a need for continuous innovation while cautioning against complacency that can arise from market dominance.

Each of these stages encapsulates a distinct phase in the journey towards a successful subscription business, highlighting the evolutionary nature of the model. The journey is characterized by a continuous process of development, adjustment, and growth, with each stage building upon the successes and lessons of the previous one. The "Journey to Usership" serves as a guide, providing best practices and highlighting potential pitfalls at each stage, helping businesses navigate the complexities of the subscription model and achieve long-term success.

Finally, in the transition from traditional transactional models to subscription-based models, it is most of the time advantageous to operate the initial "Launch" and "Iterate" phases through a dedicated business unit or separate entity. It provides a sandbox environment where new subscription offerings can be developed, tested, and refined leveraging agile response to market feedback. This approach also ensures limited constraints of existing business structures and processes, while minimizing disruption in the core business.

Spotlight: TSIA's "Swallowing the fish"

Coined by TSIA, "Swallowing the fish" is a metaphor that describes the financial trajectory businesses often encounter when transitioning to a subscription model. Originally witnessed in subscription SaaS (software as a service) models, where a company initially faces a period of lower profits or increased investments before realizing long-term gains. This metaphorical expression visualizes the company's revenue and profit curve, which dips initially – representing the fish's open mouth. Initially, the shift incurs significant upfront costs in customer acquisition, infrastructure, and product development, leading to a dip in the profit curve – akin to a fish's open mouth. Meanwhile, the spread of subscription revenues over time contrasts sharply with the immediate returns from traditional sales. However, as the subscription model stabilizes, recurring revenue begins to stack up, to then exceed the initial costs, leading the curve to rise and form the tail of the fish, ultimately resulting in sustained profitability.

This trajectory underscores the necessity for strategic patience and planning. Businesses like PTC and Autodesk exemplify how embracing this multiyear strategic transformation, ranging typically from three to six years, can pave the way for long-term success. As compared to software as a service or "pure" digital services, the shift towards subscription models with integrated hardware components becomes exponentially more challenging. Indeed, companies may not be able to infinitely stretch their balance sheet or working capital on behalf of their clients to hold the "servitized" assets nor finance it. However, the emergence of innovative financing solutions, especially in the equipment/product as a service space amid tightening credit conditions, offers a way forward. Initiatives like those from BNP Paribas Leasing Solutions, which provide flexible, usage-based financing options, are indicative of the evolving landscape to support these business models.

7. THE SUBSCRIPTION ECONOMY IS BIG, GETTING EVEN BIGGER WHILE ENTERING A NEW ERA

Let's summarize our key takeaways so far:

- The subscription economy, despite regional nuances, is a massive force within the global economy.

- Its current "modern" form started less than two decades ago, and it managed to completely transform industries.

- It is making its way into more and more use cases and industries, fueled by market trends, technological advancements, societal transformations, and the shift towards sustainable models.

- The core tenet of the Subscription Economy is to be obsessed with subscriber-centricity, and as such, grounding its growth objectives on customer lifetime value.

- Similarly to any well designed business model, a subscription offer should always start from the customer and the associated problem(s) you want to solve, and not starting from internal considerations.

- However and once done, it is key to define and hierarchize your strategic priorities as subscription models can take very different shapes and forms.

- It is important to assess across your portfolio and pipeline of products which are the right candidates to become subscription offers.

- Implementing subscription offers will require a complex 360° change across functions – requiring new practices and capabilities for success.

- Such transformations typically do not tend to happen overnight but follow a progressive "journey", with different priorities and objectives to master at each step.

That being said, we can already witness that the subscription economy is progressively entering into a new era.

Here are three recent developments as well as potential predictions:

1.   The uncertain economic climate further exacerbates customer needs for flexibility. This is why we see an accelerated adoption of flexible contract terms, associated with so-called "hybrid" pricing models that combine together a recurring subscription commitment with a consumption/usage-based pricing model. Such approaches lower buying frictions, risk perception, ultimately improving accessibility. In the SaaS space, 46% of companies have adopted either usage-based pricing or a hybrid model.[15] According to research by the Subscribed Institute in partnership with the Boston Consulting Group,[16] the hybrid model is starting to make its way across other industries as well, with an increase in adoption from 9% to 26% over the last three years.

2.   The subscription economy is the dominant paradigm and has become the new normal in many industries, such as SaaS or media. In some instances, we are reaching levels of market saturation, which forces subscription businesses to go even further when it comes to maximizing every single subscriber relationship. As a response to this, the most advanced companies are orchestrating personalized journeys for a subscriber, that is, unique based on dynamic profiling and rules – but also decide which potential subscribers to target or not based on predictive lifetime value modeling. Also, at each relevant step of the journey, they create dynamic packages and pricing. The most advanced companies in that field are media companies.[17] This is made possible and will improve in the future by leveraging data-driven approaches combined with AI. It will essentially get closer to the promise of "segment of 1", through "subscriber journey of 1" and "subscriber offer of 1" made possible thanks to the richness of the subscription economy!

3.   Finally, the subscription economy will continue its acceleration across new and existing industries, reaching further levels of maturity. This also means even more subscription offers. A direct logical consequence would be a movement of market consolidation that can take many different and combinable directions. A first direction, through the advent of subscription aggregators, that would act as one-stop-shop marketplaces for subscription offers with pre-negotiated rates for a given industry, use cases, etc. Several telecom operators or banks are already playing such a role today in the entertainment, home security, or cybersecurity space for instance. A second direction, with subscription bundlers that directly aggregate relevant offers in packages. For example, Canal+, the leading pay-TV company in France and a European leader in the production and distribution of content, has launched packaged offerings including its own channels bundled with Netflix, Disney+, DAZN, AppleTV+, etc. A third one, through extending partnerships between brands that could be from different industries sharing compatible brand DNAs within the same customer value constellation, reinforcing one another. The February 2024 announcement of a joint venture between ESPN, FOX, and Warner Bros. to build an innovative new platform to house a compelling streaming sports service is a good illustration, even though all participants in this case are from the same industry. Or a fourth one, through more traditional merger and acquisition moves.

One thing is sure: the subscription economy has a bright future. And as a pricing and packaging enthusiast, it is absolutely vital for you to build your "subscription muscle"!

SUMMARY

Subscription economy: revolutionizing business models

The chapter explores the transformative impact of the subscription economy, a concept popularized by Zuora CEO Tien Tzuo. This model has significantly altered various industries, leading to a profound change in traditional business practices.

Key points covered include the following:

- **Historical and Contemporary Trends**: Analyzing market trends to understand the rapid growth of the Subscription Economy.
- **Strategic Imperatives**: Highlighting the strategic changes required, including a shift in portfolio strategies and necessary organizational transformations.
- **Implementation Road Map**: Providing a detailed guide for businesses to successfully transition to a subscription-based model.
- **Ongoing Developments**: Discussing current and future trends within the subscription economy.

Additionally, the chapter features engaging case studies and in-depth discussions on pricing and packaging strategies, offering practical insights into successful implementation.

KEY INSIGHTS:

1. **Historical Context and Market Trends**: Understanding the evolution and growth trajectory of the subscription economy.
2. **Strategic Shifts**: Emphasizing the need for new strategies and organizational changes to thrive in this model.
3. **Practical Road Map**: Outlining steps for businesses to adopt and succeed with subscription-based models.
4. **Future Trends**: Analyzing ongoing developments to stay ahead in the subscription economy.

NOTES

1 "The Beginnings of Subscription Publication in the Seventeenth Century", 1931, Modern Philology, Sarah L. C. Clapp.
2 "Netflixisation: Vers une généralisation de l'économie de l'abonnement pour toutes les industries?", 2022, Faber Novel & Zuora
3 Excerpt from "How Inflation Can Unexpectedly Boost 'As-a-Service' Opex Models", February 2024, Subscribed Institute, Hoffmayer, Mansard
4 "End of Ownership", 2020 Report, Harris Poll & Zuora
5 "Recession-Proofing the Subscription Economy", August 2020, INSEAD Knowledge, Mansard, Ulaga
6 "Subscription Impact Report: COVID-19 Edition", 2020, Zuora
7 "The Subscription Economy Index", March 2023, Subscribed Institute
8 It's important to note here that there are powerful frameworks, such as the business model canvas, that can aid in the strategic design and analysis of business models. However, the focus of this chapter is not on these tools, but rather on the strategic implications and applications of subscription models.

9   These three plays are inspired by those found in "Reaping the Recurring Benefits of Industry 4.0", 2019, Zuora & Roland Berger, Cagin, Mansard[10] www.al-enterprise.com/en/solutions/collaboration-solutions

10 Such changes can drive material impacts for the company operations, financials, and risks. This will be addressed in the next section[11] www.al-enterprise.com/en/solutions/network-as-a-service[12] www.al-enterprise.com/en/solutions/purple-on-demand

11 "The Subscription Economy Index", March 2023, Subscribed Institute

12 "Who Owns Renewals and Upsells?", May 2023, Technology & Services Industry Association, Steve Frost

13 "Cost of Acquisition (CAC) Trap", May 2023, Elena Verna

14 Summarized extracts and selections from "12 Data-Driven Pricing and Monetization Strategies for B2B", Mansard, The Subscribed Institute

15 "The State of Usage-Based Pricing: 2nd Edition", 2023, OpenView

16 "How Consumption Models Contribute to Business Success", 2023, Subscribed Institute & BCG

17 "The New York Times: Creating the Essential Subscription", it is a good illustration of what a leading player is doing in 2023, video on demand on Zuora's Website

2

Pricing insights unlocked
The strategic shifts behind Philips Healthcare's success

Daniel Cho

I am Daniel Cho, the head of the Strategic Pricing Centre of Excellence from Philips. I started my career as a management consultant for PriceWaterhouse in Sydney shortly after I graduated as a computer scientist. I then moved on to work as a software engineer for a telecom company. I started my healthcare journey after I joined a distributor company for HP Medical selling medical equipment in HK. Selling with the consultative approach was easy (that was also my first experience of value-based selling; I focused on the outcome and not on the equipment and technology). HP asked me to join them as an account manager and later promoted me to become the sales development manager for the entire Asia Pacific (from China, Korea, down to Australia and NZ) mainly focusing on sales enablement, competitive intelligence, and capability development. There I learned a lot about competitive selling, competitive pricing, tendering, different reimbursement models, etc. Philips acquired HP Medical in 2002, and I have been working for Philips ever since. I was invited to join the headquarters of Patient Monitoring in Germany as a product manager back in 2004 and stayed in Germany until now. As a product manager, I learned how to conduct market research, host customer panels, write business cases, create need-based segmentation, and create solutions to serve them; had my first value-based pricing experience; and launched one of the most profitable healthcare products in Philips – the Intellivue X2 transport solution. I then moved on to become the head of Market Intelligence for the Patient Monitoring business and invested a lot of energy to build up our competitive intelligence network and platform. I also collected and distributed market size, market share, and customer insights to all marketing teams to support their work. My most memorable moment was to support the acquisition of Respironics (a 4B Euro+ acquisition). I was tasked to prove that we do not have a monopoly in both patient monitoring and ventilators in any of the EU States (I think 28 of them) within 48 hours. That was the longest 48 hours of my working life. The head of marketing met me taking some fresh air in the car park minutes after I delivered the report. She thought I was about to collapse. Forty-eight hours of no food and no sleep had become my own record. I later changed my role to support all launches of New Products and was responsible for training all salespeople to sell, both hard and soft skills, including competitive selling and consultative selling. I moved to pricing in 2012 for the Patient Care and Monitoring Solutions business (later becoming the connected care). I was asked to double-head the Diagnostic Imaging pricing leadership role and soon after was the head of the Strategic Pricing Centre of Excellence for the entire 13B Euro

DOI: 10.4324/9781003535966-4

global healthcare business. I graduated as a humble computer scientist, ending up leading pricing for a multinational company without any education background in business or marketing. My motto to young professionals is, do not put a box around yourself based on your education or ethnic background. We can be who we want to be if we keep learning and keep working towards it. Do not be trapped into a self-limiting belief. Most of the time you are better than you ever imagined.

To continue, I would like to share with you three short stories that hopefully can inspire your future work.

STORY ONE: THE POWER OF PRICING ANALYTICS

I was tasked to set up a pricing function in 2012 by the CFO of the Connected Care business (was called Patient Care and Monitoring Solutions at that time). I asked Toine, what do you need to achieve with that function? He paused for a good minute, and then he said, "I need to stop having surprises. I need to better predict how my margin will look like in six months, in a year, and how can I influence it if I am not happy with the forecast? I need to have visibility of how well we are doing and the transparency of where the leakages are, and once we know about it, there is someone ready to fix it".

So in a nutshell, he needed strong analytics to diagnose where the problems were located. He needed a process to take this diagnosis to someone who could derive a plan to fix it, and then he needed us to track if that fixing was working, then based on our ability to see the trend and believing the leakages are fixed, to provide the best possible forecast of how price will move and what margin he could expect.

I was given a modest budget to start this function and a 250K Euro investment for us to set up the analytics platform. We had selected a very powerful data visualization tool that we had already used for another purpose since 2008. So we have a ton of experience, and we quickly had it built up and started our analytics.

Toine had set up three KPIs to measure my work, which still drives everything that I do today. First was Price Realization, he needed to make sure the price I set was achievable by the markets. Second is Net Price Improvement at Order Intake, which is an average selling price improvement taking out the impact from configurations, cost of the configuration, and channel mix. Net Price Improvement is a great early indicator and the closest proxy to gross margin at Sales. Third is the Integral Gross Margin, which is the total margin we can get from both the factory and the market. IGM is the best indicator for EBITA or profit.

One of our biggest wins for pricing analytics was in 2016, when the CEO (Carla Kriwet) decided to turn around the business in India for the Patient Monitoring business. To help them to return to profit from a negative double-digit EBITA margin performance. Since I owned both pricing and IGM, I was tasked to lead this project. After a week of deep dive, we discovered that India did not have any pricing issues, their general price realization and margin were great in the majority of deals, but they have

Figure 2.1

The diagram shows the EBITA will return to positive just by removing small deals with big discounts. Minimum impact on total sales.

Initial scenario simulation of sample deals from 2015. What if we can take out the deals inside the red rectangle?

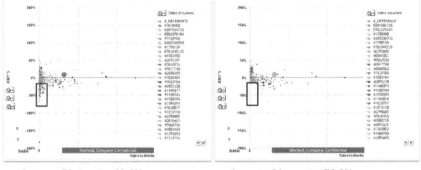

Average Discount = 69.4%   Average Discount = 70.0%
EBIT % = -3.3%   EBIT % = +3.2%

Figure 2.2

The discount behavior improvement after one year of intervention.

India Patient Monitoring Discount Distribution post-intervention. Significant reduction of discount above 70%.

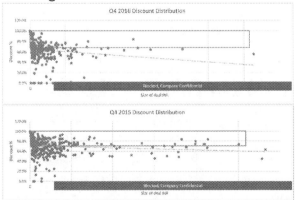

a clear discipline problem. They accepted too many small deals with big discounts, which pulled down their overall performance.

The actions we decided together were to change the target price of two products and create a policy that small deals do not get special discounts. Every quarter we create

Figure 2.3

An example of one product shows how the price was improved between the two years. Units were dropped by design; these units were shifted to a more profitable product.

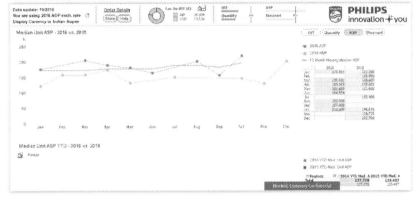

Product X Average Selling Pricing Development
2015 (grey) vs 2016 (blue) with 37% YoY improvement.

Figure 2.4

The slide shown was an actual review slide with the Indian team at the beginning of the project.

2016 Jan Deep Dive Action Review
Thank you for your active improvement

Jan Deep Dive Action	Status
Take out Suresigns off price list ASAP	Done
Improve Pricing for CM10 & CM100	Done
Improve Pricing for DFM100 & TC20, and try not to sell them in same order	Done
Try to limit discount for small deals (For example < 50,000 Euro)	No evidence
Try to simulate EBIT loss for large deal (For example >300K Euro)	No evidence
Please re-visit the Highend Intellivue Monitor	Done

Other Recommendation	Status
Better Product Positioning for the Efficia Product	No evidence
Fix Pricing Positioning for Intellivue MX400	Done

one new action, and we close one old action. And in 16 months, we managed to get them into a positive single-digit EBITA margin. They now know how to use analytics to create powerful actions, and to this day, they are still running at a healthy EBITA margin.

Few tips I like to give to people that want to start:

1) Never wait until the data is perfect. You will never get perfect data. It is better to develop a mechanism to filter out garbage data so you have clean data to drive your decisions. You do not need to have 100% data to get started. Work with whatever you have, as improvement within 20% today is much better than no improvements at all with 100% of your business.

2) It is much more important to understand the behavior that drives the leakage than the leakage itself. Just like the Indian example in the previous section. As you cannot influence a price easily, you can influence how a discount is being applied much easier and faster. I always start by looking at discount behavior, then try to understand why and if it is curable. Most of the time, it is just a matter of coaching and training.

3) Do not generate reports. No one will read your report, and no one will take action on your reports. If you are a doctor, do not just do an X-Ray; throw it at the patient and say to him, "You have cancer, very bad, you are likely to die in a year, good luck". This is how your internal team thinks when they receive your reports. "Yes, I know I am bad, but if I could fix it, I would have done it". My philosophy is, do not produce any report unless you are ready to provide a treatment. That means, you work with the internal teams on different treatment options and make sure actions are performed and impact is seen. Remember, I will say it again: do not create reports unless you are ready to treat the problem!

4) You need a tool that can provide you very high-level view and then allow you to drill down to the highest degree of details so you can dive into the real problems to be solved. Why high level first? As you would like to fix the 20% of problems that drive 80% of your leakages. These leakages may come from a market, a sales manager, a salesperson, a product line, a product, or options/ configuration of products. It can also come from a purchasing group, a customer, a deal, a contract, or a tender. It can be caused by inflation, competition, or changes in reimbursement or payment schemes. A price change can be observed and leakages detected, but treatment only comes when you find the root cause. So your analytics tool must give you the flexibility to look at your problem in many dimensions, for us, we can view our problems in over 40 dimensions on the same table and chart. This is the power of strong data visualization tools.

5) You cannot and should not solve world peace in one go. Focus on max one to two problems to be solved by each team you are working with. Give them clear guidelines of what actions they need to take (co-create this list with them so they are willing to own it), a maximum of between 3 to 5 actions. Less is more if you want to see impact because focus is what brings impact. Track their actions

and their results together, and show them their actions now bring the cure, and they are the heroes of their own success. Then celebrate like crazy once the target is reached. (Cancer-free celebration!)

6)   Never be a policeman in pricing. Showing red flags in front of executives and shaming your colleagues is not going to make you popular. Be the doctor and consultant that helps them to perform. Only show executives after they had fixed the problem and generated fantastic growth and margin. This will make you the most popular function in the company. When we worked with the Indian team, we only shared the interim results within the working team. But once the EBITA turned positive, we advertised it like crazy and shared it with all executive teams including the CEO herself.

STORY TWO: VALUE-BASED PRICING IN A HEALTHCARE B2B ENVIRONMENT

I have heard of value-based pricing from a dear colleague, Steve Pierson (who was the head of pricing for our Imaging Business at the time), and it fascinated me. I decided to invest a lot of time and energy to learn more about it, and eventually, I supported Steve in running internal training inside Philips. That was about the year 2010.

I decided to step up our effort once I became the leader in the Strategic Pricing Centre of Excellence in 2020, so I hired a very experienced value-based pricing consultant and trainer, Erica Cheng, from the European Pricing Platform. She helped me to build from scratch a training program, which trained within two years over 250 product managers and 50 other functional leaders on the concept and execution

Figure 2.5
The diagram shows a typical 12-hour training for product managers to learn how to apply value-based pricing to their innovations.

Product Manager Capability Development
Philips Value Based Pricing Training (4 x 3Hrs)

Value Assessment Day 1	Offer and Price Structure Development Day 2	Price Setting Day 3	Value Communication Day 4
• Value-based pricing in Product Development Lifecycle process • Value identification • Value Quantification • C-Sense example • Customer value case • Breakout Session	• Value validation • Apple Watch case study • Offer configuration • Breakout session • Price metrics • Price segmentation and fences	• Pricing setting • Pricing strategy • Testing & refinement and pricing over lifecycle • Breakout session • How value propositions evolve from VPC stage to launch	• Value communication best practice • 3 types of VB selling in B2B • Breakout session • Value Calculator • Value story • Wrap-up

of value-based pricing. The NPS score from the 250 product managers was 84%, which means with every ten trainees, eight of them will tell their other colleagues they must come and take the training. We literally sell the training like concert tickets. Whenever we open the registration in Philips University, we have 50% of the seats taken within the first hour, then all filled within four hours. This is the only training that we do not need to assign to any product managers, and they come lining up to take part.

I know a lot of companies struggle with value-based pricing, as it is not the easiest concept to learn, not to mention to implement. Many companies cannot differentiate between features, benefits, and values. They tend to stop at benefits and wonder why customers cannot perceive their values. In B2B, the strongest value driver is quantifiable economic value, which is the way your solution could help your customers achieve better financial results by helping them improve their revenues or reduce their costs. I can give you an example: we have a technology called Compressed Sense, which could reduce an MRI examination scanning time by as much as 50%. The feature is the AI algorithm that speeds up the scanning.

The benefit is a faster scanning. Most companies will stop at faster scanning and use that as value. Some customers are very intelligent, and they can link the faster scan to their own operations and work out their own economic values, but most cannot. There are many segments in the markets. Let's look at two typical groups. One that has a long waiting list. Each scan is reimbursed by the payor (insurance, or government). If we can shorten the scanning time, they can scan more patients in a day and get more revenue using the same resources. This has a strong ROI and can be easily quantified. For example, scanning two more patients a day $= 250\ Euro \times 2 = 500\ Euro \times 200$ working days $= 100K\ Euro$ a year $\times 8$ years of the useful life of the scanner €1 to €100. This is the quantifiable value you can

Figure 2.6
How compressed SENSE is driving value for customers.

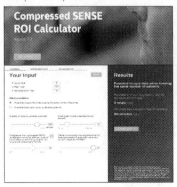
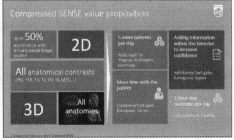

Communicate Value Drivers

Philips Compressed-SENSE Customer Facing Tools

deliver to your customers as compared to your competition or your older technology. The second customer has a fixed annual budget to treat all patients within the region. They do not have the budget or capacity to treat more patients. So faster scanning will only help them to reduce their workload. They can reduce costs by cutting down overtime salary and perhaps reducing energy costs due to shorter working days. It will have mainly cost savings instead of revenue improvement. Saving 1 hour a day for 2 operators $= 160$ Euro/day $\times 200$ days $= 32K \times 8$ Years $= 256K$. We can do a similar exercise with energy. But you can see the value perception of customer 2 is much less than customer 1, even using the same feature and having the same exact benefit. The ability to segment your customers into such categories by deeply understanding their operations and their KPIs is key to finding the best way to simulate and calculate the value you could deliver to them, and then link that value to your price.

Most companies also do not have any concept of what value drivers are available and struggle to find ways to communicate such values to their customers. I strongly recommend you define a strong but small list of value drivers, as less is more in communication.

Avoid overcommunication as that only confuses your customers. I always tell my internal teams that trying to solve all problems for all customers only makes your solution look like a Swiss army knife.

The Swiss army knife approach looks great but is never the perfect solution for a particular problem. Imagine cutting Japanese sashimi using a Swiss army knife. In B2B healthcare, Philips had decided to focus only on five value drivers: financial (improve revenue, reduce cost), operational (how to do more with less, reduce error, automate

Figure 2.7
These are the five value drivers Philips has adopted for value-based pricing and value communication.

Philips decided to focus on 5 Healthcare Value Drivers

Economic Value	How much can we help you save? How much can we help you earn?
Operational Value	How can we help you work more efficiently, reduce errors, and do more with less?
Clinical Value	How can we help you drive health outcome and improve clinical efficiency (e.g. first-time right diagnosis, first-time right treatment)?
Emotional Value	How can we help you make your work safer, feel satisfying?
Societal Value	How can we benefit the society as a whole (e.g. reduce carbon footprint, wastage, energy consumption)?

repeatable tasks), clinical (first-time-right diagnosis and treatment, earlier intervention and better outcome), emotional (cyber safe, patient satisfaction, staff experience, and not burnout), and sustainable (less energy, less waste, more recyclable). This helps us to have very sharp and precise communication with our customers.

STORY THREE: NEED-BASED SEGMENTATION

For the last story, you can see that the ability to differentiate customers on how they perceive your values is the cornerstone for value-based pricing. I dare to say that if you are not capable of segmenting your customers based on their needs and their KPIs, you will never be successful in B2B value-based pricing.

My segmentation story starts when Apple first launched its Apple Watch back in 2015. I literally bow to them with absolute respect. This is the ceiling of anyone in the world of pricing who could implement segment-based pricing to that perfection, and they managed to pull it off. It was a real-world miracle and still affects how I do things now in 2023.

Why was it so shocking? They managed to use a single technical development to serve three distinctive groups of customers and set three distinguished price levels that no one questioned. They are all happy to pay the allocated price, even when they are ridiculously different. Imagine, one watch with the same features, same user interface, same technology, and same cost to build, and the most expensive model was sold 50× the price of the lowest price model. This is the biggest price disparity I have ever seen for a single product.

It started with their immense focus on the customer's needs, and they segmented these needs into three major groups and served them with these three watch models.

This is what I believe how they designed and decided on the segmentation approach:

Figure 2.8
This is likely segmentation they had done planning for the launch.

Best Practice Value-based Pricing

Needs-based Segmentation

Fashion & Health	Personalization & Trend	Style, Superiority, Exclusivity
Needs: Conformance, part of the clan, fitness	Needs: To be respected, be part of an elite tier in society	Needs: To show wealth, and "I can afford what you cannot"
Market 1.2B units (95%) @ $349 - $1,000	Market 50M units (4%) @ $1,300 - $5,000	Market 12M units (top 1%) @ $5,500 – $15,000
Competitors swatch fitbit GARMIN	Competitors GUCCI TAG Heuer MONT BLANC	Competitors Cartier ROLEX OMEGA

And this is how they priced the models at the time of the launch:

With this approach, assuming they could only sell 1% of the Edition, 29% of the Watch, and the rest of the 70% of the Sport, then they could have achieved an ASP of $628, which is almost equal to the price of their iPhone 5, which was launched at the same time.

I referred this back to our own market and found that is also highly applicable to a healthcare B2B market. The difference in perceived value can allow us to operate on two segments with different pricing strategies.

Figure 2.9
This was the summary of their pricing during the initial launch.

Best Practice Value-based Pricing

The same product- 3 price levels

Figure 2.10

Best Practice Value-based Pricing

Clear Pricing Strategy - EDITION Skim for profit, SPORT shoot for volume and share

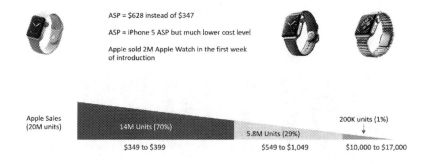

This is one example from Philips, which was selling the exact same technology development into two distinctive markets (in and outside of the Hospital). Notice the features, technology, and even cost are the same across the two models (with the exception of a low-cost plastic handle).

The difference in need between the In Hospital and Out of Hospital segment allows us to create two selling models (MP2 and X2) and carries a 15% price premium for the In Hospital model. That premium was successfully captured throughout the entire 12-year lifetime of the products. In fact, the product had zero price erosion for the first ten years due to the strong value it generated for the customers and only came down with the new platform X3 introduced during the last two years.

I keep stressing that segmentation should be based on need, and not demographics. Only need-based segmentation can group customers with similar perceived value together and that value perception is what drives their willingness to pay.

How can a company implement a need-based segmentation and value-based pricing culture? I do it by asking five simple questions to my product managers.

A lot of companies fall into the trap of asking customers what they want in the new products. First customers will tell them they want faster horses (read Henry Ford's quote if you do not know what I mean). Secondly, willingness to buy does not warrant willingness to pay. A classic example is I can convince 80% of the car drivers that the second car should be a Porsche as it is fun to drive and it looks so cool. I believe I will fail to convince 90% of them to pay 150,000 Euro for it. Having the customer agree this is what they want and not checking if they are willing to pay a lot for it is the reason why a lot of innovations failed.

Figure 2.11

This is the Philips example on segmentation. Same technology and product sold at a price difference of 15% based on delivering different value to each segment.

Philips Example:
One Transport Monitoring Solution Technology serves 2 Segments

Patient monitoring decided to put a fence between In-Hospital and Out-Hospital customers and drove a 15% price difference of same device. Sometimes it is necessary to create different product identifiers to make the fence simple to apply.

Out of Hospital Transport Segment:	In Hospital Transport Segment:
Ambulance, Helicopter, Military	Anesthesia, Imaging, Neonatal, OB
Customer needs: Rugged, Water/Dustproof, Long battery life, Certified for flying, Lightweight	Customer needs: Easy to disinfect, Easy to use, Efficient, Lightweight, Contain all major measurements
IntelliVue MP2 for Out of Hospital Transport	IntelliVue MMS X2 for In Hospital Transport

Price of X2 = MP2 + 15%

Figure 2.12

To be able to answer these five questions, the product managers must be deeply involved in solutions, segmentations, value propositions, pricing, and business models.

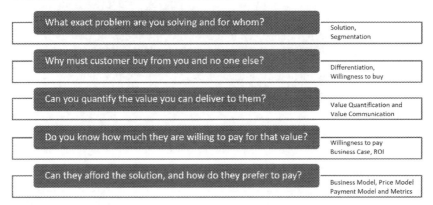

The second biggest challenge most companies face is their lack of understanding of their customers' KPIs, operation model, and revenue models. Most companies asked their customers what they wanted but failed to see how that solution linked to the operations of the customer, how it builds up revenue and reduces cost, how it reduces errors and risk, and how they help to improve throughput, yield, quality, etc. Not being able to link what you sell to the KPI of your customers risk communicating the wrong value messages to your customer. You have seen my example of out-of-hospital and in-hospital customers. If I share the value of the out-of-hospital to the in-hospital customers, they will not perceive it and will not agree to the 15% premium. I used this with my internal team: if you try to sell the highest quality Kobe beef to your vegetarian customers, you will not get the price you need.

The ability to serve the needs, able to link them to the KPIs of your customers, will make your B2B value-based pricing and selling a lot more successful. Last but not least, the key to value communication is to be credible (there is a reason for your customer to believe in your claims, that require customer testimony, white paper, actual clinical research, etc.), simple (less is more), quantified (saving life is good, but are you saving one life or 100, 1,000?. Saving cost is good, but are you saving $1K, $100K, $1M? These will give completely different perceived value to your customers and drive completely different prices. My experience is that if you claim something without the ability to quantify it, customers will treat it as zero value), and relevant (link to their KPIs).

I hope you enjoyed these three personal stories and were able to apply some of my learnings to your future work. Good luck!

Figure 2.13
Communication for success in the B2B world.

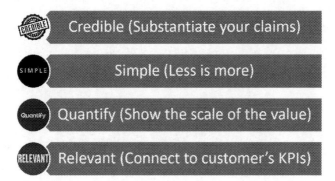

Communicate for success with B2B Value-Based Pricing

- Credible (Substantiate your claims)
- Simple (Less is more)
- Quantify (Show the scale of the value)
- Relevant (Connect to customer's KPIs)

SUMMARY

A Strategic Pricing Centre of Excellence (CoE) is a part of the company that helps to drive standardized processes, tools, and capabilities across all businesses. The main purpose of the CoE is to help businesses minimize the overall investments and delays of implementing world-class pricing and profit management capabilities.

In this segment of the book, three such capabilities were discussed:

1. The Power of Pricing Analytics

   o How a company can apply pricing analytics to tackle growth and profit challenges.

   o A case study on how to improve the EBITA margin for the Indian Patient Monitoring Business within 16 months.

   o How to focus on the behavior instead of the actual prices.

   o A few tips and advice that can advance the analytics for any company.

2. Value-Based Pricing in a Healthcare B2B Environment

   o Share a short story about how Philips started the journey of value-based pricing.

   o What a typical training would look like.

   o An example of the same technical products can generate a completely different value for different customer segments.

   o How the five value drivers that Philips is focused on for the B2B environment.

3. Need-Based Segmentation

o Gave an Apple Watch example of what a great need-based segmentation should look like and the impact in pricing and profit this can generate.

o How Philips applied the same learning and achieved similar results in the healthcare B2B space by focusing not on the technology and features but on how to drive customer values.

o Share a set of five questions to allow the product manager to place more focus on the customer's willingness to buy, willingness to pay, and ability to pay.

o Finally how to communicate for success in B2B using value-based pricing.

3

Revolutionizing revenue at Google
Advanced digital pricing models for SaaS and beyond
Mariusz Gasiewski

DIGITAL PRICING MODEL

Digital pricing models are a unique set of strategies used to price products and services delivered electronically or online. They differ from traditional pricing models in several ways, requiring careful consideration of factors like accessibility, data-driven insights, and dynamic adjustments. Digital technologies give totally different possibilities to adjust prices to different audiences and products.

Subscription model

The subscription model is a popular way for businesses to generate recurring revenue by providing ongoing access to a product or service for a regular fee. Instead of a one-time purchase, customers pay a subscription fee, often monthly or yearly, for continued use. This creates a predictable income stream for businesses and fosters long-term relationships with customers.

Whether the subscription model makes sense for your business depends on several factors, including your product or service, target audience, and business goals. Here are some key indicators that the subscription model could be a good fit:

- Provides ongoing value: Your product or service should offer ongoing benefits and updates that keep users coming back and justifying the recurring fee.

- High engagement potential: Users should have a reason to interact with your product or service regularly, creating a sense of dependence and value.

- Scalable and customizable: You should be able to offer different subscription tiers with varying features and benefits to cater to diverse customer needs.

- Digital or consumable: Subscriptions are well-suited for digital products or services that can be easily delivered and consumed repeatedly.

Often businesses have different types of subscription packages:

- weekly subscription
- monthly subscription

DOI: 10.4324/9781003535966-5

- quarterly subscription

- yearly subscription

Most often longer subscription plans are in case of products, services where after initial excitement, engagement there is potential decrease in usage of a service/product – that is why often language courses often focus on yearly packages. In other variations, longer subscriptions have much better price to value than shorter subscriptions – that is, yearly subscription has the same price as 5× monthly package.

In some cases subscriptions are designed to direct users to choose specific packages. By usage of contrast between packages, some packages have higher price-to-value than other packages (i.e. a package A has much higher value than package B and is just 20–50% more expensive).

Examples of subscription models:

- Media and entertainment: Streaming services like YouTube Premium, Netflix, Spotify, and Amazon Prime.

- Software and services: SaaS platforms like Slack, Norton Antivirus, and Dropbox.

- Fitness and health: Gym memberships, fitness apps, and wellness services.

In many use cases an important part of the subscription model is free trial.

A trial is a limited-time period where a potential customer can access the full features of a subscription-based product or service for free. The goal is to let them experience the value before committing to a paid plan.

Key characteristics of trials:

- Limited Duration: Trials usually last anywhere from a few days to a month.

- Full Functionality: Most trials provide the same experience as if you were a paying customer. This lets users try all the features of the service.

- Credit Card Requirement (Often): Many trials ask for credit card details upfront. This is to ensure smooth transitioning to a paid subscription if the user doesn't cancel before the trial ends.

- Automatic Renewal (Usually): Subscription services often automatically renew your subscription and charge your card when the trial ends unless you actively cancel.

Tiered pricing

Tiered pricing is about having different pricing plans with varying feature sets and price points cater to diverse customer needs and budgets. In some way it is a variation of a subscription model.

In tiered pricing we are providing multiple plans with varying price points and feature sets. This goes towards diverse customer needs and preferences, allowing users to choose the plan that best aligns with their usage requirements.

In some cases, packages can have huge difference in prices once they are created for different target groups that have totally different needs and different price sensitivity. Often the case is as follows:

- package for individual people vs packages for companies
- package for small business vs package for enterprise customers

This form of pricing is quite often met in software as a service (SaaS) products when it employs tiered pricing, with basic, standard, and premium plans offering different storage capacities, functionalities, and user access levels.

Freemium model

Freemium model offers a basic version of a product or service for free, with premium features available for a paid subscription. This is a good way to attract a large user base and convert a portion of them into paying customers.

That models works especially well in the following conditions:

- Once premium tier has strong value proposition. The freemium model focuses on convincing users to upgrade to the premium tier. This means the premium tier needs to offer a compelling value proposition that significantly enhances the user experience. Basic tier should be enough to feel the value of the product/service, although premium tier should give enough reason to upgrade to it. This could be through additional features, functionality, content, or other benefits that are highly desirable to a subset of users.

- The addressable market needs to be big. The freemium model works once we have ability to attract a large user base, from which a smaller percentage will convert to paying customers. This means freemium model works generally better for products or services with a broad target market and high potential user base.

- Marginal cost of providing the free tier needs to be low. The freemium model can become unsustainable if the cost of providing the free tier to each user is high. This is especially true if the conversion rate to premium is low. Having it in mind, it is essential to have a product or service where the marginal cost of adding a new free user is relatively low.

- There is a clear path to conversion. Freemium users need to understand the value proposition of the premium tier and how to upgrade easily. This means having a clear call to action, highlighting the benefits of upgrading, and making the upgrade process smooth and frictionless.

- Good value needs to be both in basic and premium package. Freemium products need to be engaging and provide a positive user experience for both free and paying users. This will encourage users to stick around and ultimately increase the likelihood of conversion.

- It works better once there are some network effects or data advantages. For some products, the value proposition increases as the user base grows. This can create a flywheel effect where a large free user base attracts more users, making the premium tier even more valuable. Additionally, data collected from free users can be valuable for improving the product and personalizing the user experience, further strengthening the overall offering.

DIFFERENCES BETWEEN FREEMIUM AND FREE TRIAL

Both freemium and free trials offer a powerful way to attract customers by giving them a taste of your product or service before they purchase. However, there are key distinctions:

- Duration: Freemium offers a basic version of the product indefinitely. In contrast, free trials provide full access to the product, but only for a limited time (e.g., one week, one month).

- Access: Free trials give users a chance to experience all (or most) of the product's features. Freemium models limit users to a core set of functionalities, encouraging upgrades for the full experience.

PAY-PER-USE

Pay-per-use charges customers based on their actual usage of a product or service.

Pay-per-use works in the following conditions.

- Once we have measurable usage. The PPU model relies on accurately tracking and billing for usage. This is only feasible if usage can be effectively measured, like minutes used on a phone call, data storage consumed, or copies printed.

- There is some variability in customer needs: When customers have predictable or widely varying usage patterns, pay-per-use can be fairer and more cost-effective than flat fees or subscriptions.

- There is a low marginal cost of additional usage. Once the cost of serving an additional user or usage unit is minimal, pay-per-use can be a sustainable way to scale and generate revenue.

Pay-per-use model is common for cloud computing services, data storage, and online transactions.

Landing pages created to introduce and show specific pricing packages often include techniques to demonstrate the value of the service/product.

AVOIDANCE OF CHOICE PARALYSIS

Too much choice creates a lot of confusion for users. A lot of research shows that information/techniques that help to choose the most appropriate option increase likelihood of decision/purchase.

One simple technique is to avoid too many options. Such cases focus on three, max four potential choices, packages (as mentioned previously usually for totally different audiences and really different for each other).

In some cases it helps to show which choice is the most popular, most often used by other users (see further chapter about social proof). Those techniques are used especially in cases when there is a business need to create quite many packages or when there are many differences between those options, so it is important to streamline the choice for those users who are not sure which offer suits their needs at the beginning

USING CONTRAST

The many researches show that users making specific choice about product/service, they try to compare it to each other to maximize the given value from it. That is the reason why quite effective way to optimize the value of a specific offer is to show it in contrast to something else.

There are many ways to achieve this, although the most common technique is to show an offer in comparison to another one that is just a little bit more expensive, although offering much more for that price.

SOCIAL PROOF

Social proof is a psychological concept where people tend to follow the actions and behaviors of others, particularly in situations where there's uncertainty. We assume that the decisions and behaviors of the majority reflect the correct approach.

Types of social proof in marketing

- Testimonials and Reviews: Positive reviews from customers are powerful tools of persuasion and are often used in landing pages.

- Expert Endorsements: Recommendations from industry experts or authority figures build credibility.

- "Wisdom of the Crowd": Displaying metrics like social media follower counts, number of customers served, or product sales figures demonstrates popularity.

- Case Studies: Success stories highlighting how a product or service has helped others solve problems.

Pricing experiments

Combination of global business (available in many countries) with digital characteristics of specific service or product (when marginal cost of additional units in the offer can be very low) brings a lot of opportunities in testing of prices for the same offer or for different offers. In some cases lowering the price can improve significantly the conversion rate of users to payers so final revenue can be higher than in case of higher price.

Digital tools allow for testing of prices in different environments. It is valid especially for digital products and services. Those tests have a form of A/B testing where half of the audience gets price A, half of the audience gets the price B, when comparing sales volumes with margins allows to establish a good price floor for the product/service.

Now there are many tools that allow such price testing (i.e. free Firebase that via Remote Config testing can help to test prices for apps).

HAMBURGER INDEX

As more and more businesses operate with fully digital products and services, then setting the prices of those products and services for different locations is getting much more important than in the past.

This is an informal way of comparing the cost of living in different cities by looking at the price of a Big Mac burger from McDonald's. The idea is that the price of a Big Mac is based on the cost of living in specific places. So if a Big Mac costs the same in two different cities, then the cost of living should be roughly equivalent. While not a perfect measure, it can give a general sense of relative prices between locations.

How it works

- Price Comparison: The Economist compares the price of a Big Mac in different countries, converting local prices into US dollars using the prevailing exchange rate.

- Implied Exchange Rate: They divide the price of a Big Mac in a foreign country by the price in the US. This gives an "implied exchange rate".

- Over/Undervaluation: Comparing this implied exchange rate to the actual exchange rate helps determine if a currency might be overvalued (Big Mac is more expensive abroad) or undervalued (Big Mac is cheaper abroad) relative to the US dollar.

SUMMARY

A digital pricing model is a strategy businesses use to determine the value of a digital product and set a price that resonates with customers. It encompasses the core structure defining how businesses charge for their digital goods.

Several factors influence the choice of a digital pricing model, including production costs, perceived value, market competition, target audience, and the product's unique features. Popular digital pricing models include the following:

- Cost-Based Pricing: Setting the price based on production costs plus a profit margin.

- Value-Based Pricing: Pricing based on the perceived value the product offers to customers.

- One-Time Fee: Customers pay a single price for lifetime access.

- Subscription Pricing: Customers pay a recurring fee for continued access.

- Tiered Pricing: Offering different product tiers with varying features and prices.

- Freemium Pricing: Providing a basic version for free, with premium features requiring payment.

- Pay What You Want (PWYW): Customers choose the price they're willing to pay.

- Product Bundling: Combining multiple products for a single price.

The ideal pricing model depends on the specific product, target audience, and overall business goals. It's essential to experiment with different models to find the one that maximizes revenue while maintaining customer satisfaction.

4

How to win with SaaS pricing
The case of Workday

Dawid Pawlak

Hey, my name is Dawid Pawlak, and I've been working in pricing for over six years. During this time, I have worked in both revenue management consulting and in SaaS business. In consulting, I have spent many days and hours working with SaaS companies to help them understand the real value of their products. Currently, I work in value management at Workday, one of the most successful SaaS companies in the world that serves over 50% of the Fortune 500 companies.

In this text, I will share insights on how companies leverage value argumentation in subscription models. The methods described later are applicable in both B2B and B2C market, but the level of the involvement may differ depending on the companies' business models and complexity of the products. As a practitioner, I will provide ideas on implementing pricing processes and gathering the pricing data from your customers. Then, I will show you how you can convert it into realized ROI to build value-based pricing in your organization.

Let's focus on a customer base. The power of the retention and uplift in the SaaS business is often diminished in comparison to new customer acquisition. But in fact, the pricing power here may have a much greater impact. Based on research provided by Price Intelligently (Paddle), a 1% improvement there is 2× to 4× more impactful on the company profit.

In this text, I will share some simple ways to measure your product value for selected customers. This knowledge will help you reevaluate product prices for both existing and net new customers, driving your company's growth. But first, let's establish some definitions to clarify most common terms of subscription KPIs that we are fighting for. If you are familiar with subscription businesses, the following definitions and KPIs will be obvious to you (feel free to skip this paragraph). However, I feel I need to start with them to make the whole story digestible and understandable for everyone.

- LTV (Customer Lifetime Value) represents the predicted net profit a company expects to earn from a customer throughout their entire relationship. It helps businesses understand the long-term value each customer brings.

- CAC (Customer Acquisition Cost) is the total cost a business incurs to acquire a new customer. It includes marketing, advertising, and sales expenses. A lower CAC is generally favorable, indicating efficiency in customer acquisition.

DOI: 10.4324/9781003535966-6

- ARPU (Average Revenue per User) is the average amount of revenue a company generates from each customer or user. It is calculated by dividing total revenue by the number of users. ARPU is a key metric for assessing the financial performance of a customer base.

- Net Churn refers to the overall loss or gain in revenue from existing customers due to cancellations, downgrades, and upgrades. A negative net churn indicates that the expansion revenue from existing customers exceeds the lost revenue.

- Gross Retention Rate measures the percentage of revenue retained from existing customers over a specific period, excluding any new sales or expansion revenue. It provides insights into customer loyalty and the ability to maintain revenue from the existing customer base.

- Net Retention Rate is a metric that measures the overall change in revenue from existing customers over a specific period, considering not only the revenue retained from existing customers but also any expansion revenue, upsells, or cross-sells. It is expressed as a percentage and helps businesses assess their ability to grow revenue within their current customer base, accounting for both retention and expansion efforts. A positive net retention rate indicates revenue growth from existing customers, while a negative rate suggests a decline.

All these metrics are taken into consideration while setting pricing in the company. The golden rule for profit maximization in SaaS companies is to maximize LTV while minimizing CAC. The longer your customers stay with you, the LTV grows. Focus on your customer base. When they do not see the value of your product, they resign from it, leading to higher churn or diminishing the price during renewal processes. Our goal for today is to find ways to have customers renew the contract at a higher price and acquire new products/features to the existing contract increasing net retention rate.

UTILIZING DATA TO DRIVE CUSTOMER VALUE

Many experts say that the power of the subscription model is the data that you can get. You can gather many metrics, including product usage, to understand customer behavior. On one hand, you can utilize the data to find patterns and segment customers. On the other hand, finding and delivering value to the end users and decision-makers may be more challenging.

Once customers start using a new product and enjoy it, they often take its value for granted and forget the impact of the solution. After signing the contract and fully implementing your solutions, they may forget why they considered changing their provider or finding an initial product to solve their challenges. That is why, when you agree with your customer on some price based on their perceived value of your product (or price list) and seal the deal, you should start working on increasing the WTP (willingness to pay) before next renewal process.

To achieve this, revisit the sales process and understand the reasons behind selecting your product. If you are selling the product with a substantial price, the sales process will look slightly different then selling an off-the-shelf product. In the first case, to close the deal, you will have multiple strategy sessions, demos, and a lot of mundane tug-of-war with legal and procurement to set all the contract formalities. Not to mention any hectic discussions around the price and product scope. To convince the potential prospect to spend some money (put the price of your product here), you and your team will have to convince the potential users and present them with all the perks and features of your solution. Then, they will have to do the same to their managers, who will agree to spend some part of the company budget to purchase your solution. So the sales team will have to prepare the fundamentals for price justification and make the purchasing team ready to prepare their own internal business case for their superiors (or use the one that your sales team prepared for them).

Once the subscription fees start flowing into your bank account, you can begin working on the uplift in the next phase. The whole process takes five steps, and I can promise you that it is simple, but not easy.

Step 1: Know the Customer Situation Before Implementing Your Product (Status Quo Assessment)
Step 2: Implement the Product and Drive Adoption
Step 3: Reassess Company Changes and Your Product/Solution Value to the Company
Step 4: Make Product Users Your Brand Ambassadors to Close the Renew Process
Step 5: Create Benchmarking and Customer Proof Points to Acquire New Customers

Figure 4.1
Process of increasing the willingness to pay in SaaS.

STEP 1: ASSESS THE STATUS QUO

To understand the value your product brings to customers, initiate the process by evaluating their current situation. There are various methods to acquire this data. I recommend creating a universal survey that customers can complete before product deployment. Once the contract is signed, there is no reason for the customer to hide dissatisfaction with the previous solution or withhold responses. The project success is the common goal for both you and customer.

To collect the data, you may not need any sophistication solutions. Simple tools like Google Forms may be all you need. Once you identify the value in this process, explore other vendors that offer superior customization and automation for surveys.

The survey should include the single-choice grids (such as assessing the product service of your vendor or agreeing with statements on product features) with the scale (e.g. 1–10 or Agree/Disagree etc.). Additionally, incorporate open-ended questions where you can inquire about specific numbers (e.g. the amount spent on external consultants to address the same problem or number of hours needed to do something manually). Focus the open-ended questions on quantifiable aspects, as qualitative feedback is challenging to be gathered and compared efficiently. Consider including an extra open text field for general comments.

STEP 2: IMPLEMENT THE PRODUCT TO DRIVE ADOPTION

Once you have the baseline assessment, delve deeper into it. Concentrate on aspects that are crucial for each specific customer. It's possible that the product from previous vendor lacked certain features or the customer struggled to use them effectively. In such cases, the focus should shift towards the proper implementation of solutions and providing adequate training.

Alternatively, if customer service was inadequate, it may indicate the need for more frequent communication with them compared to other customers. The key here is to utilize the collected data to ensure that your customers implement the solution correctly. You do not want to miss the chance to realize the value of your product at the start.

A founder of a SaaS company once shared with me that pricing should encourage usage rather than limit it, fostering a habit of using your product. This concept can be extended to the product itself, emphasizing that proper implementation is pivotal for customer satisfaction. Therefore, it is crucial to ensure that both the product and implementation team exert every effort to successfully onboard new users.

STEP 3: PROVIDE CUSTOMER WITH VALUE REALIZED (ROI) CALCULATION

Once the product is fully implemented, and the customer is actively using it, that is the perfect time to reassess the survey conducted in Step 1. This reassessment allows us to measure progress in various criteria and quantify the value delivered by the new product or service. Single-choice questions can be employed to convey qualitative changes, while open-ended questions are ideal for capturing numerical changes that can be readily translated into delivered value.

After completing the survey, I recommend complementing the value assessment process with personal interviews and one-on-one meetings with the product users. This approach provides a deeper understanding of customer needs and the journey they have undertaken up to this point.

Utilizing the survey data yields initial impressions that not only provide information on what has changed but also offer insights into how and why. That can help you to measure common success with the user with the quantification of benefits. For example, survey data and subsequent meetings may reveal that your solution is saving 25% of time for four Full-Time Equivalents (FTEs). This translates to saving one FTE in the department, representing a cost savings of X USD/EUR/GBP, which should be considered as a burden rate for the company, eliminating the need for additional hiring or allowing to do extra things within the same team.

In certain instances, direct efficiency data may be lacking, but the scope of work changes with the new solution. Customers may shift their focus from manual tasks to leveraging the data provided by your solution for more strategic work, thereby significantly impacting the company's success. Some features of your product might expedite solving business challenges or enhance the efficiency of provided solutions (e.g. CRM solutions simplifying information flow among sellers and management, accelerating deal closures, and shortening and improving discussions with sales leaders). These benefits can be easily calculated once you have baseline data.

It's important to note that not all benefits need to be quantified. In fact, in most cases, it is beneficial to include value drivers that are easy to understand but challenging to quantify as additional drivers without numerical values. From a behavioral standpoint, these can be perceived as providing more value than they might in reality.

STEP 4: MAKE CUSTOMERS YOUR AMBASSADORS

Once the collected data enables the creation of the ROI report, you can focus on presenting compelling arguments to help customers understand the value of your products. Utilize the usage data you are collecting to illustrate how your product is an integral part of their lives. A prime example is Spotify, which provides users with a personalized "Spotify Wrapped" at the end of each year. This feature not only showcases favorite artists and songs but also reveals the time spent using the app. When users see the significant hours invested, paying the subscription fee becomes a rational decision rather than a cost that could easily be canceled.

A similar approach applies to B2B subscriptions. Making the adoption of your product a key metric for your business is crucial. High adoption not only increases awareness of the product's value but also raises the alternative cost of change, making the renewal process more straightforward. The next step is to highlight all the benefits of your solution, emphasizing the value it creates for the business. It's essential not just to focus on WHAT the product provides but to combine it with WHY it matters and HOW it delivers value for the company.

Delivering these arguments to the product users is the great way to transform them into your brand evangelists. It's important to remember that selling your product to technical experts doesn't necessarily mean they can easily convey its value to procurement and boards. While they excel in answering feature-related questions, they may struggle to explain the solution's value and defend prolonging contracts without additional discounts or at a higher cost.

This often means you'll be asked to support them in presenting the value realization report or provide training on how to do it effectively. If the product is used within a department to streamline processes, it can also serve as an evaluation of their work. Through your partnership, you enable them to shine with extraordinary results that went hand in hand with your solution. This empowerment may provide additional leverage to expand existing partnerships in innovative ways (such as adding new features/products) or extend your company's products to other departments with a smoother acceptance process from the company board and procurement.

When presented with significant expenditure, each CFO questions whether it is truly necessary, if it can be replaced, or why there is little to no discount. Preparing product users to showcase the business case as a joint success story with reliable ROI calculations based on real data makes the uplift process smoother and maintains margins at a higher level.

STEP 5: CREATE BENCHMARKS TO ATTRACT NEW CUSTOMERS

Don't limit your data collection to the renewal process; instead, utilize the framework provided for calculating value to its full extent. Use it to establish internal benchmarks and customer proof points. Leverage survey data to illustrate the average improvement within your product across multiple areas. Quote your customers to gather success stories that align with the value of your product, featuring their logos. Encourage customers who have become brand ambassadors to participate in conferences, sharing their journey with your product and its transformative impact on their businesses. They can also serve as points of contact for prospective customers seeking references from actual users.

Remember to seek permission from customers before using their logos with quotes and sharing elements of the created ROI report publicly. Keep in mind that not all customers may be eager to share their stories publicly or be featured in marketing materials. In such cases, be prepared to explain the approval process for publishing the report officially. If needed, anonymize certain metrics (for example create a report without the value quantification of your product for a customer and focus just on the general improvement) or conceal customer logos to address privacy concerns. Next, you can find an example of how Devskiller, solution for staffing, talent management and engineering teams effectively utilizes benchmarks and quotes in its sales materials.

Figure 4.2

What our customers say

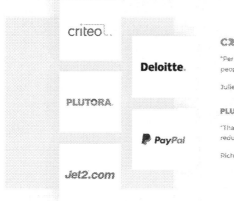

CRITEO ★★★★★

"Per hire, we've saved 2-4 days which is significant as we hire 100 people with DevSkiller every year."

Julien Gauthiez   Talent Acquisition Manager EMEA

PLUTORA ★★★★★

"Thanks to automating the screening stage, we were able to reduce the interview rate by 50%."

Richard Williams   VP of Engineering

Figure 4.3

CRITEO

IT & Solutions · Enterprise · Europe

Retargeting & internet advertising leader Criteo saves 200-400 days of work annually with DevSkiller

- **100** technical professionals hired annually with DevSkiller
- **2-4 days** saved per each hire
- **Only 3.5** developers interviewed in-person to make one hire

(READ THE FULL STORY ▷)

CONCLUSION

In the world of SaaS, it's crucial to understand and optimize your product's value for lasting success. As we've explored, the interplay of pricing processes, customer metrics, and strategic sales steps can significantly impact your bottom line.

This time, we've explored the complexities of assessing product value, driving adoption, calculating ROI, and transforming customers into brand ambassadors. Each step, from understanding the status quo to creating benchmarks, plays a crucial role in fortifying your value positioning in the competitive SaaS landscape.

Remember, the key to sustained growth lies in the synergy of your sales team, pricing/value management, and product team. By adopting the outlined framework, you empower your organization to not only meet but exceed customer expectations.

As you embark on this path, leverage the data collected not only for renewals but also as a strategic tool. Create internal benchmarks, craft compelling customer success stories, and showcase the tangible impact of your product. This not only facilitates the renewal process but becomes a powerful tool for acquiring new business.

In the ever-evolving SaaS landscape, the willingness to pay is a reflection of the perceived value your product brings to the table. Embrace the process, adapt to customer needs, and continuously refine your approach to maximize the value and the profit.

5

Clicks, cookies, and campaigns
Navigating digital ad spaces at Google
Michał Wiczkowski

PROGRAMMATIC: A BETTER WAY TO ADVERTISE

Imagine that Coca-Cola is planning to launch a new diet soft drink. It needs advertising to build awareness and convince people to buy its new product.

Before the emergence of the Internet, advertising largely revolved around traditional mediums: print, television, radio, and outdoor billboards. Ad buying was a complex dance of negotiation, long-term commitments, and manual placements.

So what did the Coca-Cola marketing team do? Once they had the ads developed, they had to predict which TV shows, radio segments, or print media would reach their target audience most effectively. For instance, they might guess that prime-time TV shows or popular sports events were the best time slots for their ads, aiming to reach a broad and engaged audience. Without sophisticated data analytics, their decisions were based largely on historical viewership data, general demographic information, and gut feeling, making the process somewhat hit-or-miss.

Next step was to engage in direct negotiations with TV networks, radio stations, and print publishers. The pricing for ad slots varied greatly depending on the medium's popularity, the specific time slot, and the personal relationships between the advertiser and the media sales teams. This process was often non-transparent, with prices fluctuating based on demand and the perceived value of the placement. Advertisers, like Coca-Cola, ended up paying premium prices for less-than-ideal slots due to lack of clear market pricing data.

Once the placements were chosen and prices agreed upon, a three-month campaign for their new soft drink kicked-off and aired during specific shows or was printed in certain publications. These commitments were often made well in advance and were based on the predicted popularity of the show or publication. Now, if the chosen time slots or mediums didn't resonate with the intended audience, or if the show's viewership declined, Coca-Cola would still be locked into their contract, potentially leading to a significant waste of their advertising budget and a campaign that didn't yield the desired results.

All companies had to navigate these challenges with limited data and flexibility, making advertising a more risky and less efficient endeavor.

DOI: 10.4324/9781003535966-7

All that slowly started changing as the internet became increasingly accessible. As more consumers began to spend time online, advertisers recognized the untapped potential of digital advertising. However, the transition wasn't smooth:

- The digital landscape was fragmented with numerous websites, each having its own audience and metrics.

- Advertisers had to manually reach out to individual websites (publishers) to buy ad space, making the process tedious and time-consuming.

- With no standardized metrics or tracking, advertisers often operated in the dark, unsure of the effectiveness of their campaigns.

Enter DoubleClick. Established in 1996, it aimed to simplify the chaotic world of digital advertising through the following:

- *Centralizing Ad Management*: DoubleClick offered a platform where advertisers could manage their campaigns across multiple websites, streamlining the buying process.

- *Introducing Metrics and Tracking*: For the first time, advertisers could track clicks, impressions, and other vital metrics, giving them insights into campaign performance.

- *Dynamic Ad Serving*: DoubleClick allowed advertisers to serve ads dynamically, meaning users were targeted based on their online behaviors and preferences.

The revolutionary idea that was at the heart of DoubleClick – instead of buying ad spaces, advertisers were now buying audiences. Ads could be targeted based on user behaviors, such as websites visited, searches conducted, and content consumed. With access to real-time data, advertisers could modify campaigns on the fly, optimizing for better performance.

But that was just the beginning. With the landscape of digital advertising evolving, the industry was poised for a revolution. DoubleClick provided a glimpse into the future, showcasing the power of centralized management and data-driven strategies. Yet advertisers were yearning for something more streamlined, more efficient, and remarkably intelligent – that's what gave birth to programmatic ad buying.

At its core, programmatic buying refers to the automated buying and selling of online ad space. But it wasn't just about automation; it was about intelligence. Programmatic technology uses data insights to decide which ads to buy, how much to pay for them, and where to place them, all in real-time (e.g imagine you're a company selling shoes. Before you would buy add this way, now you'd to it new way. And the new way is better in this way: a,b,c).

Before programmatic buying: You'd buy a banner ad on a sports website, hoping it reached people interested in running shoes. You had little control over who actually saw it and couldn't adjust in real-time.

With programmatic buying: Instead of buying space on specific sites, you target individuals. For example, your ad is shown to someone who has recently searched for running shoes, read shoe reviews, or looked at marathon tips. The system decides in real-time to show them your ad, no matter where they are online.

Why the new way is better:

> Precision: You target people actively interested in running shoes.
> Efficiency: You pay only for ads shown to relevant users.
> Real-time optimization: The system adjusts on the fly to improve results.

At the heart of programmatic buying is a concept called real-time bidding (RTB). Here's how it works. When a user visits a website, the ad space on that site is put up for auction. Advertisers bid for that space in real-time, and the highest bidder gets their ad displayed to the user. All of this happens in milliseconds, ensuring that the user experience remains seamless.

DoubleClick had already introduced advertisers to the power of data in decision-making. Programmatic took it several notches higher. With access to user behavior and demographics. Instead of generic ads, users started seeing ads tailored to their preferences and behaviors, enhancing the ad's effectiveness. Advertisers could now optimize campaigns in real-time, making adjustments based on performance metrics.

Why was it revolutionary? Because it significantly improved the return on investment for advertisers as a result of higher conversion rates (meaning, how many users clicked on the ad and then ended up buying the product).

DoubleClick's approach to helping advertisers spend their money efficiently did not go unnoticed. In 2007, in a move that shook the digital advertising world, Google announced its intention to acquire DoubleClick for a staggering $3.1 billion. The acquisition motives were clear. DoubleClick's ad-serving technologies perfectly complemented Google's advertising products, promising an integrated suite of offerings for advertisers, and with DoubleClick's data and insights, Google could serve more relevant ads to users, enhancing user experience and advertiser ROI.

But enough of the history lesson, let's dive into the pricing model. When discussing DoubleClick, or indeed any digital advertising platform, understanding its pricing model is critical. This is especially true for advertisers and businesses that seek to optimize their budgets while maximizing reach and ROI.

At its core, DoubleClick's pricing model prioritized value delivery. Instead of a one-size-fits-all approach, it adopted a dynamic model that took into account various factors, ensuring that advertisers received value commensurate with their investment, and for publishers, DoubleClick's dynamic allocation allowed them to fill their ad inventory at the best possible rates.

Before delving into the specifics, it's crucial to understand the motivations behind the pricing model. Given the varied demographics and behaviors of online users, pricing needs to be adaptable to cater to different segments effectively. With millions of auctions occurring in real-time, the pricing model needs to accommodate instant, dynamic adjustments. And given the multifaceted ad formats, from display banners to rich media and video, the pricing can vary based on the format's complexity and engagement potential.

As mentioned earlier, at the heart of programmatic (and hence DoubleClick) was a concept called RTB (real-time bidding). In RTB, advertisers bid for ad spaces in real-time, often within milliseconds. The highest bidder wins, but they pay just a cent more than the second-highest bid. Factors such as ad relevance, historical performance, and competition influence the auction. This makes predicting costs challenging but also ensures optimal value for advertisers.

You, as an advertiser, would set a specific cost target, based on one of several pricing models used by DoubleClick. The main models were as follows:

- *CPM (cost per mille)* is the cost per thousand impressions. While it's a prevalent model, its application in DoubleClick was refined by factors like ad quality, relevance, and real-time competition.

- Then we have *CPC (cost per click)*. Advertisers pay only when users click on their ads. It's especially favored when driving traffic to a website or landing page is the primary goal.

- Lastly *CPA (cost per acquisition)*. It is a results-driven model where advertisers pay based on specific actions, like sign-ups, purchases, or downloads. It requires robust tracking and is suitable for campaigns with clear conversion goals.

Alongside its core offerings, DoubleClick provided premium features that impacted the overall costs. Interactive ads, expandable banners, or video ads often commanded higher prices due to their engagement potential. While basic analytics were included, advanced reporting and insights came with additional costs. And for advertisers who preferred a hands-off approach, DoubleClick's managed services offered expert campaign management at a premium.

To give publishers control and protection over their inventory's value, DoubleClick allowed setting floor prices – a minimum threshold price below which an ad space wouldn't be sold. It also started private auctions where select advertisers were invited to bid on premium inventory, often at higher rates.

To encourage sustained partnerships, DoubleClick introduced additional products such as volume discounts to advertisers with substantial budgets and high campaign volumes, as well as long-term commitments, which basically were contractual agreements spanning multiple months or even years, sometimes coming with favorable pricing terms.

With all those products and innovations DoubleClick's pricing model became multifaceted, but its essence was rooted in delivering maximum value to both advertisers and publishers. By understanding its nuances and intricacies, advertisers could devise strategies to optimize their budgets, ensuring that every dollar spent was a step towards achieving their campaign goals. As we navigate further, we'll explore techniques and best practices to harness this pricing model effectively.

To bring the dynamics of DoubleClick to life, let's journey through a hypothetical scenario featuring two central players: "Wildlife Adventure", an advertiser, and "Forest Lifestyle", a publisher.

Wildlife Adventure, a startup specializing in hiking equipment, wishes to promote its new line of lightweight backpacks. Their target demographic is millennials with an interest in outdoor activities.

Wildlife Adventure uses DoubleClick's ad management platform to design and roll out their campaign. They opt for a mix of CPC and CPM pricing, focusing on impressions but also wanting to drive potential customers to their site. Leveraging DoubleClick's robust targeting capabilities, they zero in on users aged 18–35, frequent visitors to hiking or travel blogs, and those who have searched for hiking gear recently. They set a daily budget of $500, with a max CPC of $2 and a max CPM of $10.

Forest Lifestyle is a popular blog focusing on nature travels and outdoor activities. With a substantial monthly readership, they use DoubleClick to monetize their site through ads.

Forest Lifestyle registers its ad inventory (spaces where ads can be displayed) on DoubleClick's ad exchange. They set a floor price of $8 for CPM to ensure that the ad space isn't undervalued. For some premium ad placements, they organize private auctions, inviting select advertisers to bid.

DoubleClick's real-time bidding system identifies that Forest Lifestyle is an ideal fit for Wildlife Adventure's target demographic. When a user matching the target profile visits Forest Lifestyle, an auction is triggered. Let's say the highest bid is $9 CPM from a competitor, and Wildlife Adventure bids $9.50. They win the auction and pay slightly more than the second-highest bid, so approximately $9.01 for those 1000 impressions. For CPC, whenever a user clicks on the Wildlife Adventure ad, they are charged $2, the amount they set as their max CPC.

For Wildlife Adventure: they're charged based on the number of impressions (via CPM) and the clicks their ads receive (via CPC). If in a day, their ad gets 20,000 impressions and 50 clicks on Forest Lifestyle, they'd be charged around $180 ($2x50$ for CPC + $9.01x20$ for CPM).

For Forest Lifestyle: they earn revenue from displaying the ads. From the aforementioned activity, they'd earn the $180 minus DoubleClick's service fees.

Through DoubleClick, Wildlife Adventure efficiently reaches their target audience, ensuring their ads are viewed by potential customers. Simultaneously, Forest Lifestyle monetizes their content by displaying relevant ads, thus enhancing the user experience. This symbiotic relationship, facilitated by DoubleClick's intricate pricing and bidding system, epitomizes the platform's value proposition for both advertisers and publishers.

Measuring the impact of an advertising strategy is essential for both the advertiser and the publisher. Using a combination of analytics, reporting tools, and key performance indicators (KPIs), both parties can evaluate the success of their efforts. Here's how:

FOR THE ADVERTISER

DoubleClick provided in-depth reporting tools that allowed advertisers to analyze campaign performance in real time. Wildlife Adventure would have access to metrics such as the following:

- *Click-Through Rate (CTR):* The percentage of users who clicked on the ad after seeing it. A high CTR would indicate that the ad was relevant and compelling.

- *Conversion Rate:* The percentage of users who completed a desired action after clicking on the ad, such as making a purchase or signing up for a newsletter.

- *Return on Ad Spend (ROAS):* This metric calculates the revenue generated for every dollar spent on advertising. A positive ROAS would indicate a successful campaign.

- *Website Analytics:* By integrating tools like Google Analytics, Wildlife Adventure can track users who visited their website after clicking on the ad, monitoring actions such as product views, time spent on site, and completed purchases.

- *A/B Testing:* If Wildlife Adventure used multiple ad designs or messages, they could compare the performance of each to determine which resonated more with the audience.

- *Customer Feedback:* Engaging directly with customers through surveys or feedback forms can provide qualitative insights into the effectiveness of the advertising.

FOR THE PUBLISHER

Forest Lifestyle could access detailed reports that show the following:

- *Impression Data:* The number of times the ad was displayed on their site.

- *Revenue Reports:* Earnings from the ad campaigns, broken down by CPM, CPC, and other metrics.

- *Fill Rate:* The percentage of ad requests that were filled with ads. A high fill rate suggests that the available inventory is being effectively utilized.

- *User Engagement Metrics:* Monitoring user behavior can indicate whether the ads are complementing or detracting from the user experience. Metrics to consider include as follows:

- *Bounce Rate:* The percentage of visitors who navigate away from the site after viewing only one page. A sudden increase might suggest that users found the ads intrusive or irrelevant.

- *Pageviews and Session Duration:* A consistent or increased number of pageviews and longer session durations can indicate that users weren't deterred by the ads.

- *Feedback Channels:* Opening channels for readers to share feedback can provide insights into their perception of the ads.

- *Direct Advertiser Feedback:* Building a relationship with advertisers like Wildlife Adventure can lead to direct feedback on ad placements, visibility, and any suggestions for improvement.

Through these tools and metrics, both Wildlife Adventure and Forest Lifestyle can continually assess and refine their strategies. Effective measurement not only provides insights into the past performance but also informs decisions for future campaigns, ensuring that advertising efforts are consistently aligned with overarching business goals.

FUTURE

As we progress into an increasingly digital age, understanding the trajectories of tools like DoubleClick and the broader realm of programmatic ad buying becomes vital.

With the metamorphosis of DoubleClick into the Google Marketing Platform, its integration with Google's vast suite of tools has become even more seamless, especially with unified analytics and insights that deliver more comprehensive and unified insights by integrating data from various touchpoints, from search to display to video. Additionally Google's prowess in AI will further be embedded into the platform, enabling more intelligent targeting, bidding strategies, and predictive analytics.

While the evolution of tools like DoubleClick and the rise of programmatic ad buying have revolutionized digital advertising, the journey has not been without its obstacles. One key challenge was transparency. Advertisers often struggled with a lack of clarity regarding where their ads were being placed, which sometimes led to ads appearing on inappropriate or low-quality sites, harming brand reputation.

Moreover, the complexity of automated systems posed problems. Many companies lacked the internal expertise to effectively manage these new platforms, leading to inefficiencies and wasted ad spend. This is especially true for smaller advertisers who found the learning curve steep, as the AI-driven strategies could require fine-tuning that wasn't always straightforward.

Programmatic buying, once a buzzword, is now an industry staple. As it matures, the following trends are likely to manifest. With the surge in over-the-top (OTT) platforms like Netflix and Disney+, programmatic advertising will expand its foothold into these realms, offering advertisers new and compelling avenues. As cookie-less browsing becomes more prevalent due to privacy concerns, real-time contextual targeting (analyzing the content of a page to serve relevant ads) will gain prominence.

In the wake of GDPR, CCPA, and other privacy regulations, what we should expect is that advertisers will prioritize first-party data (data directly collected from customers) over third-party data, ensuring more transparency and compliance. With cookies becoming less reliable, the industry may shift towards universal IDs – a consistent identifier across platforms, ensuring user privacy while still offering personalization.

The frontier of digital advertising will be revolutionized by immersive technologies. Imagine trying out a dress using AR before clicking on an ad, or exploring a hotel room in VR before booking, or using AR, ads can be contextually placed in users' real world, like showcasing furniture in a user's actual living room.

Similarly the decentralized nature of blockchain presents intriguing possibilities. Every ad buy could be recorded on a transparent ledger, ensuring fairness and combating ad fraud. Automated contracts could guarantee that ads are only placed once specific criteria are met, enhancing accountability.

While the horizon looks promising, there are challenges. As ads become more prevalent, there's a risk of users experiencing "ad fatigue", leading to banner blindness or increased use of ad blockers. Also, as technology advances, the complexity of the ad ecosystem may become daunting for some advertisers, necessitating more straightforward tools and platforms. I believe the future will necessitate a more holistic approach. It is likely that brands will integrate programmatic advertising with other marketing channels, ensuring consistent messaging and more profound engagement. Also, instead of bombarding users with ads, the focus will shift towards fewer, more meaningful, and engaging ad experiences.

The nexus of DoubleClick and programmatic ad buying stands at a crossroads of innovation, challenge, and immense potential. By anticipating and adapting to these shifts, advertisers and publishers alike can navigate this evolving landscape successfully, creating resonant and impactful advertising experiences for users worldwide.

SUMMARY: PROGRAMMATIC ADVERTISING AND REAL-TIME BIDDING: REVOLUTIONIZING DIGITAL AD SPACES

The digital advertising landscape underwent a significant transformation with the advent of DoubleClick in 1996. DoubleClick streamlined the chaotic process of digital advertising by centralizing ad management, introducing vital metrics and tracking, and enabling dynamic ad serving. This evolution set the stage for programmatic ad buying – a revolutionary concept that automated the buying and selling of online ad space, using data insights to enhance efficiency.

At the heart of programmatic advertising lies real-time bidding (RTB). RTB allows advertisers to bid for ad space in real-time, ensuring ads are targeted based on user behavior and preferences. This approach drastically improved the return on invest-ment (ROI) for advertisers by enhancing ad relevance and conversion rates.

DoubleClick's integration into Google's suite of advertising products further amplified its capabilities, combining robust data insights with intelligent targeting strategies. This evolution paved the way for programmatic buying to become an industry staple, with future trends pointing towards increased use of immersive technologies like AR and VR, and a shift towards first-party data in response to privacy regulations.

By understanding and leveraging the nuances of DoubleClick's pricing model, which includes CPM, CPC, and CPA, advertisers can optimize their budgets and achieve their campaign goals. The integration of advanced analytics and real-time adjust-ments ensures that advertising efforts remain effective and aligned with business objectives.

Part II
Price setting

6

Is the definition of pricing strategy in a retail company enough? On the essence of its implementation

Anna Sokólska-Krzemińska

If you are reading this book, you probably don't need to be convinced how important role pricing plays for a retailer. Price is a key profit lever in any retail organization, so it is important that a pricing strategy is part of every company's strategy. A pricing strategy should address, among others, the following areas:

- Definition of competition – how many competitors we have, who our competitors are, and whether it is competition in all product groups or just selected ones.

- Price positioning – what is the target price positioning in the market versus the competition in each product category.

- Price image – what the price image is and what it looks like in relation to price positioning. Price image and price positioning are two separate concepts, but both are equally important. It is a favorable situation for a retailer when the price image is better (i.e. the company offers lower prices in the eyes of customers) than the actual price positioning in the market.

A pricing strategy should take into account the target group of customers and the assortment available in the store (product and price ranges). An important additional element is also the promotion strategy itself and whether, as a retailer, we want to move more towards a Hi-Lo (high-low prices) or EDLP (everyday low prices) strategy.

The very definition of a pricing strategy, in my view, is often the easier half of the way towards an organization being able to say it has a pricing strategy. The other half is its implementation, and this is where the real challenges usually begin. As I have observed, in many organizations too little attention is paid precisely to the execution of previous decisions, strategies, various projects, and then to the monitoring of the decisions or changes made. The implementation of a pricing strategy can go quite smoothly if the company has the right software and a dedicated team of experts. However, the most typical situation I have witnessed in my consulting career is that the company does not have a well-defined pricing strategy, no (or only few) systems in the company support the pricing policy, and the pricing policy team consists of one person. Therefore, it is worth remembering that to implement a pricing strategy, you would need the following:

DOI: 10.4324/9781003535966-9

- IT software dedicated to the pricing policy, which allows different types of calculation algorithms to be set up (rather than just entering prices manually into the system)

- Team, comprising:

    o pricing policy experts (specialists and analysts) who will work with pricing software on a daily basis

    o persons who will have a technical understanding of the system and will be able to adjust the system in the event of additional requirements or failure (usually on the part of the IT team or an external company)

- Monitoring and controlling the pricing strategy through various dedicated reports but also people who will review them and monitor any deviations.

Thus, the implementation of a pricing strategy for a retailer is not only a task for the pricing department, but also for other teams, including IT, controlling, or operations. The sooner we understand that the definition of a pricing strategy should go hand in hand with an appropriate, but unfortunately often complex, implementation, the sooner we can see positive financial results from the implementation of a pricing strategy.

KEY ELEMENTS TO IMPLEMENT A PRICING STRATEGY

Software

In retail companies, it is necessary to set prices for tens of thousands of products. With such a volume of SKUs, it is critical that the execution of the pricing strategy is enabled by software that is properly configured and compatible with other key IT systems in the organization. Such systems include the POS system in brick and mortar stores, the e-commerce platform, or electronic shelf labels (ESL), if any.

A properly configured system is one that will be able to calculate and propose a price for a product on the basis of the input data together with the defined algorithms for calculation. Based on my observations, Microsoft Excel is often the main pricing tool in many companies – it is undoubtedly a useful tool for various types of analyses, but it should not be the only or the main one.

There are a number of aspects that should be addressed at the stage of selecting pricing software or creating a specification for it. Not every dimension needs to be applied for every retailer, but each of these areas is worth considering. With regard to the tool being implemented, it is important to consider whether our pricing strategy is (or will be in the future) differentiated according to the following:

- Sales channel – the basic split of sales channels is between online and brick and mortar stores. Furthermore, within the online channel, in addition to the typical online store, it is worth considering whether to allow for other sales models such as marketplace or dropshipping.

- Store format – if our store chain has different formats, for example, hypermarket, supermarket, or convenience, does the pricing strategy address them in any way, and can we expect different prices?

- Store brand – if there is more than one chain brand behind a single company, and there is some overlap in their product ranges, it is worth considering how they should be positioned in relation to each other. The question that arises at that point is how interconnected the pricing teams responsible for each brand are and thus whether the pricing systems for these brands should also be interconnected or be separate entities.

- Store location – stores (regardless of format) may be located in different regions of a country or cities of different sizes. The question worth answering is whether we want to differentiate the price of the same products according to the location or segment of the store (if such segmentation exists).

When addressing the previous issues, we should bear in mind that in the age of ubiquitous smartphones, online price comparison sites, omnichannel, or the ROPO phenomenon (research offline, purchase online), it is increasingly difficult to explain to customers (even with great salespeople who know what a value selling proposition is) why prices differ between sales channels or store formats. Or why a product ordered online and picked up in a store is cheaper than the one on the shelf in a store. This is particularly difficult in industries where purchases are not made on impulse and customers have to make a larger one-off payment, for example in the consumer electronic industry.

In addition to the purely consumer aspect, there is also the issue of implementing, operating, and maintaining such a system – the more complex the pricing strategy (e.g. through various price differentiation options), the more complicated the pricing system we will be dealing with on a daily basis.

When considering how pricing software should be structured, it is important to focus on the three main areas illustrated by the following scheme.

1. Input data – that is, what information from other databases should feed into the pricing system to enable appropriate pricing decisions to be made
2. Functionalities and calculation algorithms – that is, the "heart" of the software which, through the available functionalities and defined calculation algorithms, will be able to calculate the correct product price
3. Output data – that is, what data, where, and how often should be exported from the pricing system

Figure 6.1

| Input data | Functionalities & calculation algorithms | Output data |

Input data

Costs

The cost of a product (purchase price in the case of a retailer or manufacturing cost in the case of a manufacturer) is an extremely important piece of information that should be included in any pricing system. The cost can be used for many activities when making pricing decisions, some of which being:

- calculation of product margin
- setting a minimum price for the product below which we will not sell (the minimum price may be the cost itself or the cost plus a certain buffer)
- pricing using the cost-plus method (if the organization uses this method)
- performing financial simulations

It is important for the pricing department not only to know about costs, but also to understand how they are calculated, as usually there are different types of costs that might be considered. This aspect should be consulted with the team that is responsible for this area – such as the finance or controlling team. Issues that are important to understand from the pricing department's point of view include the following:

- How is the cost calculated – is it the average cost or the last purchase price? If average cost, are we talking about an arithmetic average or a weighted average?
- Is the quoted cost really the final cost including all elements (e.g. logistics costs, possible bonuses from suppliers for sales, etc.)?
- Is the cost affected by, for example, display products or demo products for stores, which can sometimes be purchased at different purchase prices than others?

These are only examples of issues to be analyzed, there may be many more depending on the specifics of the company or industry. It is a topic that needs to be properly understood so that one is able to make optimal pricing decisions that can contribute to maximizing the company's financial performance.

Competitors' prices

Another essential element in the pricing system is the prices of competitors. In industries such as grocery, beauty, or consumer electronic, where the same products are found in different retail chains, it is quite easy to compare prices (e.g. using EAN codes). Keep in mind that this is done not only by competing retail companies but, above all, by customers – especially when dealing with expensive products or purchases planned over time.

Prices can be collected with the support of internal resources and tools or through external companies that offer such services. Nowadays, there are many companies on the market that offer crawling of online competitor price data through different types of tools. It is recommended to analyze the offers available on the market and choose the one best suited to your needs. When we mention the collection of competitors' prices, we are primarily referring to the online channel. It is much more challenging to collect prices from competitors in brick and mortar stores, particularly if it involves a large number of product prices to be matched. Price lists collection without the approval of the store manager have little chance of success – you can only try to do this on small product groups or based on receipts from the store. This is obviously the case for competing retail companies. Manufacturers who sell their products through various retail chains are in a much better situation – a price audit in this case is easier to carry out and justify. Therefore, when working with any third-party company that specializes in price crawling, it is advisable to find out which sales channels they can analyze and how these prices are actually collected (especially in brick and mortar stores).

By having pricing information directly in the pricing system, pricing decisions will be quicker and more efficient. Such information can be part of the algorithms for setting the prices (if we want to always be cheaper or more expensive than a selected competitor). Finally, be sure to validate your competitors' prices before entering them into the system – particularly if your competitors' prices directly affect our price level. Experience shows that even the best companies and crawling tools are not infallible.

Price elasticity

Price elasticity of a product is an indicator of how much demand for a product will change if the price is changed. With calculated price elasticity, it is possible to estimate the impact on future volume, revenue, or profit with the given price change. Calculating the level of price elasticity is a challenging task for many companies. It is quite a time-consuming task that also requires data validation, so retailers either use external companies and models provided by them or employ analysts and data scientists who are dedicated mainly to this task. Due to the complexity of price elasticity calculation, it is usually calculated in a separate systems. However, as mentioned earlier, it also should be included in a pricing system to facilitate the pricing decisions.

Other data

In addition to the parameters described previously such as costs, competitors' prices, or price elasticity, there is a lot of other valuable information that may be relevant to the pricing department, and it is worth considering having it in the pricing system. Examples of additional information to consider include:

- Information on the number of products in stock with their ageing
- Information on orders currently placed with manufacturers or wholesalers

- Product life cycle to know whether we are dealing with a product that is relatively new or "exiting" the market

- Product categorization, that is, the classification of a given SKU into specific product groups and subgroups, together with information on product branding

Please remember that it is not an art to collect all possible batch data in one system. The trick is to analyze it on a regular basis and for the system to work effectively despite the large amount of data. Therefore, every organization should examine its needs and analyze the system possibilities.

Examples of functionalities and calculation algorithms

In a pricing tool, it should be possible to implement different types of calculation algorithms that are able to reflect the company's pricing strategy. There are many possible algorithms, but three basic pricing approaches can be a good starting point:

- Cost-plus pricing – this method involves adding an agreed percentage mark-up or mark-up in absolute value to the purchase price of a product (retailer) or the cost of producing a product (manufacturer). With this method, the key is to properly calculate the costs incurred by the organization and then determine the appropriate mark-up levels. Estimating the total costs may seem like a trivial task, but in reality, it can also be a daunting task for many organizations: particularly if we want to take into account, for example, logistical costs or additional bonuses which are dependent on a retailer's purchases or sales and are paid at a later date than the time of purchase. It is therefore crucial to establish what level of costs is calculable and then set a target mark-up on the product.

- Competitor-based pricing – a method of pricing based on the prices of competitors. The first step is to establish a list of competitors against whom you want to position yourself. It may turn out that the selected competitors will be important for us only in selected product categories. Then, depending on our position in the market, the dynamics of the industry or what our objectives are as an organization, it is necessary to determine our price positioning relative to this competition (i.e. whether we want higher, the same, or lower prices). In practice, price indices or so-called price corridors are defined along which we want to move in relation to the competition. The final element is to determine how often we want to collect and analyze our competitors' prices.

  Please note that if you choose the competitor-based pricing method, the system should provide an easy way to change all of these parameters: list of competitors, price indices, or frequency of price crawling.

- Value-based pricing – a method that involves setting prices based on the value we deliver to the customer. Ideally, the value to the customer should be estimated at the stage of product creation and development by the manufacturer to avoid

Figure 6.2

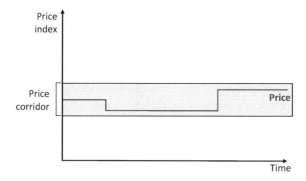

a situation where the costs of product manufacture and development exceed customers' willingness to pay. In the case of retail chains, this method may be most applicable when the products sold are not entirely comparable between chains – for example in the fashion, jewelry, or furniture industries. In such chains, the products may be similar to each other, but if they are not the same, then the customer's preference (i.e. additional value) may prevail whether a given product will be purchased.

Price corridors

A price corridor can be understood as the price range within which the prices of a given product should be set. This can be illustrated with a simple graph presented here.

Even if retailer's pricing policy is not complex and prices are set in a relatively simple way, for example:

- the price is the same as that of competitor X or

- the minimum/average/maximum price from a specified number of competitors, or

- the price is equal to the purchase cost plus a % mark-up

then it would be beneficial if price corridors functionality could be implemented in the pricing system for each product within which the system can navigate.

A simple price corridor could be the difference between the minimum price and the maximum price of a product so that the price never exceeds the maximum price or is lower than the specified minimum price.

The minimum and maximum prices of the price corridor can be defined analogously to the pricing policy, giving a greater space for price fluctuations.

For example, the minimum price may be equal to the following:

- the purchase price or manufacturing cost of the product
- the purchase price or manufacturing cost of the product plus a % mark-up
- the selling price at the selected competitor or competitors

The maximum price, in turn, can be defined as follows:

- recommended retail price (if exists)
- the purchase price or manufacturing cost of the product plus a % mark-up (greater than in case of the minimum price)
- the selling price at the selected competitor or competitors (different set of competitors than in case of the minimum price)

The previous examples are very trivial and are intended to simply illustrate the point. In practice, much more complex mechanisms can be built for price corridors, for example, the price proposed by the system will maximize profit but will move along a price corridor that will be defined bottom-up by a minimum price and top-down by a maximum price. Both prices would be based on competitor prices (either directly or competitor price + mark-up).

The way the price should move within the price corridors should be defined with specific rules illustrating the pricing strategy. There are many possibilities for creating price corridors, so it is important for a retailer to consider whether and to what extent it wants to use this functionality in the system before implementing a pricing strategy into the system.

Scoring models

One of the important functionalities in the pricing system is the ability to create scoring models. A scoring model can be used to evaluate products (and rank them) in terms of predefined variables for a specific purpose. For instance, a scoring model can be used, among other things, to determine a list of the best products for a price reduction or increase, or to define the product roles within product categories.

Let us analyze an example. The retailer sells certain product category ABC that consists of 100 SKUs. The company wants to know what are the product roles of all SKUs within this product category in order to determine importance of products, its impact on price image, and set the price (as a final step).

Scoring model may help to specify these roles and assign proper pricing strategy. Required steps:

1.   Define variables for the scoring model that may impact on price image and collect necessary input

2. Set weighting for each variable in the model (the higher the weighting, the more significant the variable is in the model)
3. Calculate final score for each product (having clear assumptions, e.g. the higher the score, the higher the impact on price image)
4. Split products into product roles within each product category based on the score

In the table you can find general data structure for such model.

Each retailer should define their own product roles depending on the specifics of their business. The most typical (but not the only) product roles that we can distinguish are image products or profit generators. Image products are price elastic products with the highest impact on price image, usually requires aggressive pricing policy which can result in a lower margin level. Profit generators are products that are out of the radar of customers where companies gain profits. Various companies may call them differently, but what matters is what these products stand for. As a result of this exercise, the company receives product roles of 100 SKUs to which the appropriate pricing strategy should be assigned by a pricing department.

Depending on the complexity of the issue and the amount of data involved, it may be decided that such models should be created outside the system for pricing policy. From a retailer's point of view, when selecting or building a pricing system, it is worth considering whether such scoring models will be needed – and if so, for what specifically and how you want to use them.

Family pricing

In a good pricing system, we should also be able to set prices for families of products. By family I mean the same products that differ from each other by one feature that can affect the final price. Such a family could be three sizes of frying pans, for example, 24, 26, and 28 cm. It is logical that the price of a pan with a diameter of 28 cm should be higher than one with a diameter of 26 cm, and that a 26 cm pan should be more expensive than a 24 cm pan. A similar example would be a 1 m, 5 m, and 10 m cable. It is logical that 1 m of cable should be cheaper than 10 m of the same cable. Of course, there may be situations where one product in a family is on promotion,

Figure 6.3

Weight (%) →	W1	W2	W3	...	Σ = 100%
Products ↓	Variable 1	Variable 2	Variable 3	...	Final score
SKU 1	Normalized values, without outliers				
SKU 2					
SKU 3					
...					

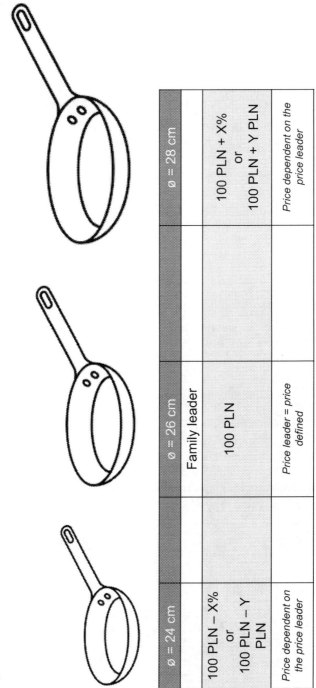

Figure 6.4

ø = 24 cm	ø = 26 cm	ø = 28 cm
	Family leader	
100 PLN − X% or 100 PLN − Y PLN	100 PLN	100 PLN + X% or 100 PLN + Y PLN
Price dependent on the price leader	*Price leader = price defined*	*Price dependent on the price leader*

and for example, a 55-inch TV can be bought for the price of the same 50-inch TV. The important thing is to do these promotions in a fully conscious way, being able to explain the given price to the customer and not as a result of pricing errors.

A slightly different example of family pricing functionality could be products for which you would like to set the same price, for example, three different types of fruit yoghurt or different colors of the same headphones. In this case, the same functionality can also be used, but the parameters should be set so that the prices of the products are the same (no mark-ups between products).

In each case described previously, it is necessary to establish the lead product and how the prices of the other products will behave in relation to the lead product, that is, how much more expensive or cheaper they would be – please check the next example.

Price endings

Any price entered or calculated in the pricing system should be reviewed in terms of price endings. It is a good practice for a retailer to have an established list of possible price endings or a clear way of determining them. By price endings, I mean both the two decimal places, but in the case of more expensive products (costing hundreds or thousands) also what occurs before the decimal point. Let us analyze this with an example.

The retailer sells the ABC product category, where the price range of products varies between PLN 1 and PLN 10. The company decides on price endings of "9" as a general rule. Examples of questions the retailer should consider:

- Do prices just above the price threshold, for example, PLN 5.09, make sense? In the case of prices just above the psychological threshold, it is worth considering whether a price of PLN 4.99 or PLN 5.19 would not be "more appropriate". In the case of a lower price of PLN 4.99, we can theoretically count on a greater volume of sales (we do not exceed the psychological barrier of PLN 5), and in the case of a higher price, which is PLN 5.19, we can theoretically count on a greater profit. Of course, this is a purely theoretical assumption, illustrated here, which should be verified preferably by market tests.

- What should be the spread between the different price points?

  o Are the following price points every 10 grosz (subunit of PLN) necessary: PLN X.09, PLN X.19, PLN X.29, PLN X.39, PLN X.49, PLN X.59, PLN X.69, PLN X.79, PLN X.89, PLN X.99?

  o Will a smaller number of price points suffice, for example, X.49 and X.99?

- Above what price level should the products have no longer grosz after the decimal point?

- Can price endings negatively affect our price positioning on price comparison websites or marketplace platforms (where a customer sorts by price)?

Figure 6.5

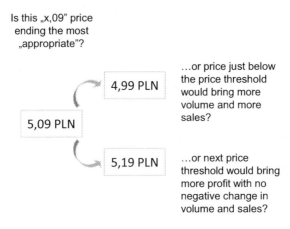

With price thresholds, it is worth recalling how important price elasticity is with any price change. Adjusting or changing price endings is a common and easy quick win to implement in many organizations. If changes to price endings are "cosmetic", it is usually possible to count the potential financial effect without using price elasticity – we then assume that a cosmetic price adjustment will not affect sales volumes. The pitfall can be the online channel, where by making price increases we can weaken our position on the price comparison websites. In addition, we need to be very vigilant in adjusting price endings when we go through significant price thresholds. This means that the same product may have a completely different price elasticity when we raise the price, for example, from PLN 4.89 to PLN 4.99 (this change may be relatively imperceptible), and when we change the price from PLN 4.99 to PLN 5.09.

Once the right list of price endings has been created, the list should be implemented into the system in such a way that, in the event of any changes, there is no need to manually change prices for thousands of products, but the system is able to recalculate this itself.

It is also worth remembering that in case of significant changes in price endings, for example, from 0 to 9 or from 5 to 9, it is worth remembering to prepare coins in stores to give change to customers; otherwise, real change may be harder to notice.

Promotion mechanisms

Another broad area to look at when implementing a pricing strategy is promotions. The possibility of programming promotions should either be addressed directly in the pricing system (as a separate module, if the system is efficient enough to process such an amount of data) or in a dedicated system, which will directly cooperate with the pricing system. Nowadays, you can see a lot of different promotion mechanisms on the market, and after the implementation of the Omnibus Directive in Poland, I have the impression that there are even more of them (or additional conditions that need to be fulfilled for the promotion to be active). Examples of promotion mechanisms:

- Promotion with percentage or absolute value discount
- Promotion with additional discount code that must be entered in the online shopping basket or given at checkout
- Promotion with a PLN 50 discount for every PLN 500 spent – discount directly on the bill or refund to the gift card
- Multibuy – first product –10%; second product –20%, third –30%, etc.
- Bundle – buy product X and get product Y cheaper
- Buy product X and get a service at a lower price (e.g. buy a TV and get a calibration at half price)
- Buy a product in installments and get 1 installment free or X instalments with an interest rate of 0%
- All kinds of promotions, but only for loyalty club members

Each such promotion may be subject to additional conditions, such as a minimum purchase amount or number of products purchased. For promotions that fall under the Omnibus Directive, it is necessary for the retailer to show a minimum price from the previous 30 days. The need to show it also means that price history should be stored in the system – at least from the last 30 days. In the case of a small number of products, this should not pose a big problem, but when you have tens of thousands of products on offer and a price history should be stored for each of them, the matter becomes complicated and can overload the systems. It might be advisable to consult IT specialists on this aspect, who will be able to advise on where such large databases should be stored.

Output data

It is clear that what should be exported from the pricing system is the selling price of the product. If a promotion can be programmed in the pricing system, then in addition to the selling price, the system can also export the strike price (if there is one) and the information about the minimum price for the past 30 days in accordance with the Omnibus Directive, if needed.

When exporting prices, it is also important to decide how often should prices be updated and at what times. There are many possible scenarios:

- Continuous price changes, which can be the result of a recalculation in the system, for example, due to changes in competitor prices or cost levels
- Price changes at specific times during the day
- Price changes once a day/once a week/once a month

Sending prices to the online channel is relatively straightforward as it does not require additional work. However, for stores that do not have electronic shelf labels (ESL), it is important to bear in mind that printing a price tag, cutting it out, and replacing it with the existing one is an additional workload that needs to be considered within existing processes in the organization. Conversely, for stores that have an ESL, it is necessary to consider at what times we want to change prices so that the customer does not hesitate when they are standing in front of a store shelf and the price suddenly changes right in front of their eyes.

The previous description of sample functionalities, algorithms or aspects to be considered when implementing a pricing policy system is not exhaustive. Every company, before deciding to implement a pricing system, should do the following:

- analyze the scale of the investment – not only the financial aspect (the real cost of purchasing and developing the software including maintenance), but also how many people and teams will have to be involved

- have a defined pricing strategy (or at least be in the process of defining one), which would give a direction for further implementation

- gather the requirements and functionalities that a particular system should address, which can then be "translated" into a suitable pricing program.

SUMMARY

Every retailer should have a defined pricing strategy that addresses areas such as competition, price positioning, target group, price image, or promotional strategy. However, we cannot forget that implementation of the strategy is as important as its definition. There are several elements that are required for a proper execution and further governance, for example, pricing software, pricing team, or monitoring and controlling processes.

In this chapter, we focused on the areas that are crucial to create and maintain an efficient pricing software:

- Input data that feed into the pricing system

- Functionalities and calculation algorithms that should be tailored to the needs of the organization and may differ depending on the company or industry specifics

- Output data exported and sent to other system within the organization

The description does not exhaust all aspects of an ideal pricing system, but it indicates crucial areas from the retailer perspective.

7

The price of innovation
Steering through value-based pricing at Assa Abloy

Karl Holm

SCENE SETTING

Let's say you find yourself in a position as a pricing professional where you speak to a colleague who is about to launch a new product, asking for input on his idea for pricing of this new product. The product manager in question, let's call him Sonny, tells you that this new version of his product is better, faster, and stronger than the existing model. He is also proud to say that thanks to great work by the engineering team and the sourcing department, the cost to produce the product has reduced considerably for this new version. These are of course two very good things – a better product which can be produced at a lower cost. His plan based on that is to launch the new model as the same price as the current version, with the rationale that the reduced cost will make us earn more money per unit compared to current version.

That is typically the time when I insert some heat into the conversation, a shame when me and Sonny were having such a good time. I strongly challenge this notion (and I've heard it many times) and push to decouple the added value of a new product, with the reduced production cost. Sonny sees the reduced cost alone enough reason to keep the price unchanged. I see the recued cost also as something great. But I also understand that if we offer more value in the new product, then customers are likely willing to pay for that, and we should be able to charge for it, otherwise we are just leaving money on the table. This is value-based pricing at its core – not charging based on our cost, but on the value we deliver.

My go-to model in these cases is to perform a value analysis. So not me telling Sonny and his team how much they should charge for their product, but instead us together with other team members in a structured way understanding the value we offer with this product and what price point that value warrants.

There are several benefits to spending time on such an analysis. First, we build an understanding of what customers care for and do not care for. Second, we analyze how we compare against the competition with those criteria. And finally, as a result of the analysis, the process will guide us to the optimal price range for the product in question.

DOI: 10.4324/9781003535966-10

THE A-TEAM

So how does one go about this in practice? My experience is telling me that this is best done in a workshop setting. And in that workshop, different views are important. With only Sonny and his team members included, they will likely be biased in their views on what customers care about. Your customer service team are likely to have a different opinion, as does the sales organization. So make sure you included them in the work, to use all their experience.

The first step to do is to start understanding the value. In this process this means in concrete terms listing all the things the customer in this certain segment and that certain vertical values. Naturally, product features will be top of mind for many here. Steve Jobs called it "speeds and fees" or "bits and megahertz" in that famous speech on marketing, meaning the technical specifications of a product. Some of these *are* of course important to customers, some more than others. But this is also where we as pricing professionals have a role to play, to challenge this a little. Surely our customers also care about other things, such as product quality, our ability to offer technical support post-sale, and our company's great sustainability engagement? The job to iron this out requires a strong pricing facilitator leading the workshop, allowing for the different viewpoints in the room to be heard while at the same time moving the conversation along forward. In an ideal world, there is also actual customer insights available either going into or to be collected during such a workshop, to reduce the risk of internal bias.

The outcome of this first step is basically a list of value drivers, things which customer care about for the product in question. A simplified example of how this could look for Sonny's product is listed in Figure 7.1.

As can be seen, the drivers listed first are linked to product features, while others are more related to the supplier of those products. And it's important at this stage to not just list things that "we are good at", as that may the first thing which comes to mind. The purpose is instead to fully list all the things our defined customers care about – whether we excel at them or not.

Figure 7.1
List of value drivers.

| Speed of operation |
| Product design |
| Ease of use |
| Security level |
| Product certifications |
| Ease of ordering |
| Technical support quality |
| Delivery reliability |
| Sustainability profile |
| Financial stability |

Once that is done, you want to define a scale for each of the value drivers, defining what is "great" and what is "poor" and in between. This will later be used to score all products against, so it is important to get it right.

NOT ALL ARE CREATED EQUAL

Once the workshop members have agreed on which value drivers make the list and not, it's time to assign weighting. Even though all drivers on the list are things which matter to the customers for this segment, they are not equal in importance – some things make a larger impact in how a customer values a certain offering.

This will of course differ between different segments and can also differ between different channel approaches for the same product. If you are doing business through one or more channel intermediaries, it is critical that you in this work define who is the "customer" you're looking at. Meaning is it your partner through who you are selling your products, and sending your invoices to, or is it the end user who will actually end up using your product. Again, in an ideal world, you want to do both analyses separately, to see how both values your offering. In the real world, with sometimes short deadlines and conflicting priorities, I find that if you need to focus on only one: focus on the end user as your customer.

Some examples from our industry which may change in relative value are as follows:

- Product design. In my experience this scores higher in a B2C than a B2B setting, for example, of course depending on the type of product and the segment.

- Financial stability [of the supplier]. This is something which larger B2B customers care about and value. They want to make sure that you as the supplier stay in business in the future, to continue to offer support, spare parts, new products, etc. Consumers, at least in some segments, do not value this as high.

- Ease of ordering. If you're in B2C business running e-commerce, having a website which allows for easy choice and ordering of your products is key. In B2B, there are often other factors which matter more.

SCORE!

Then, on to the next step, to score! Now it's time to – as a team – agree on how all products included in the analyses score against the criteria we defined in the previous step. In practical terms, to go through each value drivers one by one, product by product, and assign it a score from poor to great. The sum of all scores for all value drivers will then generate a value score, which represent the value of that product in the eyes of the customer.

This work will require a substantial knowledge of both how customers view our products and us as a supplier, but also (as we have hopefully included competition in the same analysis) that of our competition. The technical features if you have included such are often easy to find, and compare product vs. product, yours, and competitors'. The other values are sometimes harder to agree on without data around. I think in very simplified terms there are three levels of knowledge one can hope to achieve here, with the corresponding efforts matching (see Figure 7.2).

Presenting the value drivers

Now, you will have scored all the products in your agreed dataset, against all the value drivers defined as a team. There are several options for reviewing the outcome at this state in the process before we reach the next and often final outcome: the value map.

Option 1 is to simply list the value drivers and products in a matrix, with some sort of coding for great/average/poor, such as color green to red. To help visually, I tend to list the value drivers in order of importance, from top to bottom. An example with the high-level value drivers listed earlier in this chapter could look like what you see in Figure 7.3.

The second option for visual will zoom in our [relative] performance only, in combination with the importance of each value driver (the weighting). You can visualize this using a matrix of competitive advantage, to see where we perform strong/weak, and which areas the customer cares about or not (see Figure 7.4).

Taking the same data shown in the previous table, displayed in a matrix of competitive advantage, the output could look something like what you see in Figure 7.5.

Figure 7.2
Three levels of customer understanding.

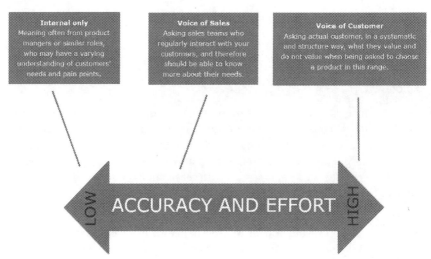

Figure 7.3

The high-level value drivers.

Value driver	Weighting	Our new product	Our predecessor	Competitor product A	Competitor product B	Competitor product C
Ease of use	20%					
Sustainability profile	18%					
Product design	12%					
Product certifications	10%					
Speed of operation	10%					
Security level	8%					
Ease of ordering	8%					
Technical support quality	5%					
Delivery reliability	5%					
Financial stability	4%					

Figure 7.4

Performance vs. importance matrix.

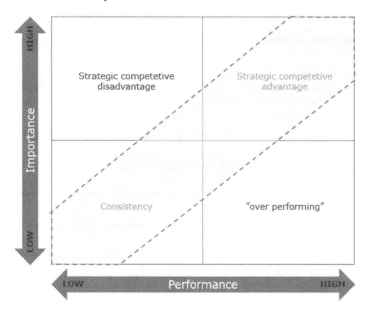

This view alone, without any pricing data inserted (this will come in the next step), will be very helpful for us. It will tell us what we are good versus poor at, in relation to how much the customers care about that specific area of our offering.

As an example, if we look at this graph and look for input on how we should market our new product, this data would indicate that we should do the following:

- Push strong for the "ease of use" dimension of our offering, since (A.) customers in this segment seem to care about that a lot, and (B.) we seem to be performing well.

Figure 7.5

Performance vs. importance matrix displayed in a matrix of competitive advantage.

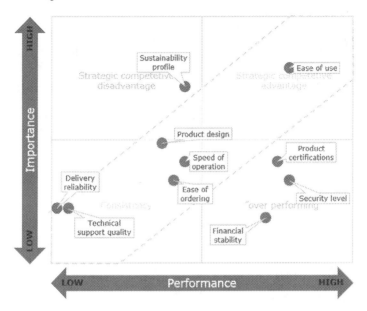

- Increase our efforts in sustainability, as customers do seem to value that, but we currently only have an average performance.

- Perhaps consider not focusing too much on our financial stability, security level, and certifications, since – even if we perform strong – customers in this segment seem not to be attracted by those things.

VALUE AND PRICE COME TOGETHER – THE VALUE MAP

Whether you are using this method to evaluate your optimal price point for a future product to be launched later or want to understand your place in the current competitive landscape, this method will produce a value map. This map (see Figure 7.6) shows all products in the range defined, with price of each product on one axis and customer value as defined in the workshop on the other.

The gray regression line represents the optimal value/price combination. Meaning that in the eyes of the customer, products located **below the regression line** are potentially underpriced, meaning offering too much value for money. This is not generally an issue for customers, of course, but it is an issue for us as a supplier, as we

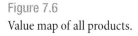

Figure 7.6
Value map of all products.

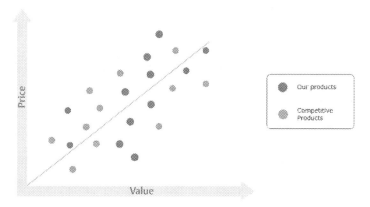

are then leaving money on the table. On the opposite end, if the analysis tells us that some products are positioned above the regression line, they are offering poor value for money, and we are potentially losing volume due to this.

In case one wants to align one's offering to be closer to the regression line, there are two levers to pull: price or value. If a product is offering poor value, one can simply decrease the price, to try and gain volume. Same in reverse for too much value, an increase of price can be the solution. But the more interesting aspect that I usually try to get my team to focus on is the value aspect. How can we move products to the left or the right in the graph, meaning changing their value, to optimize the portfolio.

This can be achieved short term by, for example, adjusting some technical specifications of a product, increasing or decreasing its performance. Longer term actions we've looked at is how we can increase our delivery quality, to over time improve the customers' perception of our services, and thereby increase the value of our offering.

What about Sonny?

Let's head back to me and my conversation with my colleague, the product manager Sonny. He has a new version of a product in an existing range and market he is about to launch later in the year. And as you may recall, his plan was to introduce this new model at the same price as the predecessor since we've been able to reduce the direct material cost by x%, rewarding us with additional contribution margin compared to the former product.

Figure 7.7
New value map with Sonnys new product.

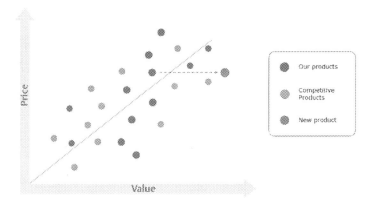

Assuming we've done all the steps described in this process thoroughly, and we have proper knowledge of what the customers value and not in this segment, we can now plot where Sonny's new product would end up in the value map (see Figure 7.7).

As can be seen, it seems that the new product is offering great value in the eyes of the customers, while the price is inherited from the predecessor, the blue product directly to the left in the graph of Sonny's new model (in green).

This outcome is telling me that with the current assumptions, we stand a good chance of leaving money on the table, since we offer very high value, in fact we seem to offer more than any other product in this dataset, but we currently plan to sell the product at the legacy price point. I then work with the team to understand if the price point itself has a strong psychological importance, for example going over 100 USD or some number which could form an obstacle to pass.

If this is the case, I proceed to work with the team to focus on the value of the new product. Is there a way we can reduce the value of the product, to provide a better value/price relationship? For example, reducing or removing certain features in software, or in hardware, or some other kind of reduction of functionality (= value).

If the price point is not psychologically important, I then work with Sonny and his team to rethink the price. Many times Sonny and his peers may be on board after such a workshop, but they require help to build the business case internally, to get senior management buy-in to increase the launch price (sometimes quite aggressively). One good thing here, coming back to the optimal A-team for such a workshop, is to have sales leadership involved. If they are involved throughout in agreeing on the value, and then subsequently to analyze the output, it makes it much harder for them to push back on the price being too high once product is starting to be sold.

In some cases we've done both. Meaning we have adjusted price level, of the new and also some existing products, and then introduced a tiered new offering, good-better-best, to align better with the regression line in the model.

That is a main takeaway of mine: if you are doing this to gain insights on where to price your new product, make sure you do it early in your development process. This way, you can use valuable insights gained to change the specification of your product (meaning adjusting its value). If you do this once your [hardware] product is already designed, procured, and stocked, price is your only level.

THE PROCESS END TO END

The workflow of doing an analysis like this will differ a little bit depending on what your scenario looks like:

- If you have access to competitive price data or not

  - If yes, then you can use the output of such a workshop to guide you to your optimal price point.

  - If no, you can do all the steps apart from the final value map as that requires pricing data to be produced. The output will instead then be a better under-standing of how we perform against the competition in terms of value (but not value/money).

- If you want input to how to price a new product, or if you want to review your current pricing model (or both).

This workflow (see Figure 7.8) will assume we have pricing data readily available and that we are using the model to help guide us where to price a new product, just like Sonny and his new product in the example earlier.

Figure 7.8

Workflow diagram that outlines a process for using pricing data to guide product pricing decisions.

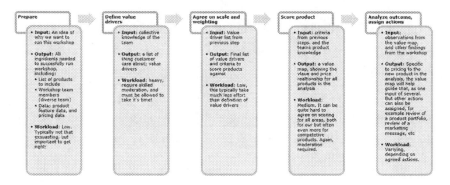

Figure 7.9

List of a few common issues encountered and the strategies to mitigate them.

What went wrong?	What does it mean?	How to mitigate?
Positive bias	Sometimes, the team consists of a tight group of product managers and marketing people. If they are about to launch a new product and have worked with this project some months or even years, its likely they will have a soft spot in their heart for the product and are used to speaking about all the great things about the product. By default, when asked to build a list of drivers, they will tend to list the areas where the product excels.	Two tips: 1. Make sure you have diverse team. I find that sales representatives are good at countering a positive bias in this setting. 2. Make sure the team is moderated and challenged when defining value drivers: to not just list the things we do well, but actually put ourselves in the shoes of the customers and understand their gains and pain points.
Value map used an only input	I've seen examples where the value map produced by a workshop like this is used as the only input to a price setting decision. That to me is not optimal, as there are many other factors not captured in this method. Also, this view in itself is static and does not show the development of a competitive landscape over time, which likely changes.	While this is a very good method, it should only be considered one of many input to any decision of a pricing action, such as setting or adjusting a price. Always make sure you have other inputs, such as the expertise of the sales team, who likely have an understanding of how the competitive landscape is evolving over time.
Too little time	In my experience from our business, this workshop is done best in person in a room, with a whiteboard and loads of post-it notes, and should be allowed to take 1,5-2 days. I've seen examples of where some teams have tried to get this done virtually, in just a few hours end to end. Needless to say, the outcome of those workshops was not very reliable.	Before committing to running and moderate a process like this, make sure you have the buying of all key stakeholders that this will and should take up a few days' time of some key employees.
No good at all	If you have a team of product people looking for help on where to price their new, completely revolutionary, product, this may be the wrong method altogether. This is because this analysis and the value map will guide you on the optimal price point, given that you have a set of equivalent products in your input data. This could be your own predecessor products, and/or competitive products. If your product is completely new, let's say you have invented something brand new and creating a new market, there is likely no existing products to include in the analysis.	Consider using other pricing tools or methods instead.

What can go wrong?

After running quite a few workshops with this method, I've seen things go wrong. Even with a great team, with a great product offering and access to all kinds of data, the process and/or it's outcome can sometimes fail. Figure 7.9 is an attempt at listing a few of the things which I've seen go wrong and how to mitigate them.

8

Artificial intelligence in pricing at online retail

Vladimir Kuchkanov

Getting the pricing right is one of the most challenging and at the same time misunderstood concepts in business management. And for a good reason – there are a handful of pricing-related problems and effects that make managing it a prohibitively complex task for a human mind.

To mention just a few:

- Different reaction of demand to price changes of even seemingly similar products; this effect is known as own price elasticity;

- Variations in demand elasticity depending on the context, that is, the same product may demonstrate different reaction of demand to price changes at different times (think about seasonality of the ice-cream sales, or high demand during the Black Friday);

- Even the reaction of demand is impossible to measure precisely because of a lot of noise in demand numbers, driven by the nature of demand itself and by other important factors influencing it;

- Because similar products in the same category can be substitutes, a change in the price of one product can make customers switch to another product, which can dilute the average profitability of a category; this effect is known as internal cross-price elasticity, or spillovers, or sales cannibalization; on the opposite side of things, there are complementary products, for example, shoe polish to leather shoes, wherein the cross-price elasticity effect results in the price of the anchor product influencing the demand for the complementary ones;

- When a new product or service is launched, or in case we need to change a price on a product or a service whose price never changed, there is no historical data to reason about a potential impact of a price change on its demand; this effect is known as "the cold start problem";

- The difference in price positioning with larger competitors can influence own demand even stronger than own prices. This effect is known as external cross-price elasticity;

- In many industries, the supply of certain goods or services is limited, which needs to be taken into account; this problem is known as the "finite stock

DOI: 10.4324/9781003535966-11

constraint", with the key question to be answered being "Shall we sell an item now, or later at a potentially higher price?";

- Finally, besides the purely mathematical aspects, there are also psychological effects in pricing, "price thresholds" being one of the most prominent ones; the price thresholds are typically round price points that shoppers tend to notice and care about, for example, €10, $50, €100, etc.

Luckily for us contemporaries, we're living in the times of a scientific and technological breakthrough in machine learning algorithms widely known to the public as artificial intelligence, or AI.

In application to pricing, we can define artificial intelligence as computer algorithms and capabilities that can effectively replace humans in strategic and tactical pricing management. These are some of the most important attributes of "AI in Pricing Management": automation, data-driven decisioning and execution, algorithmically performed tasks.

How exactly can AI help with getting the pricing right? Before answering this question, there is a more important one to be answered, which is, what does "right" mean in the first place?

For this, let's review typical tasks performed by humans, and then we'll review the AI capabilities that can potentially replace humans in these tasks.

1. Pricing target-setting – identification, prioritization, and target setting on business KPIs;
2. Pricing strategy – identifying the most relevant pricing method addressing the KPIs and the specifics of demand and supply in a given industry; identifying and prioritizing core competitors and selecting the competitive pricing method; defining the optimal price positioning; defining the roles of groups of products or services in progressing towards the overall business KPIs;
3. Pricing tactics – given the defined strategy, model the impact on the KPIs of different price adjustment scenarios, and optimize prices in a way to increase the likelihood of hitting the target;
4. Pricing execution – setting the prices (and here, even more importantly, price reductions) and making sure that they're available to and relevant for customers at the moment of decision-making and purchasing;
5. Measurement – estimating the impact of adjusted prices on the selected business targets and the probability of hitting a selected target in the future.

Target setting is still largely the prerogative of humans, as we haven't reached the point yet where an artificial general intelligence (AGI) will be able to set long-term goals better than humans. It is hardly likely in the near future either, as for an AGI to beat humans on the above, the artificial intelligence decision-maker needs to possess motivation and intentions aligned with those of the human decision-maker. Another reason (this one can be gone in the future) – humans can set goals and judge on the probability of success in achieving it without having complete data on the environment and the historical data, purely by applying judgment and some intuition. Artificial intelligence still needs historical and current data (the more, the better), to be able to compare different strategies and judge on the probable outcomes.

Thus, let us delve into pricing strategy, tactics, execution, and measurement to identify the use cases where AI can actually do a better job than us human beings.

And we start with the **pricing tactics**. Converting even the smartest pricing strategy into everyday pricing decisions is a real stumbling block that many businesses face. Besides many technical reasons like the number of products to optimize prices of and the lack of scientific capabilities, few businesses realize.that they should target neither the lowest nor the highest prices on the market. There is an *optimal* price value for each product or service. In this sense, you cannot really drive price positioning or average price level without understanding the rationale behind. In any case, certain price points need to drive profit, or revenue, or sell-through rate, or several of them at the same time, to a possible maximum. Moreover, since the price affects many business indicators at once, it is important to maintain a balance of two or even more of them when changing prices.

This is what the science of price optimization is about – given the primary business target to drive and the ones to protect, executing tactical price changes to actually drive the selected target to a possible maximum while obeying the constraints.

It is via the concept of price elasticity that it does so. Price elasticity of demand describes how much demand will change in case we change the price of a certain product or service by 1%. Demand here stands for the number of items, or volume units of goods sold. As the main business indicator to drive with the help of prices, demand is used mainly by manufacturers who are focused on building their market share. Indeed, growing demand means that a manufacturer has more customers, and existing consumers buy more. This means that, most likely, the manufacturer's market share is growing or, at least, not declining, which in turn guarantees a certain workload at the factories.

Revenue, or merchandise value, is another important indicator that companies, whose goal is primarily growth, are excited about. For manufacturers, this indicator is again important from the point of view of the balance of working capital and fixed costs, the so-called overheads. For retailers, this indicator is important primarily from the point of view of working capital – no one wants to "freeze" in warehouses the significant amounts of money spent on purchasing goods from manufacturers.

In the majority of cases though, profit (i.e. what remains after deduction of COGS and logistic costs from the revenue) is the ultimate goal of price optimization.

And finally, marginality, also known as the margin percentage, or profitability margin. It is advisable to maintain profitability at a fairly constant and sufficient level to make sure that the business is not in the race to the bottom, from which it is incredibly difficult to get out. If we want to fix the marginality by changing prices, this is relatively easy to do. To do this, you need to calculate how the share of costs in the selling price will change as a percentage and pick a price point that satisfies the target or minimal marginality requirement.

In all other cases, this is much more difficult to do. For this, you need to calculate, or in some cases to assume, how the demand for the product will change when the price changes by a certain percentage. And this is a real art, the secret sauce that can lead to businesses' success or failure, known as the price elasticity of demand.

There are two approaches that have gained prominence in enterprise of how to calculate the price elasticity of demand, and both benefit greatly from applying advanced algorithms:

1. Explicit price elasticity coefficients – those are price elasticity coefficients calculated separately from the price optimization and are typically expressed as a one-number coefficient;
2. Implicit price elasticity coefficients – inferred as one of the arguments in the function of demand with the help of machine learning algorithms trained on time series, whose complexity has earned them the name of "black boxes"; as apparent from this name, there is no single price elasticity coefficient that can be "extracted" from the model, and you need to pick a price level or several price levels for the black box to predict the demand reaction to the price change.

1. Let us start with the **explicit price elasticity** coefficients use case. The core assumption here is, no matter how much we change the price, and regardless of other circumstances like the season or the competitors' pricing strategies, the price elasticity, or the ratio between the demand and the price change, remains constant, or at least that demand can be described as a function of price and only price.

For the moment, let's assume that this is the case. How do we calculate the price elasticity, and as the name of this chapter advises, how can "AI" help here? It depends on your tolerance level as to what can be called AI and what cannot. To many, any algorithm that deals with regression or classification tasks can hold this title. And (multi)linear regression is no exception. Indeed, regression is arguably the simplest way to build a demand model that can yield price elasticity coefficients in the context of other important business drivers. It describes demand as a function of price in a form of $Q = a - b * P$, in which Q is the expected demand in quantity terms, P is the selling price, a is the intercept that takes care of the difference in scale of quantities vs prices, and b is the slope that shows how strongly the demand is dependent on price changes.

You can think of the linear regression analysis as an attempt to draw a straight sloped line in the "cloud" of points in such a way that the sum of the distances from the points to the straight line is minimal. In this cloud, X values correspond to price points of a certain product, whereas the Y values correspond to the items sold. Accordingly, if we have a new price value (X-axis) we need to predict the demand for, we can roughly calculate the sales value (Y-axis) for this price.

Next are examples of correlation between prices and items sold, and absence thereof:

1. Prices and quantities sold of a product are uncorrelated.
2. Negative price elasticity of demand – the higher the price, the lower the quantity.
3. Positive price elasticity of demand – the higher the price, the higher the demand (could be the case in case of some luxury products etc.).
4. Nonlinear dependency of demand on price changes.

A disclaimer – in most cases, there's a nonlinear dependency of demand on price changes. In any case, price elasticity coefficients have the highest values (in absolute terms) within a narrow interval from the current price point (ca. −15%/+15% either from a discounted price or from a full price). The further we get with a price change, the less elastic in relative terms the demand gets. Indeed, given an average price elasticity coefficient of −2, and a price increase of 50%, we cannot expect the items sold to go down to 0 (−2*50% = −100% demand decrease). In order to address this, a power demand curve is used to estimate the demand at a certain price point instead of the linear one. In this case, the demand curve is described by a power curve of the form $q = a*P\^b$, in which $a > 0, b < 0$.

POWER PRICE RESPONSE FUNCTION

However even this approach doesn't completely solve the problem of the demand reaction attenuation after a certain threshold of price changes. Indeed, at some

Figure 8.1

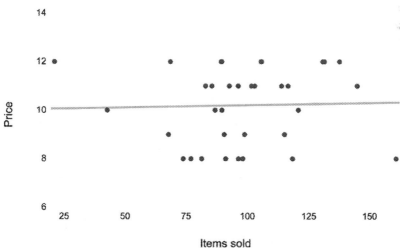

Figure 8.2

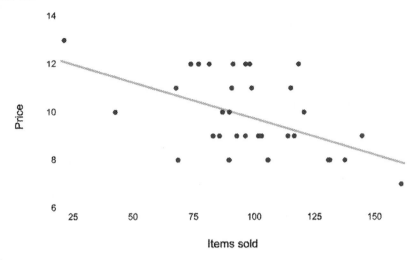

2.

Figure 8.3

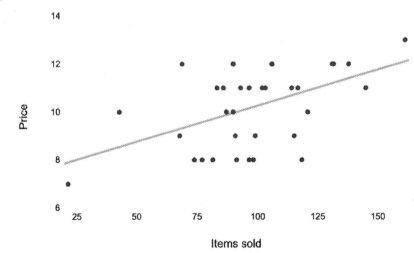

3.

point it doesn't matter whether we give a −70% price reduction or a −80% one, the demand uptick will be roughly the same. To address this, the sigmoid demand curve, also referred to as the logit demand function, is used. It can be specified as follows:

Figure 8.4

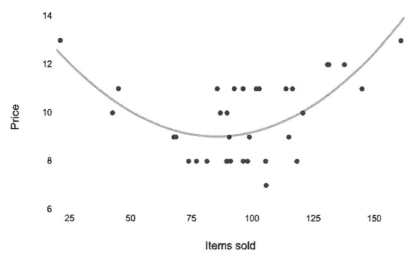

4.

Figure 8.5

Figure 8.6

$$q(p) = Q_{max} \cdot \frac{1}{1 + e^{a+bp}}$$

Figure 8.7

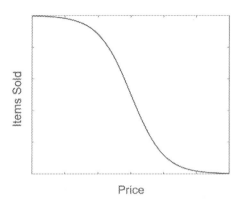

Figure 8.8

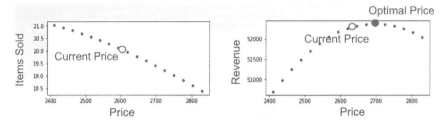

in which Q_{max} is the maximum achievable demand, and b is a parameter that controls the steepness of the demand curve. Next is an example of a sigmoid demand function with respect to price.

SIGMOID PRICE RESPONSE FUNCTION

Another way to estimate the price elasticity of demand in an explicit way, that is gradually becoming the best practice, is with the help of so-called "causal inference" methods that attribute changes in demand to changes in price in a statistically robust manner (two-way fixed effects, a.k.a. TWFE, and PCMCI are examples of such algorithms). Given that price elasticity is still calculated in the form of a single coefficient, the transformations described previously (transforming the linear function into a power or a logit one) also apply here.

Now that we have calculated the price elasticity, we need to decide how to use them in the **price optimization process**. The task here is to find the price point that is expected to yield the maximum possible demand, or a derivative thereof such as revenue or profit.

Let us take a look at some examples of how optimal prices may look different depending on the target of optimization (sold items vs revenue) and on the price elasticity of demand of different products.

Figure 8.9

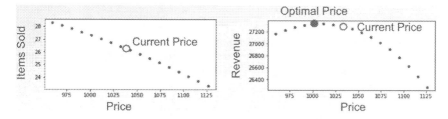

Figure 8.10

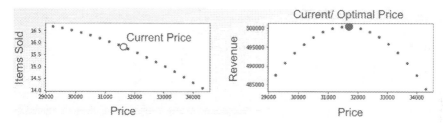

In the first case, in order to achieve the maximum possible revenue, you need to increase the price.

Here, you need to decrease it.

And here it needs to be left unchanged.

As mentioned previously, revenue is not necessarily the ultimate goal of price optimization. In many cases, it is profit.

We need to assume how the demand (Q) will change in respect to a price change (P), given the constant relationship between the two, to calculate what the optimal price is that maximizes gross profit on an individual product level:

$$\text{Piopt} = \text{argmaxPi Qi (Pi)} \cdot \text{(Pi} - \text{Vi)} - \text{Ci}$$

in which Vi is variable costs (e.g. wholesale product price), Ci is fixed costs associated with the product, and Qi (Pi) is our assumption of how the demand (Q) will change in respect to a price change.

For the explicit price elasticity coefficients, predicting demand is less important than for the implicit elasticity ones, for a couple of reasons. First and foremost, the explicit price elasticity coefficients are only applicable to a narrow interval of possible price changes, and are valid in the context where they were calculated. You cannot really assume what the impact on demand will be in case of non-typical price changes applied in the context that's not in the historical data. Secondly, explicit price elasticity coefficients have a strong assumption behind that demand is only a function of own price elasticity, and the values of other parameters, including relative price positioning to substitutes or competing propositions, are disregarded. Thirdly, given that the price elasticity coefficient is given, price optimization calculation in case of profit can be reduced to a formula not requiring demand estimation. After certain transformations of the optimization formula in the previous section, we can arrive to the optimal price with respect to profit being

$$\text{Piopt} = \text{Vi} \cdot \epsilon\epsilon - 1$$

in which Vi is variable costs, and ϵ is the price elasticity coefficient, that is, the ratio between the quantity sold change and the price change, expressed in %.

2. In case of **implicit elasticity** coefficients, as you can imagine, there are upsides and downsides in comparison with the explicit ones. So why the hassle? In comparison with the rather simplistic approach of one-number elasticities, there are plenty of options for more accurate price optimization. The "black box" models can treat demand as a function of a lot of factors influencing it in reality, and the most exciting part of it is that they can produce context-aware price elasticities. For example, if the reaction of demand to price changes of a certain product was different in high and low season, when a big competitor ran a discount and when it didn't, a complex enough model trained on a large dataset can capture such differences. Assuming non-linearity of demand beyond the observed price changes is also not a big deal for these algorithms. Finally, such models can assume elasticity of products that are very new to shelves, based on their similarity to products sold in the past. Sounds like a lot of advantages. So where is the catch? The thing is, accurate prediction of demand is essential for such models. As well as they need to be suitable for efficient price optimization purposes. Let's consider several examples of AI algorithms capable of producing demand forecast, and taking the impact of prices on it into account along the way:

- Gradient boosters, for example, AdaBoost, Gradient Boosting, XGBoost, LightGBM, CatBoost; these algorithms produce so-called discrete demand predictions for specific price points, separately by season and other contexts, which tends to be quite accurate and detailed. However, they do so by producing and comparing the quality of many possible decision trees, which limits their applicability in price optimization to the cases where there are few products to optimize prices for, the precision of a price point is not too important, and the spillover effects are negligible.

- Time series forecasting (auto-)regression models; such models aim to describe the autocorrelations in the data and thus can forecast demand for the coming period based on past trends in demand and the factors influencing it. Contemporary time series forecasting algorithms, for example, Prophet can beat many other algorithms on the accuracy of demand prediction, but due to their high dependency on past demand trends and low dependency on exogenous features, they are likely to ignore the impact of prices on it. And this artifact is very challenging to overcome.

- Neural networks (NN) are worth mentioning for the price optimization use case. A neural network can be thought of as a network of "neurons" organized in layers. The input data are stored at the bottom level, and the outputs (forecasts) form the top layer. There may also be intermediate layers containing hidden concepts of how to use inputs in combination to produce accurate forecasts of the target. Neural networks represent a sweet spot for price optimization in a sense that they are capable of both producing accurate estimation of demand and its reaction to price changes, and producing output in a way it can be used for price optimization.

- Reinforcement learning (RL) is a rather recent addition to the army of AI methods used in price optimization. It is a machine learning technique that allows an agent to learn how to behave in an environment in order to maximize a reward. The agent does so by interacting with the environment and observing the consequences of its actions. The agent starts with a random policy, which is a set of rules that determine how it will act in different situations. As the agent interacts with the environment, it learns to improve its policy by trial and error. The agent receives a reward for taking actions that lead to a desirable outcome, and a penalty for taking actions that lead to an undesirable outcome. The agent uses these rewards and penalties to update its policy, so that it is more likely to take actions that lead to rewards in the future. Due to this fact, such algorithms can develop quite complex pricing strategies stretched in time that resemble Hi-Lo "human" pricing strategies. The problem with application of RL algorithms in pricing is that the response of the environment necessary for an agent's learning is incomplete, delayed, scarce, and blurred. MoviOnline stores and marketplaces are also examples of environments where RL has some potential. However, there were no success stories of its successful implementation in the latter at the time of writing.

The table summarizes the pros and cons of different AI algorithms in price optimization:

	Accuracy of demand forecasting	Applicability in price optimization	Interpretability/ explainability
Gradient boosters	High	Good	Good
Time series forecasting models	High	Poor	Moderate
Neural networks	Moderate	Good	Moderate
Reinforcement learning	Not proven	Limited	Poor

The core advantage of using implicit price elasticity approaches is that one process can combine both the elasticity estimation and the price optimization. Lack of immediate explainability is one of the key disadvantages mentioned with regard to these methods.

Any demand model can only be as accurate and complete as the data that it has been trained on. A good train dataset for a demand-predicting algorithm that is at the same time good at inferring price elasticities could benefit greatly from having the following features in it:

1. Price-related factors:

    a. Own full price

    b. Own discounted/reduced price without personal incentives applied

    c. Price change vs previous period

    d. Cumulative price change over a period

    e. Promotion mechanics

    f. Promotion reach/coverage

    g. Price indexes vs "true" competitors

    h. Price indexes vs categories that a product belongs to, substitutes, and complementary products

2. Non-pricing factors:

    a. Temporal (week, month, year, etc.)

    b. Description of categories that a product belongs to

    c. Representation of a product in respect to the cluster of similar products, substitutes, and complements

    d. Availability (e.g. weighted distribution of an SKU)

    e. Events calendar

    f. Weather anomalies (temperature, precipitation, etc.)

    g. Advertising investment, reach, and share of voice

    h. Advertising efficiency indicators (CTR, VTR, etc.)

    i. Out-of-stocks

After the algorithm is trained, it also needs to have complete data on the constraints that need to be taken into account within the optimization process, such as stock availability in total and by market/warehouse/segment, end of shelf life date, legal constraints such as EU Directive on Unfair Commercial Practices, business constraints such as minimum marginality allowed, etc.

Let us now return to the list of typical pricing tasks, and pick **pricing strategy** as the next use case where AI can be instrumental. Two sub-tasks catch our eye here: identifying and prioritizing core competitors, and defining the roles of products or services in progressing towards the overall targets. Imagine you have a dozen of potential direct competitors, and hundreds of thousands of products that are not unique to your portfolio. Such a situation cries for prioritization. Which competitors are the "true" ones, meaning that they do have (negative) impact on your rate of sale? Which products are "true" key value items and thus have to be priced competitively? What is the most meaningful way to cluster substitutes and complements together? Finally, how can these effects be taken into account in price optimization, that is, how does one embrace the external and internal cross-price elasticity mentioned previously, in the price optimization process?

There are traditional non-AI methods tackling these aspects, of course, but these are the new machine learning algorithms that take the quality of pricing strategy insights to the next level. For starters, you can take competitors' price changes, their ranking in search engines or reviews – assuming that you have them – and your own sales, for the past three months or so, and visually inspect the time series. You can probably see for yourself that in the case of some competitors, surges in their popularity in a search engine or deep discounting periods coincide with drops in your rate of sale. This way you can reduce a list of competitors to only those who have at least visible impact on your sales. Besides, you can ask your field force or your customers directly who the true competitors are. Better still, you combine the mentioned sources to arrive at a more or less robust conclusion on who your most fear-worthy competitors are. The only remaining thing to do is to build your competitive pricing strategy around this priority list.

However, when getting to executing this strategy, one can easily face the wall when choosing which products to competitively price against the shortlisted competitors. Segmenting your products is a non-trivial task either. This is where the AI will extend a helping hand. The so-called causal inference algorithms mentioned previously are capable of establishing a cause-and-effect relationship between a price change by competitor or on a substitute, and the demand change of a product in question. This discipline has evolved a lot in recent years, driven by significant progress in algorithms and by high investment of flagship businesses like Amazon and Google in it. A concept of interaction between demands for products (a.k.a. interference) and between prices and demand for the same products by different competitors is key. Estimation of the causal relationship is largely based on experiments (when one actually runs an experiment) and quasi-experiments (when experiment-style analysis is performed on historical data). There is another group of methods that make attempts to represent causality in a probabilistic way. Here, one can name Granger causality and its descendants like tigramite or PCMCI. However, they are not considered "gold standard" anymore.

In short, by establishing a cause-and-effect relationship between price changes by competitors and demand for a certain product, you can prioritize two things: (1) competitors causing most of your products to underperform in sales can be treated as "true" competitors; (2) products whose sales performance is the most impacted by the competitive price moves are the "true" key value Items. You then prioritize investment in competitive pricing accordingly: price-match only the true competitors, and only on true KVI products. In a similar fashion, causal inference can help with aligned pricing of products whose demand depends on each other's price levels. For this, proving that price points of so-called "anchor" products influences sales of substitutes can be instrumental in building pricing architecture within a category, that is, which products need to be priced together so that their relative price positioning remains unchanged. This prevents within-range sales cannibalization.

Further on, once you have localized parts in your portfolio where internal and external cannibalization may occur, it becomes just a technical matter to use the internal and external cross-price elasticity effects within the price optimization process. However, one needs to keep in mind that technicalities do matter here. Measuring cross-price elasticity is a much more advanced topic in comparison with calculating own price elasticity and is not nearly as impactful as the latter. Therefore, we often have to use simpler approximations, such as the ratio of the price in a given segment to the average price in other segments. Another challenge is that the dependencies between different products can make the optimization problem computationally prohibitive.

Still talking about pricing strategy, imagine that we have a proven true competitor whose prices are worth matching or even undercutting. The following issue related to execution arises then – how do we know whether a proposition by competitor is identical or at least similar to mine to be worth price-matching? The task here is to find an identical or a very similar product in a competitor's range. Traditionally, this task has been outsourced to so-called matchers or annotators, that is, humans who either find exactly the same product by searching a webshop, or validate that a pair of products is exactly the same. With the advance of natural language processing and computer vision algorithms, however, it has become a matter of time for these tasks to be outsourced to algorithms. Current state of the art in these two disciplines allows for producing so-called embeddings, or vector representation of images and text descriptions of products, that are accurate enough to predict with high accuracy whether two embeddings belong to identical products, or they are far off from each other. Out-of-the box CV and NLP algorithms such as CLIP (https://openai.com/research/clip) or MUSE (https://ai.meta.com/tools/muse/) are accurate enough to be considered for producing a solid baseline. AutoML packages, for example, AutoGluon (https://auto.gluon.ai/stable/tutorials/multimodal/matching/index.html#) require a bit more effort but can produce an even better baseline.

In fact, the product similarity estimation technique has multiple applications. Solving the so-called "cold start" problem is one of those. This problem is prominent in the introductory pricing, where the task is to define the optimal price for a product that is newly listed and has not yet sold a single item. Beyond that, there can be long-tail products whose typical days consist of mostly zero and scarce one-item sales. In addition, especially in the pre-COVID world, in many cases a price for a product has never ever changed, and it is impossible to tell from the historical data how the demand would react to a possible price change. Specifically to B2B environments, one-for-all promotions are few, which makes it challenging to determine which items should be price-discounted.

Finally, **measurement** of the impact of execution of certain pricing strategies and tactics is where data-driven algorithms can surely help. Suffice it to say that the 2021 Nobel Prize in Economic Sciences was awarded to David Card, Joshua Angrist, and Guido Imbens, who laid the groundwork for natural experiments, a.k.a. A/B-tests. The science of randomized experiments is currently undergoing a renaissance, driven by the likes of Amazon, who find it particularly important to be able to measure the impact of their initiatives in pricing and other retail operations. Advanced statistical methods helped to make it a real science rather than a toy that can help justify someone's wrong decisions. For A/B testing, the following concepts are critical:

1. The basics – parameters of the general population and the treatment and control cells
2. Experiment design – the null hypothesis (sometimes neglected for "learning" reasons but important to have even if learning is one of the test's goals), the metrics, and the decision-making principle upon the test results, randomization unit, interference
3. Statistics – confidence level, margin of error, confidence interval, Type 1 error, Type 2 error, p-value, statistical significance, statistical power, minimum detectable effect, practical significance, sample size, and experiment duration in relation to the minimum detectable effect
4. Artifacts – unexpected environment changes, for example, own or competitor's promo, short-lived effects that vanish after the ab-test is over, for example, novelty and primacy effects, spillover effects between the treatment and control groups.

Hopefully, this chapter has had you excited about implementing artificial intelligence in your pricing processes. Now what?

There are four important aspects to consider that can make or break it.

1. Data preparation:
    Data preparation and collection can be a surprisingly challenging task. The data is often unstructured, stored in different sources, and contains many errors. "Data swamps" rather than data lakes have become the real nightmare of many enterprises and smaller businesses. This can make it difficult to cleanse and prepare the data for machine learning. The process of preparing and collecting data can take several weeks or even months. In some cases, it may be necessary to hire a contractor with expertise in data management. However, the good news is that even if you plan to use machine learning to automate multiple business processes, such as logistics, inventory management, and algorithmic pricing, you only need to prepare your data once. This is because the data will have a similar structure regardless of how you use it.

    Here are some specific challenges of data preparation and collection:

    - Unstructured data: Unstructured data is data that does not have a predefined format. This can make it difficult to process and analyze (e.g. internal trackers in spreadsheets, free text, images, etc.)

- Data silos: Data silos are data repositories that are isolated from each other. This can make it difficult to access and integrate data from different sources.
- Data errors: Data errors can occur during data collection, processing, or storage. These errors can lead to inaccurate results
- Data streaming vs data batch processing: These are two very different data engineering solutions, so it needs to be considered carefully and well in advance whether price calculation needs to happen in real time, or within a day or two after the fresh transactional data become available.

Despite these challenges, data preparation and collection are essential steps in the machine learning process. By taking the time to prepare your data properly, you can improve the accuracy and performance of your machine learning models.

2. In-house vs external vendor solution:

There are pros and cons of developing your own price optimization solution, and the optimal decision here largely depends on the size and maturity level of the business you are in. Businesses need to be good at many different things in order to be successful. These things may not be directly related to their core competency, but they are still important for achieving success. For example, you may be able to offer all customers low prices and negotiate good purchase prices. However, your profits depend not only on low purchase prices, but also on optimal shelf prices. This means that you need to learn how to set prices that are neither too low nor too high. This is a new skill that requires a significant investment in research and development (R&D). Whilst investing in R&D is overall a great long-term idea, you need to be realistic about the time and money you need to invest in developing an in-house solution that is stable and delivering successful outcomes. As a rule of thumb, you can think of a three-year and several-million-dollar investment to achieve a good enough state of things. However, for enterprises it still makes sense, as developing in-house products catering for business critical processes allows them to avoid the so-called vendor lock, that is, over-dependence of critical business processes on an external agent.

3. Educating your team:

Once your AI-enhanced pricing system is ready, it is important to train your pricing and category managers. They need to understand how the system works and why it makes certain price recommendations. The logic behind the recommendations may not always be clear, but the managers need to trust the system and be willing to experiment with its suggestions. By working together, the managers and the system can achieve better results than either could on its own. The system can provide the managers with insights that they would not have otherwise had, and the managers can help the system to avoid making mistakes.

Here are some specific things that you can do to train your pricing or category managers:

- Explain to them how the pricing system works and why it makes the price recommendations that it does.

- Show them how to use the system to set prices and track their performance.
- Encourage them to experiment with the system's suggestions and to put guardrails on the system as needed.
- Help them to understand the limitations of the system and how to avoid making mistakes.
- Communicate regularly with them about the system's performance and how they can improve it.

By taking the time to train your pricing or category managers, you can help them to understand and trust the system, and you can achieve better results.

4.   Ongoing improvements:

You need to have a pricing strategy in place and provide the pricing system with a set of goals that it needs to achieve within this strategy. You should be able to monitor how the system is performing and make adjustments as needed. If your goals or strategy change, you need to adjust your pricing system accordingly.

It is impossible to review in proper detail in a single chapter the plethora of AI algorithms used in pricing nowadays, as their number is growing by day. However, hopefully, the author has managed to both inspire the reader and to provide her with sufficient starting points for the most important use cases in pricing where implementation of machine learning algorithms can be very beneficial for business.

SUMMARY

Pricing is a complex task for businesses due to factors like variations in demand, competition, and lack of historical data for new products.

Artificial intelligence (AI) can automate pricing decisions and improve accuracy through machine learning algorithms.

There are two main approaches to calculate price elasticity of demand (PED), which measures the impact of price changes on demand:

- Explicit price elasticity coefficients: These are one-number coefficients that assume a constant relationship between price and demand within a specific range. They are calculated using regression analysis.

- Implicit price elasticity coefficients: These are inferred from complex machine learning models that can handle nonlinear relationships and consider various factors affecting demand.

AI can be used to optimize prices for different goals such as maximizing revenue, sold items, or profit.

AI can also help with other pricing-related tasks like identifying key competitors, defining the roles of products, and segmenting products. Matching competitor products and solving the cold start problem (pricing new items) are other areas where AI can be applied in pricing.

Implementing AI-powered pricing comes with certain challenges:

- Data Preparation
- In-house vs External Vendor
- Team Education
- Ongoing Improvements

However, given the business benefits that it brings along, any challenges are worth overcoming.

9

Price management success across sectors
In retail at Nike vs in hospitality at Hilton
Mohammed Ahmed

Mohammed Ahmed is an expert pricing strategist with cross-industry experience in airlines, hospitality, and retail. For the last years he is lead of revenue management for Hilton for a group of hotels across the Middle East, Africa, and Turkey. He shares his interesting journey from help desk to head office and offers helpful insights into pricing strategies used by these different industries.

Thanks for joining me, Mohammed. You have a very interesting story. To begin, perhaps you can let our readers know how you got started with pricing? What caught your attention and interest?

My career in pricing started completely by accident. I graduated in 2009 during the recession and found myself working for Virgin Atlantic airlines in my hometown in the UK. I worked in their call center for around one year, and then I was promoted to team leader.

One day a customer complained to one of my agents that their flight had been booked incorrectly. I needed to change their flight back and wasn't able to do so because of some system constraint. I was told I needed to phone revenue management as they control the flight bookings.

It was the first time I had heard this, so I phoned them, and they changed it. At that moment I realized, okay, revenue management are the decision-makers, so I need to find a way to get to that department. I found an organizational chart of the company and mapped out a plan of how I would get there.

My plan worked. I started by looking for a position in the audit department. I chose this auditing role because I knew they audit the work of revenue management. After nine months of doing auditing I secured a role in revenue management, so that was when my first venture into pricing really began.

For Virgin I was pricing for the interline and offline market. Virgin Atlantic used to fly from London to mostly transatlantic destinations and had a few other stopovers in Africa and the Middle East. I had to connect people such as from Madrid and Amsterdam, from places that people would then connect through to London. I needed to price fares based on what information the airline would give us as well as be sure fares were competitively priced so that people would book them.

DOI: 10.4324/9781003535966-12

That was my first sort of real foray into pricing and basically I've been doing that type of job ever since, so we're looking at about eleven years now.

Can you tell me why you moved to Dubai, to Emirates airline, and now to Hilton, and what were your decision points or what made you choose to change your assignments.

Virgin Atlantic is a small airline in the grand scheme of things, so I had been doing the pricing job for just under a year with Virgin. At that time, the Emirates were going through a massive expansion plan, and I received a sponsored ad in my LinkedIn from the Emirates saying, "apply revenue management pricing professionals." For me Emirates was the "Real Madrid" of airlines, and you don't want to say no if they come looking for you, so I applied, thinking, okay, let's just see what happens.

They were looking for a candidate with seven years' of documented experience in pricing, and here I had only one year. Nevertheless, I managed to make it to the interview stage. They had a very thorough assessment process which took roughly six hours and involved about five tests. If you passed those, you moved on to day two where it was face-to-face with the revenue management department. I managed to get through all that and was offered a pricing management role, so I moved my family to Dubai and began working with Emirates.

When I first arrived at Emirates I felt like I was drowning, as I was moving from pricing from four origin points to about twenty destinations with Virgin to being given six origin points and needing to price to over a hundred twenty destinations on a daily basis for Emirates.

There were a number of other strategy tactics to grasp as well, and that's when the real learning kicked in. I learned how to manage multiple currencies from multiple origin points from different markets as well as needing to understand the sales conversations and reasoning behind why you need to price fares a certain way.

After around three years I was ready for a management opportunity. However, my expectations coincided with Turkish Airlines and Qatar Airways starting to emerge, so for Emirates, naturally pricing in the market took a downward swing, which meant profitability and the opportunity for growth started to be limited.

I began looking for a pricing role outside of the airlines industry as I wanted to find something that was more strategy based. With airlines you have a certain strategy, but it's quite reactionary as you need to react sometimes twice a day to what the competition is doing as well. It's a very price-driven industry on a consumer basis.

An opportunity with Nike emerged out of nowhere. They were based in the Netherlands, and within two weeks they arranged for me to be flown there. I did the interview and got the job.

They have a distributor model which includes the Middle East, Eastern Europe, and North Africa which was what they had in mind for me to oversee for pricing. Nike had decided they wanted to focus more on consumer-value-based pricing rather than cost-plus, which is what their distributors were doing. My task was to turn things around into more of a consumer value sort of perspective, and it was a good role, which I enjoyed.

However, we can't always rely on our career choices. Sometimes you have to use family as an indicator of the direction things should take.

I fully understand, as we are expecting our second kid.

Congratulations on that! My first son was born in the Netherlands, and my wife was expecting our second kid, but she just wasn't happy there. I thought, okay, we were happy in Dubai, so I'll arrange to get us back to Dubai, and I found an opportunity with Hilton Hotels, so that's where I am now.

Would you be able to share how pricing is integrated into these different companies' strategies? What would you see as the differences and similarities of how they approach pricing from a strategic perspective?

Airlines and hotels are quite similar in the way they can control pricing and profit from it. You have much more direct-to-consumer influence, so that's your strategy. It is more of a channel distribution strategy where you want to drive direct sales yourself, and you can capitalize on that. So your revenue management is basically capitalizing on that demand. You can only sell so much of your inventory on a certain day, and once that day is gone, your opportunity to sell goes with it.

It's more about building relationships with people that can expand your distribution, so you have your online travel agencies and boutique style agencies for certain destinations as well. And then you have the corporates that probably make up between 20 to 30% of your customer base so you're able to switch between them depending on what's happening in the overall market. For example, during COVID, with hotels we were able to pivot and take advantage of government contracts, and quite a few of our hotels were used as quarantine properties welcoming people as a quarantine business.

Whereas with retail, you need to be a bit more strategic because the majority of your business is going to be booked before the season kicks off. A buy-in will be made perhaps six months before the product launches. Commitments will be made so you don't have the opportunity to really capitalize as much because you're probably selling 10% directly to consumers and the rest as a wholesaler, which is one way in which the business objectives are kind of different.

With retail businesses you have a bit more say in cost-cutting for increasing your own profitability whereas with airlines and hotels you're more at risk to the elements. Essentials such as fuel and electricity may increase, and your cost base will increase, but you can offset that by increasing your direct-to-consumer price as well.

That makes sense when you think about how pricing was integrated into the structure of the corporations. Do you see any differences in any of those pricings which would have a stronger sway? What do you see as the differences?

With airlines, front and center, pricing is everything whether it's cargo or the passenger side. They know this is what will make or break the business. Hotels are slightly backseat from this, but it's still quite to the core. With hotels you may have some more operational elements because hotels offer FNB opportunities. You may have a restaurant space which you may be able to lease out to an external provider, or host weddings, conventions, and so forth, so there's a few more elements that you can depend on outside of the normal pricing. So hotels probably rely a bit more on sales than an airline does in that way.

As far as retail, when I joined Nike, pricing seemed to be more of an afterthought. I was part of a team tasked with bringing a greater focus on pricing. At that time, because it was more cost-plus, it was more like, okay this is the margin we need to be profitable, so this is the amount that we will sell it at. So if the retail price were $100 in the US, we would recommend the same price but converted to Euros in Europe. So that was more or less the basic approach.

When I arrived, the department was maybe one and a half years into the process of bringing pricing into more of an advanced sort of practice. It had been pretty much an afterthought before that.

That is surprising because I would think that companies like Nike are really proficient at pricing, and they have extensive themes, you know, tools expertise with price experiments and everything, so quite surprising.

They were good at digital direct to consumer, they were good there, but at that time when it came to setting the RRP for everyone globally, it was a bit lacking.

As you've been in the pricing business in these different industries for eleven years now, how do you see technology and the new tools have changed and evolved things in terms of pricing? And again do you see any differences between the different industries you have worked with?

As far as the airline industry is concerned, they were using mostly internal data, so we used revenue management software, and you would plug in your price points after doing your own analysis. When I arrived at Emirates, there was a tool which was used to upload the rate that the public sees, and this would take someone about two hours' worth of analysis to analyze from different sources.

I created an Excel template because I had to get the competitors' data, plug it in, and plug in our market share from another data resource and then upload everything after making a decision. So my program reduced that time from around two hours to only minutes, so at that time there wasn't much market intelligence coming in real time.

The focus was mostly about how is the airline operating and what's the capacity from London to Dubai and then what is the capacity from Dubai to Thailand and so forth, which was how we arrived on the prices based on these few elements.

Things have changed greatly in the last few years. If I compare things now to how the hotel industry worked at that time, there have been many changes. When I first arrived at Hilton four years ago, it was more or less the same story. Pricing was based purely on how the hotel you're looking at was running in terms of occupancy and rates and what you've said should be the rate.

In the last two years there's been much more advancement with AI so that we now have intel coming from the market in real-time, and there's also a separate tool that scrapes websites. For example, I can select Booking.com, and it will scrape for my chosen destination, and then it will feed that into the revenue management system, and every four hours it will reassess the market pricing of what is the properties occupancies based on this pace and what is the expected occupancy. It will continue to perform estimated price experiments throughout the day, so prices will increase and decrease in accordance with the latest data. So things have moved now to using more dynamic real-time pricing software, so I imagine if hotels are doing this now, I'm more than certain airlines have probably started doing something similar as well.

Can you speak more about the application of AI in pricing. How do you perceive the application of AI in pricing, and how will it help you or change your job?

For now what it has done is remove the manual element. It's become more of a help to assist with pricing. An example would be if a hotel lets me know they've received a sales inquiry for 20% of their inventory to be sold for a conference that's taking place. I can literally put that info into the revenue management system, and based on the trend that it's seeing at the time, it calculates what it estimates the property will finish with, and then it gives me a figure that mitigates any displaced customers if we receive this group. So for me it's been a positive aid.

Right now I'd say it's a help, but I remember two years ago when we first started to use these enhancements, it was more of a hindrance because it was giving us prices that were double that for which we would rationally sell. It has definitely improved as it has learned. After training the AI, I have seen the learning of the system itself go to a more reasonable pricing point, so now I rarely have to influence it. The way it has changed my role is I'm spending less time doing analysis and more time influencing the system to get it to where I want it to be, but overall it's reduced my time of analysis.

So you now see your role as a pricing manager/pricing executive in terms of shaping or changing these tools to your needs. Do you have a road map for the future?

For me it's more about what is the desired result and weighing that up with what the market is doing at the same time. So if I'm seeing a slowdown in demand, but I'm not seeing the system learning that these units are going to be selling at a much lower rate in the real world, I need to influence the system to rationalize with what we know, but the system doesn't know.

I'd say overall the relationship for me is to coach the AI into what's realistic and what isn't. If I do see an exceptional event that maybe causes the prices to sell at a much higher rate than is reasonable, I know this was an exception. For example, if there was an election in Nigeria last year that caused much higher rates, I need to make sure the system doesn't think of that as the new trend, so I just need to insert some parameters to disregard the data from these particular dates but use the trend from the last three months to estimate for January next year. So for me I'm basically training the AI at the moment.

In the next three to five years, do you see investments in pricing at Hilton will be more with people or with technology? Will you spend more money hiring new pricing people or developing that technology?

Currently the technology is something that's being developed more. I think the good thing about technology is it can give you consistent results, whereas as far as pricing as practitioners, I don't believe there's ever a wrong or right answer. We don't know until we've done the work. So if you're investing more in technology, you can take the learning of seven or eight people or even more and apply that, so technology is probably the direction where investment will go.

Perhaps we can change gears and ask if you could describe a particularly challenging pricing decision you faced and how you navigated through it.

Yes, I have one from the retail space. I was taking over the Middle East, and over here they have one particular company that are selling at wholesale to all other retailers, but they are also retailers themselves. With them it was a cost-plus model, and I had to try to give a consumer-based pricing approach to them and try to sell them on this strategy.

For my approach I used basketball shoes as an example. A basketball shoe retailing at $100 in the US was probably retailing for €110 in the Netherlands, and the price in Italy was maybe €98, so there was a kind of a regional difference. Then I looked at how the UAE was pricing, and there was about a 30% increase in price from Europe to the UAE, but the landed cost was less than what it was in Europe, so I was able to see that there's a big cost-plus element to this coming from the distributor as I was advised they have influenced the pricing heavily over the years.

What I discovered was there was a trend emerging of people becoming more savvy as shoppers as they realized they were able to buy from other countries and get shoes delivered for next to nothing or have someone go on holiday to London to pick them up. Also what was happening in the UAE was people were getting used to waiting to buy until an item went on sale.

This was the problem of the distributor. After I looked into the basketball category I found competitors like Adidas and others were pricing around a 15% increase versus Europe. I came up with a pricing plan and told them we actually need to drop our rates quite heavily and that we need to go to about 15% less on their retail price. Their main argument against this was their margin would be reduced because of the wholesale price that we were selling to them for.

We negotiated and I used their own data to show them from their own stores that when they were making their final sales, their end price was not at the profit margin that they were aiming for because the majority of their shoes were being sold once they discounted them heavily. They might have been retailing the shoes for $140, as an example, but when they actually sold, their average sale price was about $110.

I told them this shows that your pricing was wrong from the start. As basketball isn't a big category, I suggested we can at least run this experiment in that category and measure the results, and after much discussion they finally agreed. After running the experiment we did find that they actually improved their profitability in that category by about 7% from season to season. That allowed us to roll it out on other categories over time, but that was their first initiation into cost-plus not always being the best, and perhaps consumer focus is a better way to go.

That's a very interesting story of looking at pricing from a totally different angle. Especially when I think about airlines or hotels, you always have to balance the competitive pricing with maintaining a healthy margin. So how do you approach this challenge because most of your costs are set costs. Let's say on the one hand you want to have the capacity and you want to have the volume, but on the second, you want to make as much money as possible, so how do you balance those two out?

Personally, when I take over a project like that I will sit down with the finance person on property who's most involved with balancing the books and will ask them to tell me what is the minimum amount we need on a daily basis for this hotel to break even. They'll break down the bills that they need to pay for staffing, everything that covers the maintenance of the hotel, etc., and they'll tell me what we need from a revenue perspective. I'll see that we need this amount of revenue, meaning the minimum occupancy needs to be X and the minimum rate needs to be Y.

I'll have different scenarios in mind, and over time I look at things on a monthly basis in that case, but I keep a constant eye on how things are developing. This then influences my decisions regarding which groups the sales team can sell their group rates to. If they're selling for a conference, I let them know this one needs to be at X amount, although it's mostly driven by how many rooms are already booked in the inventory.

For example, I have a particular destination in Durban, and for this particular hotel I know it's a business hotel, so they're not really going to get much leisure business Monday through Thursday, but Friday, Saturday, and Sunday they will get some leisure business because it's close to a beach. Also for this particular hotel we secured airline business for crew stopovers, so that was priced in a way where if they sell, say, an additional twenty rooms at one of our lowest prices, at that point we break even.

Then once we break even, I can then start going into more of the market positioning sort of approach where I look at what the competition is doing and how I'm pricing versus them, and I have, like, a continual experiment with the pace of bookings based on historical data. I will understand if I'm twenty or thirty rooms ahead versus the same time last year.

I'll watch how the revenue is performing as well, and I'll be looking at this continuously on a monthly overview. On a daily basis I'll be adjusting the prices so if I do increase the rates today and tomorrow and I see a pickup of, say, twenty rooms for the next four or five days and I start to see my gap between the same time last year and this year increasing in both rooms and revenue, I will then maybe push the price up a little bit more again. At the same time, if I see it going the other way, I will start to gradually bring prices down, so it's a continuous experiment in that respect.

When you make a pricing decision, you compare it to last year's occupancy level, so what is the metric that influences your pricing decision the most?

The main thing would be current stats versus the same time last year. I'll be looking at that as the main factor that influences my pricing decision. I will still be keeping an eye on what the competition are doing because I don't want to undermine myself. This would be based on, let's say, the six main competitors I look at in the area. I will price myself near the bottom, maybe in position five if I have single digit occupancy, and then I'll just climb up through that ranking as the occupancies increase.

Coupled with that is the booking pace. If it's picking up versus the previous year in a good way, I'll be increasing prices gradually, but then also I will be using other strategies. For instance, using the lowest room type as an example, in a hotel you'll have your standard rooms, and you might have deluxe rooms, which have more space and maybe a nice view. Corporates have fixed agreements beforehand whereas a leisure customer is a bit more price sensitive. So if I'm seeing demand increasing, I will close the standard rooms to the corporates off from the system so they can now only book the higher room type as an example. So that leaves the lower room type available for the more price sensitive segment, but they are also willing to pay more than the corporate, so there's different strategies for balancing that out.

You've worked for some highly famous and successful companies. What did those organizations do to promote innovation in pricing?

I would say Emirates and Nike especially encourage experimentation. At Nike I came up with a revenue management type model. Although it was never used in the end, I was encouraged to work on this model. We would then present it to the decision-makers.

It was for a shoe that Nike offers, that you can design yourself and you can customize each part of the shoe, the sole, the sides, the tongue. The pricing model I came up with was looking at data on what are the most ordered parts based on color, and I just adjusted the pricing on these different parts. If it were more highly ordered, I would increase the price, etc. Ultimately the decision was we wouldn't use it, but nevertheless, I was encouraged by my direct reporting line to pursue these sort of experimentations.

There was even a particular shoe where if I priced the running shoe range logically, the whole company would follow the same pricing structure for the same range. There were three model shoes released that year called Vapor Max. It had a clear bubble heel and these had sold out very quickly the prior season. I suggested for these three models we increase the price by another 40%, and I was able to do that and sell it to the partners with this strategy in mind. Overall sales did slow down, but it resulted in more revenue because ultimately across the board in Eastern Europe, North Africa, and the Middle East, they were able to sell more units at the full price. There was a slight drop in sales, but overall revenue left before they discounted was greater than the prior season so that 40% increase didn't negatively impact the business.

At Emirates I remember a completely out-of-the-box idea. In an airline they typically have an advanced purchase rule where if you book a flight seven days ahead, you might have a cheaper price available and then inside those seven days the rate is no longer available. I came up with an idea for the airline's private channel that is designed so that only the travel agents of your choice can see if something is available. There was a particular route between Bangladesh and Qatar at the time, and there was the World Cup building project going on, so there was a massive number of passengers flying from Bangladesh to Qatar.

Naturally, Qatar was the market share leader for this particular route because they had a direct flight. With Emirates you had to go from Bangladesh to Dubai to Qatar. I identified two flights on our network that weren't empty, but they had maybe 30 to 40% available seats by the time they departed. I picked these two flights and put in a price which was quite low but still enough to make the flight additional revenue. I picked it with the pricing distribution person that does the background work, so that if there were at least 10% seats left on the day of the flight, this particular price, which was quite low and undercuts the competition heavily, is available privately only for the travel agents serving this particular route. I was encouraged to be able to do this as an experiment so we did it because it was on flights that were otherwise going to go with 30 to 40% empty seats. We went from about 3% market share on the Bangladesh to Qatar route to about 32% in the space of three months. So yes, Emirates and Nike definitely were open to experimentation as long as it worked without too much risk.

That's quite impressive. Can you speak a little about takeaways you may have regarding setting prices for new products such as shoes, airline routes, or new hotels.

With new products is always quite difficult. I had an example recently which was in Kinshasa, Congo, regarding probably the second international hotel in the market. There's only one other, so the idea with this initial pricing parameter was to see what the competition does. At the same time we're also looking at what would be considered incomparable hotels as well because the International hotel I think is about 20 years old, so it's quite aged. I noticed this and said, okay, we will set our low end to be what their average is for the public and then experiment by having about a $30 or $40 increase for the max within the parameters. Then our AI revenue management system would basically fluctuate in between those two, which allowed us to sell at a certain price, and we saw success. Then we gradually increased the flow of the pricing. This suggested we probably started off a bit low because the pace of bookings didn't slow down as I increased the flow. That's what I mean by the difficulty of pricing when you enter a new place.

Another example I've priced is where a resort has come into an environment where a resort didn't exist, so I've had to then look to a neighboring country for data. Say the countries are about 600 miles apart, and people are willing to pay X amount in the other country. When I compared the economic data, the GDPs were quite similar and spender indexes suggested a similar consumer power index, so then I would price similarly taking into account the rate of exchange. I might then just see what the rational, psychological price point is for that country. So I might have seen a hotel typically ends with a 99 on the end of their price point, so then I know, okay, customers are used to seeing 99 at the end, but the price is going to be X amount higher for the result as you're pricing based on a different country altogether.

It's quite difficult to do with hotels. For example, pricing for retail is dynamic, and you're able to adjust very quickly. At the same time that's where a mistake can be made, and you don't find out until it's too late, such as with the example of the Vapor Max shoes that Nike released, where after one season I suggested we can go 30% up on the price, and it showed that they could have so it was probably undersold for future iterations of a similar product. It gives a lesson but because there was nothing like it on the market beforehand, you had to kind of go based on similar sort of trends that you may have seen from something else.

I think with consumer products it's a bit more difficult to price at the outset if you're the first one to the market. It's similar to what happened with the Apple iPhone. Apple came out with similar price points to other smartphones when they initially launched their iPhone perhaps with a slight premium. Then over time they've pulled away as their understanding of the consumer base grew.

Okay, then your general advice would be it's better to start low then increase or to start high and then decrease?

Personally, I am more in favor of finding your breakeven point and starting lower, as long as you're making a profit. So I suggest always aiming for that by starting on the lower end and increasing over time.

A question on a different subject that is coming up is about ESG sustainability environmental issues. Do you see that those things affect pricing in your current or previous jobs?

Yes, I do think it's becoming more important. I remember in footwear as an example there was this emergence among the brands where they started using recycled plastic in the sole of the shoe. However, these were mostly boutique-style companies that had lower volumes, therefore they were charging a higher premium, but there were people willing to pay more because of that. So yes, in retail that is probably an influence so that people would be willing to pay more.

As far as hotels, I haven't seen the evidence to suggest that it does. There is a bit more of a push when I look at what the competition's doing to highlight the ESG credentials. There might be something to do with community impact, such as X amount of your hotel rate will go to the local community for schools and things like this being advertised. At the moment, personally, I don't see any impact on my market share, but I'm seeing it being pushed more as a value to the consumer base from the competition.

Do you find that pricing practitioners are evolving with the AI and related tools that now require different skills or not?

Yes, definitely, I think there needs to be more emphasis on technical expertise with new systems. When I started, pricing was more about how good you are with Microsoft Excel. Now it's about understanding how the systems themselves are working. With the revenue management system I now use, as well as the one I used at Emirates, there were different influences on which you could work. However because there were so many data points coming in, the desired outcome would take a bit of work to get to it.

Whereas, when I was with Virgin Atlantic, it was pretty much you're going from A to B. So this is the price I want, and I would just set the price to that amount, and when you get to that amount of capacity use this price. It was a bit more, let's say, very practical and set by yourself. Now we're having to work with systems that have a thought process of their own. Therefore you have to learn how to use these systems rather than just relying purely on Excel like before.

Also when I look at my friends working in other industries who are also doing pricing, they're saying they need to use other program languages now as well such as SQL. I think eventually this will enter my space as well, but yes, there definitely has been an evolution for greater technical skills.

Do you think that you will need to learn how to write code or not?

Yes, I think eventually coding may come into it to analyze larger datasets. As data continues to grow, we will need to learn to manipulate it in a more efficient way than with Microsoft Excel as an example.

To finish up, what would be your advice to younger pricing experts who are starting their careers?

I think the standard advice would be to at least know how to work with numbers. At the same time I think there needs to be an openness to abstract thinking because it's very rare that a price is wrong. By that I mean each pricing decision is going to be an experiment. You're going to learn whether the price was too high or too low, so you need to learn to be comfortable with that lack of certainty because each decision will be a learning lesson.

I recall training someone in the Emirates who had transferred from the finance department who was a trained accountant. I remember her being in tears some days because she wasn't able to grasp the concept that you and I will look at the same data but our suggested price may be different by \$20 or \$30 for the same thing that we're looking at. I think my advice would be to keep an open mind that you will not have the same answer as the person next to you. Each pricing decision is an experiment that you're opening yourself up to.

Thank you very much for your time and input, Mohammed, it's been a highly informative and helpful conversation, which is much appreciated.

Part III
Price realization

10

Customer value management
Implementation of value-based pricing at Borealis

Paolo De Angeli

Have you ever been approached by a salesman trying to sell a product or service by telling you the story of his/her company, how many years they have been around, and how many customers in many industries they are serving? Does it ring a bell?

And how many times have you instead been approached by someone genuinely interested in your business, your issues and possible solutions to help you become more profitable?

Customer value management (CVM) is a professional practice that puts customers' needs at the center and has the benefit to help suppliers build partnerships with their customers, moving away from mere business transactions.

It requires time, passion to learn about the counterpart, and curiosity to learn more about the business of other companies you wish to serve, in exchange of the fair share of the value you create together.

When working with CVM, especially, B2B companies ask themselves questions such as "Do our customers make more money doing business with us?" or "Are we consistently capturing our fair share of the value we provide?" or again "How can we grow profitably with our customers?"

In this chapter, we will first describe the four main areas of the CVM framework and illustrate why CVM has recently become more important. We will, then, review some examples of challenges and best practices observed while implementing these concepts, before concluding with an explanation on why value-based pricing should be the preferrable way of setting prices.

WHY CVM?

In hectic business environments, many companies have understood that, in order to be successful, they have to put their customers at the center of everything they do. Only by creating differential value (as well as being able to communicate it and capture their fair share), companies can win and retain business and profits.

DOI: 10.4324/9781003535966-14

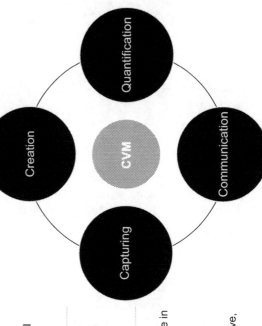

Figure 10.1
Key elements of CVM.

CVM consists of:

Value Creation: customer interviews and market research to create additional value for customers with products, services and capabilities

Quantification of the tangible and intangible elements of the differential value proposition, using value calculators

Communicating and selling-the differentiated offer vs the next best alternative in the market

Capturing the fair share of value (↑ price, volume, profitable mix; ↓ cost to serve, commercial terms leakages; defending current business)

There are many reasons why companies should focus more on CVM. To keep it simple, we will focus on the three most important ones that have direct impact on profits:

- Competitive pressure and challenging internal financial targets require focus on the value we deliver. If you are not delivering differential value compared to your best alternative solution and you are not able to explain in simple terms why someone should be interested in your product or solution, there are high chances you will lose business or will need to differentiate by offering lower prices (which is the easiest lever of differentiation – everyone can do it in a matter of seconds – and this is the worst decision you can take for your profits).

- Procurement organizations have become more professional: it's not enough anymore to have a good product and to build a strong relationship. Companies, especially in B2B, need to quantify customers' benefits and build the business case for the customer's procurement organization, in order to be successful. This is done through value creation, by engaging customers beyond procurement, and building the prerequisite to become more profitable together (it's a win-win – the one who loses is your competitor).

- Listening to customer needs and building differential value following the CVM principles improves customer experience, which has a direct impact on profits.

CHALLENGES AND BEST PRACTICES

Challenge 1: value creation – how to work on relevant customer information to create more value

Understanding what customers need to make more money and help them be more profitable is of paramount importance and one of the most interesting things a company can work on, in order to differentiate from competitors. Those who think like a business owner rather than as a supplier are able to establish immediately a profitable relationship.

Lots has been written on the concept of differential value proposition, but to summarize, if you don't have – or you are not able to successfully communicate – any distinctive elements that help your customers either:

- increase their prices and/or
- sell more volumes (incl. mix) and/or
- reduce fixed costs and/or
- reduce variable costs,

. . . then you have a problem!

You can start identifying areas of differential value creation internally, for example, by running a customer journey mapping exercise with your team and a fit/gap analysis between the "happy flow" and current status. But eventually you need to have a conversation with your customers. It is typically recommendable to have interviews or value workshops with customers, as well as to focus on understanding opportunities to create value when sending out customer surveys. It is also very important to carefully read the results of the customer engagement questionnaires, to fully grasp what customers are suggesting that their suppliers focus on, to improve the way they feel served.

This may sound too simplistic, but still too often companies do not dedicate enough time to listen to their customers, and those who establish a sound feedback process end up having a competitive advantage.

Challenge 2: value quantification – how to put value into numbers? Why should I spend time on it?

Putting qualitative statements into numbers is very important because it makes the statements concrete and credible. Many times, companies claim to have the best products, the most supportive customer service or the most sustainable solutions, but they fail to express how this turns into benefits for their customers by calculating a monetary impact. There are different ways to do it, and in any case, it's always better to keep it simple.

One can start by making a realistic estimated guess (for example, "in similar situation, we can reduce costs by x%") or by having a more precise calculation for the key variables. Typically, it is worth to start with a high level approach: if the value is not high enough, companies should not bother to enter in details, but if the value is high, then it is worth having a more detailed calculation and a detailed estimate with the commercial force and eventually the customer. Needless to say, data quality should be as high as possible, but practitioners should remember that often it does not matter if the figures presented are right to the cent, but rather that the hypothesis is realistic enough for the specific customer business, to initiate a fruitful conversation. This should also increase chances to receive open answers from the counterpart, which is often one of the most difficult parts of this exercise.

As said, value models should be simple. Often, in fact, companies tend to complicate their assumptions and calculations, creating value models that explain very carefully every aspect of reality but end up being too complicated for the majority of the stakeholders. After some time, some find themselves not able anymore to understand the thought process and the formulas used, with clear difficulties in explaining the benefits to the customers. It is recommendable to start with very simple calculations and formulas and adjust them, step by step, building on customers' feedback.

In principle, it is fine to start from a general model or template but is then of great importance to adjust it for each customer the differential value proposition will be presented to. This forces the team to think of all the customer-specific characteristics and to prepare well every time.

Challenge 3: value quantification – how to quantify the intangible elements of value (technical service, customer service, sustainability, supply reliability, brand?)

Quantifying the intangibles is very relevant but often neglected.

What are the intangible elements of value? Typically those related to some sort of "soft" differentiators (like brand, reliability, safety, technical, and customer service), and customers are often willing to pay more to avoid unknown costs in the future.

They are recognized in the market but very seldom quantified in monetary terms, because too difficult.

Why is it difficult to quantify the intangible elements of value? Because they represent services or capabilities that are often taken for granted (although making the difference), they are more difficult to be explained to customers, and as a consequence, companies fear reactions. In addition, working at this level of quantification requires curiosity, creativity, and a deep knowledge of the customer's business and problems (that sometimes companies do not have).

Nevertheless, as said, it is very important not to forget about the intangible elements of value, for the following reasons:

- It is not only what companies sell, but also *how* they sell
- The intangibles often make the difference (customers relationship)
- They are often forgotten or taken for granted
- Very few companies know how to quantify the intangibles (*opportunity*)

For the reasons explained, this topic deserves more focus from the pricing/CVM communities.

How to quantify, then, the intangible elements of value?

In this case, the recommendation is that practitioners start asking themselves a simple but very powerful question, keeping the customer constantly in focus: "*so what?*"

For example, let's suppose that a company is recognized as the most reliable in its industry when it comes to supply and is interested in quantifying its differential value.

So what? What does it mean for the customers? It means that they can trust that supplier more than others and therefore order less quantity every time and keep less safety stock. This is because they are sure that that supplier will deliver on time, and they will not be forced to stop their production due to lack of material (in parallel they have, instead, to keep higher safety stocks of other suppliers' material). So what? Less safety stock means less warehouse space they need in their premises. So what? Less warehouse space means less warehouse costs (in addition to lower opportunity costs – they can invest the money somewhere else and make a profit out of it, instead of building a warehouse to prevent issues with suppliers reliability).

This example also shows that, in addition to the figures and the calculation, it is also important to have a solid thought process to follow, when preparing and presenting the logics behind the quantification.

Challenge 4: value communication – how to establish a meaningful conversation with customers? Where shall I start?

What is typically recommendable is to start with an internal assessment and forming a "Value Team" of experts (sales, marketing, technical support, customer service reps, commercial excellence) is, in this sense, always very useful.

For this type of exercise, in fact, experts are needed, and working as a team from the beginning really makes the difference.

It's important that the team starts defining (first at a qualitative level) the areas of the value proposition where the company is providing differential (unique) value, in addition to a couple of areas where the experts believe the company is as good as the main competitors.

Once this step is finalized, CVM practitioners should help the teams transforming qualitative statements into figures. The final result of internal assessments should be a definition of the areas of differentiation and a sum of figures that explain how much more money the customer is making (typically, per year) with the supplier, if compared to the next best alternative. In addition, identifying two or three areas where the "Value Team" believes the company is as good as the main competitors helps to focus on concrete opportunities to improve (creating more customer value for the future).

In spite of the fact that, above all at the beginning, this exercise may take some time, it is typically well appreciated by the teams involved, who are put in a position to build the communication towards the customer, in a very structured way. As a result, they often also feel more confident about their value proposition and comfortable in defending it from any challenges.

After the internal assessment is complete, the team needs to meet the customer. This is very important, in order for the exercise not to remain too theoretical or based on assumptions.

It can be particularly useful to identify a person at the customer who helps organize a first meeting around CVM/value proposition and makes sure the relevant people are present. Who are the relevant people? Those that are in the position to validate the assumptions on the present differential value proposition (internal assessment) and those willing to share ideas and wishes for the future, to enable supplier and customer to work as a team and create additional value together.

There are many ways of running customer value workshops, but it is particularly useful to first show the (assumed) areas of differentiation and, after an agreement between the parties, continue then with formulas and figures, to reach a final alignment on the numbers provided.

Often the thought process is as important (if not more relevant) than the formulas themselves. Companies need to learn to think like the customer and show them they are trying everything they can to improve their customer's profitability.

When having conversations with customers, it is important to frame it properly since the beginning. It is about having a dialogue on value and nothing else. Chances of success are higher if the team approaches the customers being humble and with the goal of validating initial assumptions and asking to be as transparent and candid as possible. In addition, teams should consider focusing only on value during the meeting: often, in fact, companies tend to discuss about value together with other topics and not to invite the right people. This is a recurrent and big mistake: meetings where the value proposition is discussed need to be well-prepared, with the supplier doing the preparatory work and the right contacts at the customer prepared for a transparent conversation. No other topics on the agenda, for a couple of hours maximum. Anything else may distract the team from the main focus: agree on the current differential value delivered and make customers even more successful and profitable in the future.

Challenge 5: value capturing – how can I capture my fair share of the differential value I deliver?

There are many ways of capturing value. For example, companies can ask for higher prices building argumentations on the differential value they deliver (thanks to the work done with CVM): this is value-based pricing, the most profitable way of capturing value. Alternatively or in addition, a company can ask for more volumes, higher share of wallet, a reduction of the cost to serve (for example, reducing expensive services provided for free), etc.

What matters is that a fair share of the differential value delivered is captured by the Company creating it, otherwise it is not a fair business relationship between supplier and customer.

Experience says that is always easier and very important to start well from the beginning. When launching a new product, for example, any first element of differentiation (coming from first documented trials, for example) should be clearly considered and help set the initial price. It is also easier to start a joint value creation project with a customer and agree at the beginning how to share the additional value created, rather than trying to implement value selling after years that a product has been put on the market or a joint strategic initiative has been launched.

There are several reasons why we should price according to the differential value we deliver:

- It is **fair** (both to you and your customers) – win/win
- Customers do not (or should not) care about your **costs**
- It is **more profitable** in the long run

- It encourages your company and your customers to **improve together**
- It enables for further **value creation opportunities** and transforms suppliers into **partners**

SUMMARY

Customer value management (CVM) is the practice that puts customers' needs at the center and has the benefit to help suppliers build partnerships with their customers, moving away from mere business transactions.

To initiate a consistent sales process and philosophy, the following points shall be kept in mind:

- Value-based pricing is **easy to understand** but **difficult to implement**
- It requires **discipline, time, passion,** and **differential value**
- What makes the difference: **support** from the top, alignment across **commercial functions** and embedding value-based pricing in **key commercial processes**
- **Need to show the money!** (externally and internally)
- Your differential value can be in your **products** but also **services and capabilities**
- **Intangibles: often recognized, seldom quantified**
- Need to create a **culture** for **customer value management**

Forming and maintaining long-term customer relationships is the ultimate goal:

- Customer value management requires **curiosity, creativity, and a deep knowledge** of the customer's business and problems
- **Your differential value proposition is your reason to exist**
- Everybody can sell on price, **few can sell on differential value** created together with customers

11

How Bonduelle and Unilever manage price image for perceived value

Anna Telakowiec

MANAGING YOUR PRICE IMAGE MATTERS

Managing your price image is a strategic choice and a crucial necessity which can make or break your business.

Price image refers to how consumers perceive your prices in relation to your competitors. It is not always about actual price point, but more a psychological understanding of your position in the minds of customers. It represents the value your product or service offers, and the price you set can significantly influence consumer decisions, ultimately impacting your business performance. For global brands, the ultimate goal is to create a perception of value that drives customer loyalty and leads to business success.

Welcome to the intricate world of pricing and perception!

THE POWER OF PERCEPTION

Let's be honest, the power of perception is a force that influences every aspect of human decision-making. Consumers make their decisions based on their subjective beliefs and feelings as a response to a strong value proposition that brand or company offers. When considering a brand, consumers already have a price image in mind.

In the words of Clifford Geertz, man is an animal suspended in a web of meanings that he has woven for himself.

As a distant paraphrase of this renowned cultural anthropologist's words, I would say that a brand image is a network of meanings woven by the marketer and interpreted by the consumer. Therefore, a crucial task for a marketer is to construct a brand image, including its pricing, in such a way that the consumer willingly pays the right price for the brand or product offered. This price should contribute to the profitability of the brand and the overall company. From this perspective, the price image serves as a fundamental pillar of a company's profitability and financial stability. Viewing the price image through this lens makes it one of the key elements in shaping the company's strategy.

And so the starting point and the marketing job to be done is the fascinating journey of first defining your brand's value proposition.

DOI: 10.4324/9781003535966-15

STARTING POINT FOR THIS JOURNEY IS UNDERSTANDING YOUR TARGET AUDIENCE AND THEIR SPECIFIC NEEDS AND DESIRES

The initial step before one defines value proposition involves gaining profound insights into your target group. What are their requirements, preferences, and pain points? How do they perceive value? Adapting your price image to align with their expectations is of paramount importance.

This understanding forms the foundation of your price image strategy.

For a renowned brand like Bonduelle, which specializes in canned vegetables, the critical factors that create value for their target audience include convenience, ready-to-use products, freshness, positive health impact, and the assurance of trustworthy quality. It's worth noting that trust in the food industry represents a core category value. It's crucial to identify the core category value in your specific business sector to ensure that it's one of the aspects integrated into your offerings.

The core category value ensures that your product or service transcends being a mere commodity and becomes an essential resource that enhances the lives of your customers, positioning it as an indispensable choice in their eyes. This should be followed by the development of a robust value proposition for your business or brand.

Consumers also form their own image through the products they choose. They aim to be perceived a certain way by others, believing that their possessions communicate volumes about their identity and status. While this is evident in durable goods such as watches, phones, and cars, it is equally applicable to fast-moving consumer goods (FMCG) brands.

This underscores the importance of recognizing the aspirational lifestyles of your target audience and incorporating them into your product or brand. It involves fostering the belief that not only the product features themselves but also the brand image can support the desired image of the consumers. In the case of the Bonduelle brand, for instance, it's about projecting the image of a nurturing mother and a trusted brand that aids in her family care efforts, or the image of a health-conscious woman who demands the highest quality.

HAVE YOU CLEARLY DEFINED YOUR PRICING OBJECTIVES?

It's crucial to establish well-defined pricing objectives to guide your pricing strategy. Are you striving for a premium image, competitive pricing, or value-based pricing? Your objectives will serve as the compass for your pricing decisions.

Regardless of your pricing objectives, the fundamental task at hand is managing the price image for perceived value. It's essential to ensure that your pricing aligns with your value proposition. If you commit to offering competitive pricing, your prices should reflect that commitment. Consistency is key in building trust.

Take, for example, Bonduelle's promise:

> Like the group, the Bonduelle brand is committed to achieving the agro-ecological transition. More local, more anchored in the seasonality of vegetables, more innovative in environmentally responsible packaging, more involved in organic, it is striving towards a future agriculture that is more respectful of the planet, as well as to a delicious food offering that guarantees health and well-being.[1]

This promise implies a significant resource commitment, leading to a premium brand price objective to secure the necessary revenues. Bonduelle's pricing strategy is in line with its brand promise, and conversely, the unique and relevant promise allows them to command premium yet affordable prices.

In a competitive market context, it's also essential to consider your competitors' pricing strategies. Understand where your pricing strategy fits within the market landscape.

BUILDING A STRONG VALUE PROPOSITION

Establishing a robust value proposition serves as the cornerstone in effectively managing your price image. It's a commitment, a promise to deliver distinctive benefits and the core reasons why customers should choose your product or service over alternatives. Crafting a compelling value proposition involves a deep dive into your business's strengths and a comprehensive understanding of your target audience's needs and desires. It implies identifying what sets you apart in the market and aligning it with the solutions your customers are seeking. A strong value proposition resonates with your audience, instilling confidence and trust while enhancing the perception of value. This proposition can evolve over time.

To illustrate this point, consider the case of Bonduelle, a leading food brand in the processed vegetables sector. In the early 2000s, the brand's value proposition was framed around being the "vegetable expert providing quality vegetables", deeply rooted in a sustainability philosophy and environmental respect. However, as consumer expectations changed, the company underwent a substantial effort to redefine its value proposition towards "at Bonduelle, our firm conviction is that enabling consumers to incorporate plants into their meals every day is essential to living better. This is our way of moving towards more well-being, pleasure, and respect for the environment".[2] This updated proposition not only sounds different but also expands the company's business scope into the broader plant-based food sector. A well-defined value proposition should clearly drive your business towards growth.

Another example can be seen with the global food brand Knorr, which is part of Unilever's portfolio. Unilever's primary value proposition is to offer quality goods at reasonable prices. The phrase "reasonable prices" is relatively broad, considering Unilever's premium pricing in many countries. In terms of price image, "reasonable" doesn't necessarily mean cheap. This corporate value proposition is reflected in the Knorr brand. Additionally, Knorr aims "to be a force for good and to get food that is good for people and the planet on 7 billion plates by 2025". Knorr has made commitments to make this brand promise credible. While Knorr's value proposition may appear broad and imprecise, it is quantified with a clear business target: putting food on 7 billion plates. This sounds like a growth target and a promise to company shareholders, but it may be less focused on consumer needs. Further elaboration includes "we're inspiring everyone to eat food that is better for their health and the health of our planet". The challenge lies in whether this can be a credible value proposition for a portfolio of processed food products.

Developing a compelling value proposition requires a thorough exploration of your business's strengths while maintaining an in-depth understanding of your target audience's requirements and aspirations. It's essential for the brand to be credible and capable of delivering on its promises; otherwise, consumers will quickly react to any lack of authenticity. A robust value proposition should resonate with your audience, instilling confidence and trust while enhancing the perception of value.

SELECTING THE RIGHT PRICING STRATEGY TO SHAPE VALUE PERCEPTION

Now, let's delve into the process of setting a pricing strategy, a strategic approach that profoundly impacts the overall value perception of your product or service.

For global companies, defining the pricing strategy and desired price image is an integral part of their brand framework. A well-crafted pricing strategy doesn't just influence your revenue; it also molds the way your customers perceive the value they gain. The significant impact of pricing on perception highlights the intricate connection between what customers pay and how they assess the value of a product or service.

There are various approaches to choosing a pricing strategy.

Many companies opt for pricing strategies based on product cost or profit per unit, and these parameters are undeniably crucial and merit measurement. However, value-based pricing takes into account how much the customer believes a product is worth. In this context, the price image has the potential to elevate a customer's self-image.

To assess how much customers believe a product is worth, it is highly recommended to test the pricing strategy with customers through qualitative and quantitative market research. This helps in determining whether customers are willing to pay for the product or service in accordance with your strategy and whether you are effectively delivering on your value proposition.

COMMUNICATING VALUE THROUGH BRANDING

Your brand image plays a significant role in price perception. Strong brands possess the remarkable ability to command higher prices and profit margins in the market as well as lay the groundwork for a stable business. These brands have successfully cultivated trust, loyalty, and emotional connections with their customers. When consumers view a brand as trustworthy, of exceptional quality, or possessing unique attributes, they are often willing to pay a premium for the associated benefits and peace of mind. This premium pricing not only supports profitability but also strengthens the brand's position as an industry leader. Strong brands effectively communicate their value proposition, instilling in customers the belief that the higher price is a justifiable investment in quality, experience, and reliability. As a result, they can enjoy the advantages of enhanced profit margins and enduring customer loyalty, creating a mutually beneficial scenario for both the brand and its customers.

Building a powerful brand is undeniably one of the critical benchmarks for measuring a company's success. A strong brand goes beyond only representing a company's products or services; it conveys its identity, values, and the emotional connection it shaped with its audience. A well-established brand not only captures market attention but also cultivates trust and loyalty among customers. It becomes a symbol of quality, reliability, and consistency.

Moreover, a powerful brand often enables a company to command premium pricing, resist market challenges, and enjoy sustained success even in the face of competition. Thus, in the journey to business success, the development and nurturing of a solid brand are fundamental, being a vital indicator of a company's long-term prosperity. This is why in global companies' strategies you can find declaration: "we will win with our brands".

Knorr, a well-known brand in the food industry, has built its image through several strategic approaches:

- Emphasizing quality to gain trust: this commitment to quality forms the foundation of its brand image.

- A broad product range: this diversity satisfies a wide spectrum of customer needs, positioning Knorr as potentially comprehensive solution. Continuous product extension such as recipe modifications extend a product line, offering variety to loyal customers and attracting a broader audience.

- Expertise: the brand portrays itself as a culinary expert, providing recipes and cooking tips through various marketing channels. This expertise reinforces the idea that anyone can become a better cook with Knorr products.

- Commitment to innovation: bringing novelty is one of the key rules of the category. Knorr continually prepares new product offerings and packaging. Even minor modifications to a product or recipe can serve as a valuable opportunity for fresh communication messages, allowing brand to tell a story of evolution and improvement.

- Sustainability and responsibility is one of Unilever's commitments. It is delivered by sustainable sourcing of ingredients and environmental responsibility. This resonates with consumers who care about ethical and environmentally conscious brands.

- Global presence: Knorr has a global presence, giving it credibility and recognition on a worldwide scale. This global reputation contributes to the brand's image of quality and trustworthiness, a strong brand image, associated with quality, convenience, and culinary expertise, which resonates with consumers globally.

- Marketing investment: Knorr invests in marketing campaigns that often revolve around themes of home-cooked meals, family bonding, and the ease of preparation. The brand's consistent media investment and presence is one of strategic company decisions to deliver certain share of media investment and underscore its commitment to maintaining a strong brand image.

- The brand has often collaborated with chefs and culinary experts, further establishing its authority in the food industry.

By implementing these strategies, Knorr effectively builds and maintains a brand image that evokes consumer response on a global scale. However, the question is whether there is a strong value proposition behind this brand as the products of Unilever are imitable; they can be easily substituted with other products.

When communicating value through branding, social proof, customer reviews, and testimonials are already a common technic to influence value perception. Companies are leveraging positive reviews and endorsements to justify their pricing and build trust with potential customers.

MEASURING YOUR PRICE IMAGE – KEY METRICS FOR EVALUATING PRICE IMAGE

Evaluating the price image is a critical aspect of any business strategy, and key metrics play a central role in this assessment. It helps you determine if you are effectively implementing your strategy and how customers are responding to it. Are you genuinely delivering value to your customers?

The following metrics could be taken into account

- Price perception and positioning: assess where your products or services stand in the market in the eyes of customers, aligning with your objectives.

- Price communication: analyze how well you communicate your pricing strategies to customers, ensuring transparency and consistency. Evaluate how consistent your prices are across various channels and over time. Inconsistencies can erode trust.

- Perceived value: measure how customers perceive the value they receive in relation to the price they pay considering the impact of brand image.

- Brand perception metrics: define the desired brand image and identify key elements for creating that desired perception in customers' minds. Global brands such as Bonduelle or Knorr measure brand perception metrics on the ongoing bases in quarterly or annual surveys.

- Customer satisfaction: ensure a thorough understanding of customer satisfaction levels and how well your pricing strategy aligns with their expectations.

- Promo tracking: measure the impact and effectiveness of pricing promotions, discounts, and special offers in influencing customer behavior.

- Competitor pricing trends: monitor competitors' pricing strategies and trends, comparing your prices to theirs to determine alignment with your competitive strategy, as any competitive price moves may have impact on perceived value of your offer.

These metrics collectively provide insights into the effectiveness of your pricing strategy, its impact on customer perceptions, and how it positions you in the market relative to competitors. By regularly evaluating these metrics, businesses can make data-driven decisions to fine-tune their pricing strategies, enhance their brand image, and ultimately improve customer satisfaction and loyalty. The way to measure price image can be conducting customer surveys or studying customer reviews. Some companies like Bonduelle would run annual surveys to understand several metrics, while some metrics, such as promo tracking or competitor pricing trends, would be evaluated on a more frequent or even ongoing basis.

Depending on your industry and specific business goals, you may prioritize and customize these metrics accordingly.

ADAPTING YOUR PRICE IMAGE – REPRICE STRATEGICALLY

Repricing is a critical strategic consideration in today's dynamic business environment. To maintain control over your price image, it's essential to approach price adjustments strategically, focusing not solely on cost changes or inflationary factors. While monitoring competitors is important, the decision to reprice should align with your desired brand image.

For some companies, consistency in pricing is of paramount value. Their pricing strategies need to reflect a stable and dependable image. However, in rapidly evolving business environments, there's also merit in demonstrating agility through frequent price changes.

Managing price changes can be a complex process. In consumer packaged goods (CPG) companies these changes are often influenced by various factors, including annual negotiations of trade terms with retail partners. While CPG companies often rely on various partners to grow their business, they must proactively manage these relationships to ensure that the protection of their brand image remains a top priority. Clear communication, strategic partnerships, and monitoring are key elements in achieving this balance.

Regularly assessing and adjusting prices enables companies to ensure that their offerings remain attractive and aligned with customer expectations. Furthermore, repricing can optimize revenue by identifying pricing sweet spots that strike a balance between attracting customers and maximizing margins.

In essence, the key takeaway is that repricing should be a deliberate and well-considered part of your pricing strategy. It's not solely driven by external factors like cost changes or competitive moves but rather should align with your brand image, business goals, and the ever-changing needs of your target audience.

EMERGING TRENDS IN PRICING AND PERCEPTION – PREPARING YOUR BUSINESS FOR WHAT LIES AHEAD

Emerging trends in pricing and perception are reshaping the way businesses approach their pricing strategies. The following emerging trends are worth mentioning:

- Real-time price changes. One of the most notable trends is dynamic pricing, enabled by advanced data analytics and AI algorithms. This allows companies to adjust prices in real-time based on factors like demand, inventory levels, and even individual customer behavior. Already well-known in the airline or turistic industry, it is surprisingly also found in alcoholic beverage bars in France and Spain.

- Personalization. This trend reflects a shift towards more customer-centric pricing strategies as businesses seek to tailor pricing to the specific needs and preferences of individual customers, enhancing their perceived value. Using data analytics and artificial intelligence to personalize prices for individual customers. This allows them to offer discounts, promotions, or dynamic pricing based on a customer's past behavior, preferences, and willingness to pay. Personalized pricing can create a stronger perception of value as customers feel they are getting tailored deals.

- Sustainability and ethical pricing are gaining traction, with consumers showing a growing preference for products and services aligned with eco-friendly and socially responsible practices.

- Subscription-based pricing model, which involves customers paying a recurring fee at regular intervals, typically monthly or annually, in exchange for continued access to a product or service. This model enhances the perceived value by providing convenience, continuous updates, and access to premium features. It also builds customer loyalty. It may aim at creating more personalized value as it often includes personalized tiered pricing plans to accommodate different customer needs, providing ongoing services such as streaming platforms, software as a service (SaaS), and subscription boxes.

- Pay-as-you-go models are becoming increasingly prevalent, offering customers more flexibility and predictability in their spending. It allows customers to pay only for what they use or consume, with charges calculated based on usage or specific transactions. This model offers flexibility and cost-effectiveness, as customers are not locked into fixed payments and can scale their usage up or down as needed. The value, among others, is created by affordability and customer cost control in this model. Often used in cloud computing, telecommunications, and utilities, where usage can vary widely.

- Gamification of pricing. Some businesses are gamifying their pricing strategies, for example, Penny Auctions is an example of how companies use a competitive, game-like approach to pricing to engage customers and create excitement around the buying process. This not only creates excitement but also enhances the perception of value for customers.

- The transparency of pricing, including simplified pricing structures and the elimination of hidden fees, is also a rising trend, helping to foster trust and brand loyalty.

In this evolving landscape, businesses must adapt their pricing strategies to align with these emerging trends, making sure that they stay competitive in a dynamic marketplace while delivering value in line with customer expectations.

Remember that managing value perception, building and maintaining a strong price image is an ongoing process. Price image cannot be captured in one concrete rule. It's the combination of many factors that go through a customers' mind. It requires a deep understanding of your customers, market dynamics, and a commitment to delivering on the promises made through your pricing strategy. If we do not build the image, the brand's activities become more and more transactional, which leads to commoditization and, consequently, the erosion of business profitability.

Pay attention to what makes up a price image, and stay true to your brand, and you're on your way to creating the image you want.

SUMMARY

Welcome to the essential guide on managing your price image, a pivotal factor that can make or break your business. In today's competitive landscape, price is more than just a number – it embodies the perceived value you offer to customers. Whether you run a small business or manage a global brand, you will find practical tips and inspirations that will help you achieve success.

This chapter

- explores the strategic importance of managing your price image to influence consumer perception and drive business success

- reveals how to strategically shape your price image to attract customers, foster loyalty, and distinguish yourself from the competition

- discovers how brands use their price images to build strong, trusted relationships with customers

- offers practical strategies and insights for creating a compelling price image that aligns with your brand's value proposition

- presents emerging trends in pricing and perception

Understanding how consumers perceive your prices relative to competitors is crucial for building value, trust, and profitability. Prepare for a journey that will transform the way you think about pricing and the value you offer your customers.

Unlock the power of perceived value and master your price image.

NOTES

1 Bonduelle, "Bonduelle Pioneer in plant-based food", Available at: https://www.bonduelle. com/en/activities-brands/bonduelle
2 Bonduelle, "Bonduelle Pioneer in plant-based food", Cyrille Auguste CEO Bonduelle Europe Long Life, Available at: https://www.bonduelle.com/en/activities-brands/ bonduelle

12

Proud pricing in the facility management industry at Coor

Jerker Johansson

Often, to price more based on customer value than of cost is met with skepticism.

> It is complicated, it is difficult, it does not work in real businesses, my customers are always asking for the lowest price, value based is a myth. And if not a myth, you need advanced calculations, rigorous surveys and use advanced systems.

Maybe so.

But in this case, I think Coor, the leading provider of facility management services in the Nordics, did very well. Also, working with value-based pricing, Coor also discovered that delivering customer value makes you proud. Not knowing customer value, but only your costs, does not.

We learned how to listen to customers' perception of value, inviting customers to tell us how they wanted things to be handled. And the key, when being proud of your service delivery and understanding what value the customer gets from it, it becomes natural and easier, with greater confidence to ask for a price that reflects that value. In this case you will also find how Coor succeeded, through empowering their staff, moving pricing decisions closer to customers, where value is delivered and perceived.

When introducing the concept of value based in the rollouts, we used the next statements as kind of a requirement to understand value based. If you do not agree, you probably do not want to try the mindset or the ideas we are about to share.

- Different people/clients value the same service or product differently.
- The same person/client values the same service or product differently in different situations:
  - *Sometimes we used the willingness to pay for an ice cold beer at the workshop vs the same beer in the sauna at midsummer – quite a difference!*
- There is not *one* objective correct price when selling a unique service to a unique client.

DOI: 10.4324/9781003535966-16

If you agree with the previous statements, you get it. Maybe you see similarities between your business and that of Coor. Hopefully this case inspires you to start on your own proud/value-based pricing journey. Customer value is so much more fun than costs!

Probably you discover that your company, more often than not, base pricing on cost and has different opportunities in different parts of your business. Start small, keep it simple, master the basics first, and discover the relation of customer value and being proud. It doesn't have to be complicated to be successful. Be wise. If your current cost pricing culture is strong and you are aiming for more value-based pricing – do not forget you are initiating a cultural change.

With a smile,

Jerker Johansson

BACKGROUND: COOR AND THE FACILITY MANAGEMENT INDUSTRY

Industry overview

The business-to-business facility management (FM) industry encompasses a wide range of services aimed at ensuring the functionality, safety, and efficiency of built environments and its surroundings. These services range from building maintenance (HVAC, electricians, caretakers, etc.), landscape maintenance, security (access control, installation, guardians, etc.), and cleaning to energy management, real estate, front desk/reception, catering services, and more.

The business model is based on being a one-stop-shop delivering FM services with higher quality at lesser cost than customers themselves could do (having their own employees or managing many different contractors). Lesser costs and higher quality are achieved through specializing in these services (effectiveness), economies of scale, and people management.

Often, contracts include outsourcing where the FM company takes over personnel from the customer. This means that personnel before being employees to the client now are employees of the FM company, a contractor charging for services. This explains some of the later described hesitation for new staff to charge their former colleagues for work previously "done for free". Now, "if it's not included in the subscription, it should come with a fee".

Traditional pricing in the facility management industry

Normally, a customer asks for a number of services to be performed with a certain frequency with a certain level of quality. For this the customer agrees to pay a fixed fee. This is called subscription. Some services are hard to include in the subscription, often because the usage/consumption/costs are hard to foresee/budget/calculate. These are called additional services, not included in the subscription agreement.

The majority of contracts, and especially the large contracts for subscription services are highly competitive and are traditionally won by the contractor that meets the quality standards of the RFQ (request for proposal) and detailed SLA (service level agreement) with *the lowest price*. The bidding therefore includes detailed calculations, large amounts of data as square meters and windows to be cleaned, number of people in the facility, experience-based productivity data, materials needed, consumables, risk and associated costs, and a lot more.

Of course, there are exceptions to this general description. Today, we see sustainability and quality requirements getting higher weights in evaluations, and some of the large contracts are going towards higher degree of collaborations, advisory services, and partnering.

Together with the detailed planned service (subscription) provided periodically every day/week/month/year for a fixed fee, the contract includes an agreement on how to regulate prices for services not included in the planned service – this is called *additional services*.

Additional services could be close to what is within the subscription (extra cleaning due to the customer hosting a conference) or anything related to the facility, for example:

- Repair of HVAC and electrical installations
- Projects for building modernizations
- Installation of energy-saving LED lighting in the whole factory
- Eight hundred birthday cakes for the corporate anniversary

Usually customers experience great value out of the simplicity of receiving additional services from the provider already present. Most often, prices for additional services are regulated in the agreement by prices for time/labor and materials (products, often cost-plus). Sometimes there are preset prices including both labor and materials for specific deliverables, as for example: "setting up a workstation for a new employee", "fixing a broken <any type of item>".

Coor: a positive people business company

Coor is the leading provider of integrated facility management (IFM) and facility management services in the Nordics, offering all the facility management services necessary for a company or public body to work smoothly and efficiently. Besides commitment to quality, innovation, and sustainability, Coor stands out for its people-centric culture. Decades ago, and even today, many of the services FM companies provided were regarded as simple, not sophisticated or advanced. Coor has continuously worked to change this view. The company focuses on the following:

- People-Centric Approach: Coor is a people-intense company and is committed to creating a positive work environment where employees feel valued, respected, and motivated.

- Innovative Solutions: Coor continuously invests in the latest technologies and best practices to offer innovative solutions to its clients.

- Sustainability Focus: Coor commits to sustainable practices. The company has initiatives aimed at reducing its carbon footprint, was one of the pioneers in the industry with green certified operations, promoting energy efficiency, and ensuring that its operations are as environmentally friendly as possible.

- Client Relationships: Coor prides itself on building long-term relationships with its clients. Their focus is on understanding the unique needs of each client and tailoring their services accordingly.

INITIATING VALUE-BASED PRICING

After decades of perfecting cost-effectiveness and lowering prices to customers every year, Coor top management in Sweden under the current Nordic CEO AnnaCarin Grandin initiated a pricing assessment study.

The reason, explained by AnnaCarin Grandin, was that the focus on cost-effectiveness and productivity initiatives, although successful, might have had some negative effects:

> We saw that we could do better at listening to customers' other needs besides lowering costs. Always focusing on cost had affected our courage to charge, to ask for a reasonable price. Also, as we found out later, all discussions of cost sometimes made people feel like costs, a burden rather than a proud provider of customer value.

Figure 12.1
Cost and value.

Understanding pricing was an opportunity, and most probably a journey, top management searched for external experience and support. I had previously been developing pricing capabilities with other large companies in nearby service industries. The straightforward, change management based approach attracted Coor. With a smile, I got the assignment to deliver the assessment of pricing opportunities together with the head of sales and business development, Daniel Stigberg. The journey started as it should, with top management commitment.

Different pricing situations

To better understand opportunities, we analyzed the landscape where Coor set/communicated prices. We found several *different* pricing situations in the company pricing landscape. For simplicity reasons here, we divide them in two categories.

1. Large FM/Outsourcing deals in fierce competition doing a predetermined scope of work for a fixed fee (subscription).

   o Dedicated experts in pricing and calculations working several months to complete a bid/price
2. Many smaller *additional services* (assignments) done to clients when the predetermined subscription scope will not cope.

   o Pricing done either on a running bill with prices for time and material regulated in the subscription frame agreement or as a calculated fixed price

   o Often team leaders and managers do the pricing

Also, the hourly rates and the costs per hour used for pricing the large contracts had created a *negative price anchor*[1] of hourly rates for additional services. The low hourly rates that were top of mind in Coor were "the rates necessary to win in fierce competition when a large customer commits to buy 10 000 hours a year". The same rates were top of mind even when selling new services when "a customer has something to be solved the same day for something not previously negotiated".

Figure 12.2
Pricing in different situations.

Large FM Subscription contracts	Additional Services in current contracts
1. No (or limited) customer relationship	1. Active relationship, agreement, dialogue, on-site
2. Selection criteria - Lowest price	2. Delivery time higher priority
3. Large amounts (>> $100 000 annually)	3. Smaller amounts ($300-$10 000/work order)
4. High competition	4. Less competition
5. Limited opportunity for communication & dialogue	5. Good opportunities for communication and dialogue
6. Long foresight, 3-9 months	6. Short foresight, days
7. Decision-makers often procurement professionals	7. Decision-makers often have responsibility for client operations, or running the facility
8. Same playing field/conditions as competitors	8. Cost advantage compared to competitors due to on-site location, knowledge about the facility and ongoing work

Despite the significant difference between quoting for large contracts and additional services, the difference in guidelines, objectives, support (tools), culture, and mindset is often minimal

The pricing culture

Customers rated Coor services high in quality. Employees generally felt strong about the quality provided. However, almost all pricing was based on cost and the strong low-cost culture.

The focus on costs over a long period of time had indeed negatively affected the courage to charge, even what was supposed to be billed according to the customer agreement.

Time used to understand, design, price, plan, perform regulatory risk assessments, procure the materials, schedule the task or perform quality control were seldom found on the invoice. These are certainly valuable activities that reduce total cost for the customer and enhance the quality and speed of delivery.

Also, if performing additional services, one used consumables, materials, and machinery calculated for the subscription services free of charge "because they were already on-site". Not taking into account that restocking and extra service of machinery would increase at the cost of Coor (in the subscription agreement). In one interview we even heard "the contract regulates that materials should be invoiced with the cost of the invoice and the agreed added percentage. If we do not have an invoice, we cannot charge". Therefore, when using materials, consumables, or machinery on site, intended for the subscription and the most effective way of performing the additional service, they were often left outside the bill.

Not surprisingly, and very important for the project, Coor also found managers with *very* good pricing performance where customer value influenced the pricing decision, and leakage was low.

The business case strongly supported going forward with developing the courage to charge in additional services. We also concluded that to be successful with large FM subscription contracts, pricing would continue to be best based on cost and competition, and that's fine.

The management team decided to create a project for the cultural change to support the courage to charge and to make pricing less complicated for everyone involved in *additional services*. One business unit was chosen as a pilot. The next phase, design, should develop pricing strategy, pricing structure, price management process, tools, and training.

Understanding that this was more a cultural change initiative than a pricing optimization project, an important decision was made: staffing the design project with internal business stars (role models), people in the organizations recognized for performance excellence. To have business stars as the drivers of the design phase would guarantee practical solutions and good anchoring.

Learnings initiating value-based pricing

1.   Be sure to deliver customer value before starting any pricing initiative.

   o   Going value based without delivering value will make you broke.

2.   If your current cost pricing culture is strong and you are aiming for more value-based pricing – you are initiating a cultural change.

   o   Change management is essential, and you will need a solid business case.

   o   Consider using external experience – but engage your business stars from the start.

3.   Pricing is top management top priority.

   o   Price is not cold and objective; price is filled with emotions, also with senior executives. Working with pricing without top management commitment may end up as waste.

4.   Make an assessment and understand your whole pricing landscape.

   o   You will most probably have different opportunities, models, requirements, and pricing situations in different parts of your business. In *some* areas most probably you will find that either cost or competition will continue to be the best base for your pricing. That's okay.

5.   Beware of negative price anchors.

THE DESIGN PHASE

The project for the design phase was set up to deliver explicit deliverables needed to change the culture and the mindset for pricing of *additional services*. We continued to engage business stars (role models, managers, and experts renowned for performance excellence) together with experts on support systems, invoicing, and business control to create working solutions. Top management was deeply engaged and responsible for all final decisions.

The core of proud pricing, people are vessels of value

Although profitability is of great concern for the company, profitability was considered not to be the most positive driver, engaging all employees. Neither would it fit the overall people centric culture. Coor, building competitive business by giving opportunities to people from different backgrounds, *choose to base their pricing strategy on people being proud of their service delivery.* People are not simply a cost; *people are vessels of value.*

Coor understood that when people realize, really understand the value their services have to their customers, people feel proud of the delivery. Being proud of what one does eight hours a day is essential for happiness. When we are proud of what we deliver, it is easier to talk and listen to the customer. Focusing on value instead of cost makes us more receptive to evolving for different customer needs. Talking to your customer about how they value your service makes your customers happy. The happier the customer, perceiving value delivered – the more of that value you may retain. Also, when understanding that results and profits are the ultimate customer expression for gratitude, this boosts pride even more!

We named the project Proud Pricing, aligning the improvement of people's happiness with business goals.

Figure 12.3
Proud Pricing.

Deliverables from the design phase

The design phase was carried out in seven half-day workshops during 12 weeks, together with our business stars and experts. Not rushing was a conscious decision; change takes time, for all of us.

The deliverables in summary, some of them presented later on.

- The Proud Pricing mindset – the vision
  - Exemplifies the previous cost-plus mindset and describes future value-based mindset and daily habits, fortunately in some cases current best practices
- Pricing strategy
  - Establishing the foundations for pricing of *additional services*
- Proud Pricing principles
  - Describing how dialogue and customer value comes first and how this is good for both customers and Coor
- Pricing structure
  - Clarifying fundamentals of how we price in different situations, what is included or not in our prices
- Price management
  - The process and responsibilities for managing and improving prices and tools
- Pricelists
  - Better anchoring real value, including definitions, simplifying pricing
- New value-based practical practices (based on strategy, principles, etc.)
- Pricing tool for value-based pricing
  - Enables more staff to price, shortening time to price, less complicated, and with a value-based mindset, moving pricing closer to the customer and the perceived value
- Manual to make it work in current ERP- and work-order systems
- Implementation method – training

Fun fact: In the design workshops discussing customer value, we discovered that many things customers consider valuable are hard to charge with traditional pricing. Examples were as follows:

- Dialogue, contact, feedback – we are easy to talk to, and we talk when necessary, few surprises

- Time – speedy responses, arrives quickly, comes when we promise
- Trust – my customers trust me, no mess, no scam
- Credibility – we exchange when needed, repair when possible
- Availability – always available, and if necessary, we fix it immediately
- Professionalism – we suggest improved features when we are going to "fix something" anyway

These discussions concluded that providing these things is something to be proud of and needs communication to be understood and really perceived by the customer. But not all of us are confident in talking to customers. It is not always *just do it*. However, the more proud one is about the service provided, the easier it is to tell someone about it. Let's start there, help our colleagues understand the value provided and boost pride!

At the last workshop, participants, many of them site and contract managers, were asked who could consider hosting a pilot implementing all this. All volunteered! For resource reasons, two sites were selected, one multi-client site, one single client site. To be honest, several others started implementing the tools and mindset by themselves anyway! The pilots were successful and full of more learnings, improving the implementation methodology.

Eventually, the project covered all business units. Every business unit went through the design phase, engaging business stars and did their own adjustments to the design.

Learnings from the design phase

1. Engage business stars
2. Engage experts on ERP and work-order systems

    a. Find better usage of your current support systems (ERP and work-order)

    b. Often, there is no need to change or develop new systems to handle new ways of charging, or adding new simplified items

3. Do not rush, change takes time, let the discussions flow

    a. Even if the new things (e.g. value based) sounds obvious and looks great at a PowerPoint slide, new things do not automatically convert into convictions and ability to apply them in real-life situations

    b. Use all your knowledge about change management

4. Focus on the basics before climbing the more complex steps of the ladder of value-based pricing or price optimization

    a. If your staff have a hard time understanding your pricing, most probably many customers feel the same

    b. Stop leakages, discover the value provided, communicate that

FOUNDATIONS FOR SUCCESS

Next are short descriptions of some (not all) of the deliverables created during the design phase. Many of them are traditional change management tools you are well aware of. Some are pricing specific. What might differ is the focus on simplicity, we did not try to cover all details, not to out-smart each other. It is all right to have different angles on the strategy. Not all customers, not all contracts or all business, even within the same company, are exactly the same, so best application might also differ.

The vision, the Proud Pricing mindset

The Proud Pricing mindset was used to describe current state of a cost-based mindset and exemplifies how the new *more* value- (proud) based mindset would look in *daily* habits.

We put in a great effort in describing that the ambition is moving more *towards* value based. Not totally going 100% value based, excluding costs in the mindset. As you'll see later, in the *pricing strategy*, costs associated with value is still a factor. The project provided guidelines and principles more than rules and optimized prices.

The Proud Pricing strategy for empowering proud people

Although not detailing the actual strategy, we may share a few and for this case vital highlights. The strategy worked as a guideline for the design project and later for all people involved in pricing and communicating value.

- We are proud of what we deliver; we charge for the value provided and all costs associated

- Our prices are easy to understand for customers and employees; the price never comes as a surprise

- Managers responsible for profits are responsible for the price of work orders

  o This does not mean that the manager personally must control every invoice. This is acknowledging that the ones closest to the customers, responsible for customer satisfaction, profits, and staff are best at balancing these factors with price. Better than corporate staff, better than consultants

In practice, in the rollout, this was also converted to questions and statements connected to real-life situation, as for example:

- Does what you do deliver customer value? If so, communicate and charge!

- Does what you do to deliver value also drive costs? If so, communicate and charge!

- Does what you do NOT create customer value? Consider not doing that.

- Does your customer not want to pay for your value activities? Communicate, and consider not doing that for that customer. Instead, you could do more work for customers that appreciate your value delivery

Proud Pricing principles describe what comes before the price

Both during the design phase, and certainly during the implementation, there were some valid criticisms, mostly from staff very loyal to their customers.[2] *Doesn't this make it more expensive for the customer? Would not the customer get mad if we charge for this?*

Answering these questions gave birth to the Proud Pricing principles. The principles can be shared with every customer and describes what must be done before ever sending an invoice. There are five principles, and one always applies them in order.

1. **Listen and engage with your customer**
2. **Deliver excellent service and be proud**
3. **Always follow the contract/agreement**
4. **Use your best judgement**
5. **Charge for the value provided and all costs associated**[3]

Listen and engage with your customer: without talking to your customer, you will never be able to understand what and how the customer would like you to perform the service or what's most important to the customer in this unique service delivery. Most important to the customer could be anything from price, quality (extremely high or just done), time (finished not later than, not during work hours), using particular products or almost anything. Getting more information on how this *particular* customer values this *particular* assignment is essential to meet or exceed expectations. Be curious.

Deliver excellent service and be proud: if you're not proud, you're not done. By understanding and delivering to customer expectations, you will feel proud about your service anyway. Being proud of your work is important.

Always follow the contract/agreement: Might seem odd to have this statement here. The reason was not that staff were not compliant with agreements, but to underline that anything new also had to be compliant to existing agreements. Example, we introduced a more simple way of charging for road taxes during needed transportations. But if the contract explicitly prohibited charging for this, of course this should not be invoiced – even if the principle is to charge for all costs associated.

Use your best judgement: if you believe your customer will be upset, and you cannot explain the value or the reason – don't do it. Coor trusts your judgement.

Charge for the value delivered and all costs associated: the center of the strategy to charge for value and all costs comes last, when all other principles are covered.

Pricing structure for mastering the basics

The pricing structure defines the different options to price additional services, in essence on a running bill or with a fixed price. It exemplifies how/when one or the other is beneficial for the customer and the contractor, challenges, and if some things are to be regarded included in the hourly rate or not, what risk is, and when and how risk should be managed.

For many this might be common knowledge. However, I have not yet seen any company that has a *common* understanding of this, nor the ability to communicate customer value in each case.

Another common misunderstanding is when calculating a fixed price, one is obliged to use the "risk free prices for a running bill assignment from the frame agreement". Remember, many times these risk-free hourly rates in the frame agreements are discounted to be really low. First, there are seldom or no such obligations. Secondly, when the contractor calculates risk any way the contractor wants, this makes the exact price of an hour obsolete. In the rollout, this was one of the toughest things to get through. Top management explicit decisions and crisp explanations were essential to succeed.

When offering work on a running bill, it is a good thing to offer customers to choose their service level. Different customers have different perception of value. Different assignments have different needs. Not all assignments need detailed planning, consumables, transportation, etc. But if all these valuable things normally are included in the hourly rate, that means that customers *not* needing these things subsidize the

Figure 12.4
Running bill or fixed price.

Running bill	Fixed price
The final price is known only when the work is completed. Often regulated by prices in a pre-agreed frame agreement.	The price is agreed before starting the work. With a fixed price the customer transfer the risk to us. Risk is always priced.
We are loyal to the agreement, charge for value delivered and all costs associated. The customer carries the risk.	Fixed pricing means free pricing, totally unrelated to the frame agreement. Always talk to the customer before giving a price, this way you get a first understanding of how the customer values the delivery, and you may adjust the content and/or the price.
• *Customer value*: Speedy start, choose service level as you go, no risk-premium	• *Customer value*: Risk free. The client budget will not be exceeded. No surprises. All inclusive. Also, with a time-to-price in minutes, a speedy start.
• *Value for the contractor*: Risk free	• *Value for the contractor*: Opportunity to retain more value where we are very good, easy to administer.
• *Challenges*: Track, document and charge all things done, *not* all inclusive	• *Challenges*: Charge for value and risk, to specify the delivery

Figure 12.5

Let customers choose service level.

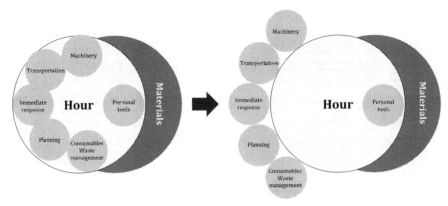

Before, much included, not billed, often with no reason or communication of value provided

Now, the customer choose service level, does not have to pay (subsidize other customers) for anything not consumed. All value provided is communicated.

ones consuming a lot of it. This makes your company's hourly rates not competitive for those customers. Also, what's "free" often gets overconsumed.

Let us clarify what is normally included in the hour and what normally should be a choice for the customer. As always, if something else is agreed in a specific contract, the contract is always no. 1.

In essence, this is not stranger than the common understanding that price (customer value) increases if you order more products. The more you consume, the more you pay. But if not clarified, there might severe leakages. Very important, when charging for any of these value items, the value gets communicated to the customer.

Price management process engaging business stars

To turn the project to business-as-usual, Coor established a pricing committee of selected business managers/stars, coordinated by a part-time pricing manager. The business managers, often a contract manager (manager of a large contract of several sites) or site managers are responsible for almost everything, including customer satisfaction, people, and profit. With Proud Pricing, responsibility includes pricing of additional services. The selected members of the pricing committee are the ones close to the customers in everyday operations and know better than consultants or corporate staff what really works. Also, *if the well-known successful business managers in the committee find these prices fine to work with, then it is probably good for me too.*

The pricing manager and the pricing committee are responsible for proposing changes in prices and tools when appropriate (minimum once a year). Top management makes the final decision and thereby takes responsibility in formal meetings.

Coor also introduced proud pricing as one of the modules in corporate training for leaders.

Pricelists better anchoring value

As mentioned earlier, hourly rates top of mind with Coor professionals were heavily affected by the prices quoted in the large subscription deals, prices that often were rock bottom to win the deal. That created a negative anchor, internally and with customers. To combat this negative anchor, Coor and the project created a new pricelist where customer value of the services and market intelligence were better taken into consideration. This pricelist created the new anchor for Coor as well as for new customers. It also became the new anchor when a current customer asks for a service not regulated in the current contract.

But as stated in the pricing strategy, it is possible for the manager responsible for profit to discount *if* needed.

Often, we are talking about customer value, and that is extremely important. But as important for pricing is to understand the *contractor* value of different agreements of different customers. This helps understand that value goes both ways and why sometimes discounting is good – and to discount based on value!

Volume is often mentioned as a value to a contractor. That is why the total price of 1,000 items often has a price per item lower than just pricing one (1) item. Selling 1,000 items at once makes sales cost per item less and fills up the order book for a longer time, both valuable to the contractor. This can be applied to many things besides volume, such as timing (do I have items/hours/hotel rooms available or not), is this small deal the wedge to land the larger one around the corner for a new customer, etc.

Coor new pricelist was created to be directly actionable and valid, without discounts, when the deal was not *very* valuable to Coor. The pricing strategy gave opportunities for the ones closest to the customer, responsibility for profit, to make discounts according to the value the specific deal/customer provided for Coor.

NEW VALUE-BASED PRACTICES, EXAMPLES

We developed a smorgasbord of concrete, actionable things, understandable and valuable to the customer that normally should be charged. We understood that not everything works with *every* assignment, contract, or customer. But for every assignment, contract, or customer *a number of things from the smorgasbord are very suitable.*

The smorgasbord contains recommendations to charge for all activities of value to the customer, such as solution design, planning, preorder needed materials, extra speedy services, etc. Also "service not regulated in the contract is apparently not regulated, and free pricing based on our official pricelist is recommended", and many simplifications for consumables, road taxes, etc. Next are a couple more examples:

Value-based pricing of consumables on a running bill

When performing almost any kind of maintenance, service, or repair, one needs small items such as screws, bolts, drills, cable, cable ties, zip ties, cleaning detergent and wipes, gloves, etc. With a cost-plus mindset, one should charge the cost of the item and an agreed percentage. But then, what is the cost of three screws, one meter of cable, and a cable tie? Let's make an assumption, buying these in bulk, the share of the cost maybe is $5. Adding the agreed percentage, we then should charge $6. However, what about time doing the procurement, attrition (wastage/spoilage), etc.?

A more important question, *what value does it have to the customer when we from experience show up equipped with the right consumables for the assignment?*

Value based compared to the alternative: we argue that the value is quite high, much higher than $6 (we also argue that the costs of providing this is higher, but that's another story). For example, without the right consumables, we need to get the right consumables. That means either travel (time 1 h and transportation) to buy, or stop the work, order online, and wait until the next day (extra travel). Either case, the work would be delayed, and the cost would be (at least 1h + transportation) more costly (let's say $100).

Customer value: if customers would choose between "*we bring consumables, for which we carry costs and finishes the job the same day for* $25 " or "*we come empty handed and get for you exactly what is needed – but that would probably cost $100 and job done tomorrow*", we think customers would choose the $25 option. But not without a proper explanation. Now, to make this easier and feel good for both the customer and the handyman, we did two things.

First, we included a new item, *consumables*, to the pricelist.

Consumables charged by usage, minimum cost $25

This makes the policy a corporate statement. This takes away the pain for the technician or anyone to estimate the cost or price of small items, just check the box. This is value based and flexible.

Secondly, we trained ourselves to focus on value, how to argue, and present this as good for the customer – and ourselves.

I will only check this box when I understand and believe in the value I provide, feel proud of my work, and know that I can confidently communicate this value to the customer. Even if this may be considered "just stopping leakages", this too starts with understanding value and being proud. How many invoices does your company send every year, how many boxes are there to check?

Figure 12.6
Consumables.

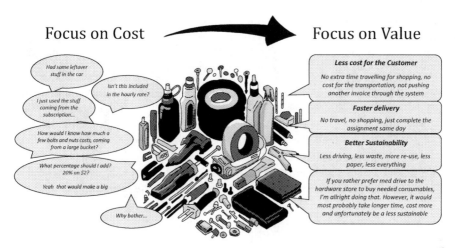

The value of immediate response

The strategy states, *charge for the value you provide and all costs associated*. Another important statement from the strategy is that *the price is easy to understand and never comes as a surprise*. One obvious and strong customer value is, if urgent, to start repairs immediately. Some, but few, contracts have complicated agreements on how to regulate this.

Before, Coor would respond to an emergency call (or just a customer calling saying it is urgent) by doing everything possible to start immediately. However, if not planned for, resources are seldom readily available. This calls for the first line manager to see who the best resource is to stop current work, maybe travel to the new site, start work and finish the work, go back and continue the original work, maybe work overtime to meet that customer's expectations.

With the culture of only charging for work performed on site, this is a loss. Also, it was hard to give the urgent customer an estimate of what this would cost. Also, even with trying to charge for all costs associated with the urgent delivery, how many hours would it take to find the right resource, would travel be necessary, would overtime with the first customer be necessary? That might end up in surprises.

We made this easier by introducing a new value-based item.

Same-day urgent response, fixed price $300, added to normal bill

Now, a customer who calls for an urgent same-day response is greeted by "Yes, of course. Be aware that we have costs to re-schedule and delay planned assignments.

This means that on top of the normal bill, we must charge another $300 to cover those costs, would that be okay with you?"

If this is really urgent, the value of immediate response is much higher than the fee. The bill will not come as a surprise. If this is not as urgent as first claimed, the customer often replies, "Well, if you come tomorrow, would that be an extra fee?" Where the answer is "No, tomorrow we can fit this into a good plan without extra costs for either of us".

Please remember, Coor created Proud Pricing around people and trust, not rules and regulations. Application of these new value-based practices is not mandatory. What is mandatory is to deliver excellent service and following the contract. The strategy and principles[4] also mandate you to *not* apply anything new you do not see fit with your best judgement. In this case for example, if Coor in the contract has several staff on-site, and the customer asks for a small assignment that could fit into the workday, no one would consider asking for an extra fee for immediate response.

Value-based pricing tool and time to price

In many companies, quoting fixed prices, even for small assignments, are normally performed by *managers* or *specialized calculators*. Calculations are often based on costs, detailed, taking days and sometimes weeks from "first question to on-site inspection,

Figure 12.7
Time to price.

calculation and quote". Questions for a price are usually vague, not specifying if the needed price is "a ballpark figure for a running bill or a fixed price transferring risk to the contractor". This, of course, could incur confusion (and risk), overcalculating and slowing down the process of getting a quote to the client. Also, days or weeks after the initial request for a price, getting hold of the client can be cumbersome, leaving the only option left to email the price. The initial urgency for service may have declined.

Understanding that shortening *time-to-price* is key to more business sold, pricing effectiveness, and profitability, together with the consultant, Coor developed a value-based pricing tool (web application). To price any assignment should not take a practitioner more than five to ten minutes!

The tool consists of recognizable items (the pricelist), value activities, reasonable simplifications (as risk), gives a good picture of profitability and an *inspirational* price. The inspirational price is what the assignment *should* cost considering the *value* provided.

With this tool, interested frontline workers (instead of managers) already on site, who know the site, the task, and most probably would perform the assignment are able to shorten the *time-to-price* to *minutes*. It enables everyone to talk with the client about value activities (some often forgotten or *thought of* as not allowed to charge for) needed to perform the assignment, to address risk, and have the value dialogue with clients – with less stress and much less time (cost). Doing this, the frontline worker often gets the order confirmation immediately. For many customers, a fixed price also eases the administrative process of getting the formal price acceptance.

Coor boosted the number of fixed priced assignments as well as profitability. Clients are happy with a price immediately, and most often also the assignment is performed almost as soon as possible. The client gets the issue off the to-do list and does not have to worry about possible price increases. Moreover, this moves pricing closer to the customer, where value is both perceived and delivered. Also, it empowers more of Coor staff to be part of the joy of doing business.

IMPLEMENTATION METHOD, ROLLOUT BY INVITATION, AND PRICE COACHING

The implementation was done, not in waves controlled by a corporate timeline, but on the *invitation* from each site manager. Timing was considered essential, since "every manager, every site has its own priorities and challenges". A manager struggling with setting up a new contract/site, recruiting key personnel, or having other challenges, should not be forced to introduce a new mindset challenging common practices. It would not stick; it would be a burden, taking focus from more important priorities.

With strong results from the pilots, tracked in the business case, the implementation was met with good expectations. The method for rollout, also tested in the pilots, was designed by the same managers as in the design project. A local rollout was done in 12 weeks and normally included *engaging the local manager, setting financial targets* (estimates). The local manager invited a *selection* of personnel to two four-hour

Figure 12.8

Rollout timeline.

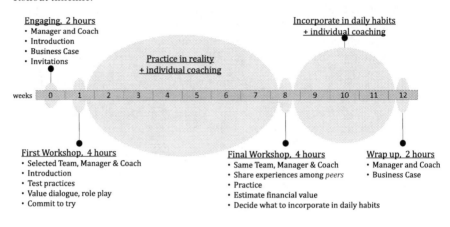

workshops, six to eight weeks apart. The personnel were normally all managers at the site, first-line workers with an interest in pricing, other key personnel, and administrative staff. With administrative staff we mean the gold nuggets of individuals who translate operational services to invoices.

Presence of the local manager at the workshops was mandatory. If the manager could not make it to the workshop, the workshop was called off.

The first workshop introduced the news, discussing the effect and practice at the site and then immediately went on practicing them in live environments. That meant helping each other out answering customer questions, calculating fixed price assignments, preparing invoices, not forgetting valuable activities performed. Estimates were done on both financial effects of the actual work performed that day and the annual effect for the site. The first workshop ended with the team, together with the local manager, selecting site-specific new practices to be tested until the next workshop.

Individual price coaching. Between the first and second workshop every participant had at least one phone call from the pricing coach, the same person facilitating the workshop. The conversation varied from 5 to 60 minutes, discussing how it went, difficulties, responses from customers, and everything else. This was vital information for the second workshop and is considered one of the true success factors.

The second and final workshop had the objective to share experiences from live practicing of Proud Pricing. Instead of a pricing expert or corporate staff telling people what works in other places/sites, now colleagues, peers, with the same customers, shared what worked (most often everything actually worked everywhere). Having a second workshop six to eight weeks after the first workshop enabled participants to invoice their customers and experience customer reactions.

Also, participants trained presenting the major deliverables (strategy, structure, principles, pricelists, etc.) to each other as well as with role plays training how to respond to anticipated or real customer questions. The workshop ended with the team and local manager deciding, *from experience* on what to have as new pricing practices on their own site/contracts.

Second wave of individual price coaching was done three to four weeks after the final workshop. This round often became more of collecting great stories to inspire others, and to help evaluate the local initiative.

Finalizing the rollout, the facilitator/coach and the local manager shared experiences, updated the local business case, and evaluated opportunities to track performance.

Next rollout at the next site now had plenty of new great true stories of success to share and serve as inspiration!

Learnings from the rollouts

1. Present managers are mandatory in change
2. As project manager or consultant in the implementation, seek invitations
   a. If you are not invited to inspire, the timing is wrong, or inspiration is not wanted or needed. That's a management issue, not an issue for the project.
3. Practice as soon as possible
   a. In the first workshop, we practiced how to respond to customers, how to register in the work order system, how to calculate fixed price for real assignments in the tool, how to describe value based to peers.
4. Individual coaching
   a. Few of us are able to incorporate new habits in our daily life after attending a class or a workshop. Not all of us are comfortable in asking the possible "stupid" question in public, or to object to corporate statements when the manager is present. Individual coaching catches that (especially if the coach is external), listens, clarifies, helps, and encourages to test.
5. Use the power of peers
   a. A colleague/peer/friend who tells you it works is much more trustworthy than an "expert" or a manager. Secure success (*individual coaching*) and have peers share their experiences (*workshop 2*).

FINAL THOUGHTS FROM COOR CEO ANNACARIN GRANDIN

Today, we still work with advanced pricing methods, often based on cost and calculated with continuous cost improvements in our assignments. We still focus on ways of improving effectiveness, lowering costs in everything we do. We use new and advanced techniques to do things more effectively, with better quality and faster. We still win many of our contracts on price, although this is gradually changing towards more emphasis on collaboration, quality, and value.

However, we have greatly improved our value-based mindset, and we definitely no longer see the lowest rates in the largest contracts as the objective value of our services.

We are better at listening to how our customers want our service to be performed, and I must say we are better at delivering on and above customer expectations. Much of this comes from succeeding in making all of us aware that customer value not just comes from low cost, but from so much more. Our Proud Pricing initiative started several years ago, and we continue to try to keep that mindset with us every day. Our principles and this mindset works.

We are more proud of our services today, a little better at communicating value with our customers, and generally that makes our customers a little more happy. And when it comes to pricing and profitability, we know that a "little" makes a huge difference.

/AnnaCarin Grandin, CEO of Coor

SUMMARY

Value-based pricing is a pricing strategy where the price of a product or service is set more according to the perceived or estimated value it offers to its customers, rather than solely on the cost to produce it, or the prices of competitors. Often, companies struggle with getting started, or overwhelmed trying to optimize a price through different segments of customers.

This case presents a practical, hands-on approach of moving towards more value-based pricing, where people and understanding of customer value are central elements. When understanding customer value (not only costs to provide the value), it becomes natural and easier, with greater confidence to ask for a price that reflects that value. This case also showed how to move pricing closer to customers, where value is delivered and perceived.

NOTES

1   The concept of a *price anchor* is a common psychological pricing strategy used to influence a customer's perception of the value of a product or service. It operates on the principle that the first price a customer sees sets an expectation of the general price range, or "anchors" them to that figure. When a customer sees a price for the first time, it creates a reference point in their mind. This is the anchor. Any subsequent price the customer sees for that product or similar products is compared to the anchor price. If they see a higher price, they might view it as expensive; if they see a lower price, they might view it as a good deal

2   Remember, in outsourcing deals, the FM provider employs staff previously working for the client

3   Directly from the pricing strategy

4   The Proud Pricing principles:
    1. Listen and engage with your customer
    2. Deliver excellent service and be proud
    3. Always follow the contract/agreement
    4. Use your best judgement
    5. Charge for the value provided and all costs associated

13

Terms and conditions excellence at DHL

Jędrzej Rychlik

Revenue management approach may differ significantly between industries. However, one of the key factors is the type of the market that company operates on. To keep it simple, let's distinguish two dimensions:

a.   B2C (business-to-consumer) where each transaction has an individual character, transaction price is linked with consumer segment, occasion. In general, the goal is to meet needs of consumer at a particular moment.

b.   B2B (business-to-business) where transactions are conducted between two parties as a part of rather long term cooperation. This cooperation is defined based on agreement (contract) with several conditions that were pre-discussed and agreed between companies.

Looking at four revenue management pillars that are in common use, we may expect that role of each individual pillar changes depends on a market type:

a.   Brand pricing
b.   Portfolio architecture, including both product and channel mix
c.   Promotions (high importance on B2C market, which are often driven by promo activity)
d.   Trade terms and conditions (increased role on B2B market where the business has long-term horizon)

Sometimes it is not simple to pick one single market type. For example, in FMCG industry a manufacturer usually operates on B2B market, dealing with retailers and distributors. However, this market more often looks like B2C as all players are responding to final consumer needs. They use framework contract, but its importance is limited often due to promo activity. Sometimes this model is called B2B2C

In this analysis let's focus on pure B2B markets where contractual terms and conditions may be the most powerful lever that company has.

Usually we play with trade terms conditions while we discuss the way to secure the margin of existing customers (to prevent the margin erosion). However, when we look at customer life cycle we may play with our trade terms and conditions even before

DOI: 10.4324/9781003535966-17

Figure 13.1

Customer life cycle.

Source: Own elaboration

Table 13.1

Trade terms framework.

Industry: services	Industry: FMCG manufacturing
• Acquisition effectiveness • Payments • Profile compliance • Business development • Brand positioning	Business efficiency • Logistics • Payments Business performance • Growth • Distribution • Shelf presentation • Promotions, temporary presentations

Source: Own elaboration

a prospect customer becomes an active one. We can design a set of conditions to support business growth and as a results margin development.

CUSTOMER LIFE CYCLE

Let's discuss a set of useful mechanisms. Next are two examples from different industries and highlighted points to be considered while designing trade terms:

a. Services industry
b. FMCG

SERVICES INDUSTRY

In services industry business efficiency is mixed with business performance factors; thus they are ordered in a slightly different way. Looking at the list: payments and profile compliance are two dimensions that can be linked with customer efficiency. On the other hand, business development and brand positioning are in business performance category. Finally, there is acquisition, which is a kind of promotional activity that usually happens at the beginning of cooperation. That is why this will be the first mechanism, then we'll go through business efficiency and finish with business performance.

TRADE TERMS – ACQUISITION EFFECTIVENESS

Acquisition in B2B services is usually a long process; thus additional argumentation in the hands of a sales representative or account manager can be very beneficial to close the deal. Companies try to forecast future profitability when signing a contract with a new customer. This profitability is based on a profile of the customer as well as agreed rates. Sometimes though the customer accepts the offer, it needs additional trigger. Source of this trigger can be out of our control, for example:

a. The customer is not fully satisfied with the quality of current provider.
b. Existing services have new requirements and existing provider is not able to meet them.
c. The customer is searching for cost optimization (and our offer gives it).

We can offer such an incentive. Here are examples of what it can be:

a. Extra rebate for our services for a limited time. This option should be tailored to an expected customer lifetime. If an average lifetime value for customer is above a year or two, we can sacrifice profitability a little in the first three months. This in fact is harmonized promotional activity. From one perspective it gives an empowerment to frontline people with limited risk on a contract from full-time perspective. On the other hand, we should have proper tracking of who gives these rebates and when to be sure they are not misused.
b. Frozen variable conditions. In some cases we may operate with modular pricing where final price is a result of several components. In logistics industry a normal practice is to distinguish base transport rate and fuel surcharge. In such case, fuel surcharge amount is linked with market conditions and reflects cost of fuel, which can change over time. At the beginning of cooperation we may offer stability and fully predictable conditions, taking this risk on us. This mechanism should be an option and not be given for free to all. We should also avoid freezing price variable in long-term horizon.
c. Investment in customer. Starting a cooperation in B2B business often is linked with additional requirements like systems' integration. In the first two examples we agreed on discounts on a potential revenue that may appear in the future. In this case we need to make an investment upfront. We can hedge the risk and include additional conditions that the customer will need to pay back the money if there is no delivery declaration.

All previous cases have one thing in common. The goal is to support acquisition process, and event they harm the profitability in the short run, they are beneficial long-term in helping to get new customers onboard and finally drive mass margin development. These mechanism are widely used in B2C world, where consumers are targeted with numerous promotions to be convinced to sign a long-term contract. Examples:

a. Rebate for first 3 months in a 24-month subscription
b. Additional gifts, items while signing a contract

TRADE TERMS – PAYMENTS

In general, payment terms are agreed at the beginning of cooperation. This is mostly about how often we invoice customers and what payment period we accept. We can invoice customers every time transaction is done, but often there are defined billing periods, for example, weekly, biweekly, or monthly.

In terms of payment period, it is extremely dependent on market conditions. However, if collecting receivables earlier has significantly positive impact, companies may decide to offer extra discount if the invoice is paid before due date. The amount of discount should be calculated in line with the cost of capital that the company has. If the company has no tangible benefits, for example, received money is kept on bank account, there is no point to offer such a discount.

TRADE TERMS – PROFILE COMPLIANCE

Based on the profile that the potential customer should provide during negotiation phase, the company offers a set of products or services to meet the exact needs at a price that, from one side, is accepted by customer and, on another side, gives the right margin level for the company.

At the beginning we define the profile based on customer's declaration and later on it may appear different than assumptions. To eliminate a need of long-lasting negotiation every time there is a deviation, we have the option to include several conditions upfront that will address them. This is definitely the most relevant lever to secure the margin. Especially if we can execute these conditions automatically.

The question appears, what does the profile mean? Depending on business complexity, we may use several options:

a. Revenue – very simple metric that we can monitor monthly or annually. This is useful when we have a single product or a set of products that have similar profitability. As very often the price that we offer to our customers is linked with its size and scale; in this case a revenue realization will simply secure profits.

b. Volume – another simple metric but we need to be more conscious while using it. If our portfolio of services varies significantly, revenue does not always mean volume and vice versa. Sometimes we need a minimum volume to have our operations efficient. To secure it should expect particular volumes across product types, and this brings us to a more sophisticated metric.

c. Product mix – offering a set of services to our customers, we should look at overall picture of revenue, profitability, etc. In most cases we have different profit margins between services. A complexity to deliver them also varies. Usually there is one or two products/services that build up scale of cooperation but we do not make much money on them. Additionally, we have extra services in our portfolio that lift up overall profitability. To have a win-win situation, our customers need to achieve a particular mix.

d. Product features/characteristics – sometimes product mix level is not enough as a real differentiation is a level down. Let's discuss this based on several examples:

   i. Offering services such as headhunting or external recruitment is completely different when searching for a highly skilled specialist (e.g. in IT industry) versus searching for blue-collar staff to work in a warehouse facility. Even in both cases, where the customer can be one company that needs 10 IT specialists a year and 200 warehouse staff, we should not treat it as 210 process contract.

   ii. Another example from logistics industry, where we can talk about shipments. As an e-commerce business we may search for a provider to serve our 2,000 shipments monthly (it can be courier services or fulfillment). Real differentiation here can be what type of shipments we have: small 1-kg packages or heavy 30-kg boxes.

In both cases we should of course secure ourselves with differentiated pricing for our services, but as long as our margins are not the same across offered services, solely pricing may not be enough.

While negotiating a contract, we should not assume that a potential customer will try to cheat on us and provide incorrect information. Currently we operate on such dynamic markets that customers' profile may change and even they might not expect it. That is why we should have full transparency and prepared solutions. With identified deviation from agreed profile, we have the following options:

a. Charge extra fee on every single unit.
b. Charge extra fee only on products that are below the plan.
c. Charge fixed money that corresponds to missing margin.
d. Start discussion with customer to adjust the profile.
e. Modify assumptions on contract terms.

These are examples to be considered. Final action should be mutually discussed as soon as these deviations appear. We always need to remember that in B2B industry, long-term cooperation always is an advantage and need to be beneficial for both parties to help them grow and improve services.

TRADE TERMS – BUSINESS DEVELOPMENT

Every company is happy when their customers are growing (assuming they are profitable for them). As mentioned before, size of the customer is one of the key price drivers. The bigger scale we have, the better price we may expect. The reason is that as a company, we have to cover amount of fixed cost, and increasing our sales volumes, we get benefits of scale. Of course, to some level when our capacity reaches the maximum, we need further investments that lead to fixed costs growth. In a short- and mid-term period we usually have the capacity to increase our sales volumes. Selling more decreases our unit cost. Having that, we get benefits and more profits. To tighten a cooperation and build even better relationship, we can share the profit with our customers. To make it happen, we can offer additional rebates under condition they grow with us. There are several ways how such a discount can be granted. First dimension is period – whether we want to settle based on monthly figures or offer annual calculation. On a monthly basis we can track current month performance and adjust trade terms for existing period. We may propose degressive approach over a year performance, and if the customer achieves a particular threshold, it gets an adjustment. There is an option for annual settlement and loyalty bonus or discount. The way we adjust trade terms is also configurable. If possible, we can simply adjust our rates and bill the customer with actually lower, better conditions. Another option is to pay back so-called retro-bonuses to our customers. Business development can also be extended to other metrics than revenue or volume. We can also offer additional incentives when customers improve their service mix or contribute to other factors that enhance our profitability. This factor becomes more and more important as currently customers have more than one provider. Trade terms that support growth and minimize additional administrational effort on our side is the way to achieve margin growth.

TRADE TERMS – BRAND POSITIONING

Building the brand, we expect it will be exposed and recognized. If we offer our services that are offered further to customers or consumers, we should take appropriate effort to make sure the brand is well communicated, presented, and so on. Our brand stands for a quality of services we offer; it should also be differentiating us from other competitors. Having a strong relationship with our customers, they become our partners. If they help us to develop the brand, we should reward them. Depending on the type of industry, brand position of the supplier can be an advantage for the customer. Let's imagine a company that is providing IT services to SME clients. One of its value proposition is the fact that they use Microsoft technology, which is considered as very reliable and a world-class solution. They are even recognized as a gold partner of Microsoft. With such a certification and meeting all branding requirements, they can expect to negotiate better rates from Microsoft. Another good example is the e-commerce sector, where selection of trusted partners really matters. Delivery and payment services options are among key factors that have significant impact on conversion rate. The right selection and presentation at the checkout process can boost the sales. From the perspective of service providers, they want to achieve the following:

a.   Default position at the checkout (or even exclusivity); first option is already proven that majority of consumers just follow the default option. Exclusivity for sure can be beneficial for service provider but not really for e-commerce as it may decrease conversion.

b.   Branding standards are another topic that makes a difference in the long run; thus, we should be eager to pay our partners.

FMCG MANUFACTURING INDUSTRY

As the main topic of this study was the B2B sector and in particular services industry, let's quickly go through another industry example – fast-moving consumer goods market, from the manufacturer's perspective. In fact, even grouped in a slightly different way, they are nor far different than described previously.

BUSINESS EFFICIENCY – LOGISTICS

Logistics trade terms are similar to profile compliance. As a manufacturer we expect level of costs to be covered according to warehousing and delivery processes. If the volume is below planned level, the company faces increased unit costs that harms profitability. In many cases manufacturers apply simple conditions or fees linked with logistics minimum on orders.

BUSINESS EFFICIENCY – PAYMENTS

In both industries the payment mechanism works generally in the same way. As mentioned earlier its importance may vary case by case. The fact that for FMCG/retail market standards are around 60–90 days, the role of payment conditions increases.

BUSINESS PERFORMANCE – GROWTH

Growth element was already well described in the section about business development related to services industry. In the case of FMCG industry its importance is pretty high as most markets are already matured and saturated. Manufacturers need to recognize customers which help them to grow. Often customers have even more negotiation power than suppliers, so they require to be paid for business continuation, not really future growth.

BUSINESS PERFORMANCE – DISTRIBUTION, TEMPORARY PRESENTATION, AND PROMOTIONS

Except form a growth factor, FMCG companies are even more eager to pay for qualitative elements that help to grow their business. Paying for distribution means additional discounts under the condition that the retailer distributes and offers the right portfolio of products across the country or defined region. Distribution goals can be defined as following: the goal is to reach a distribution of 70% retailer outlets for a premium brand. Additionally we can set a target for minimum sales value to be generated. Business performance here is mixing with profile compliance. On top of this we can define pre-conditions for additional promotional activity to be executed during the contract period. Trade terms should include the following:

a.   How many promo activities are planned (both manufacturer and retailer plan their promotional activity, so the schedule must be coordinated)

b.   What promo mechanism will be delivered (price promotion, bundling, all different types of multibuys)

c.   What additional exposition, support will be provided (extra display at end of aisle, shelf presence, etc.)

Strategy and design of promotional activity is a topic of another revenue management lever; however, designing comprehensive trade terms we should include assumptions and boundary conditions to execute promotions smoothly.

CONCLUSION

All previously mentioned mechanisms and examples are not exhaustive. The goal of this chapter is to give inspiration on how to apply logic of "pay for performance" into your trade terms. They are not static notes that easily become outdated. It's the way to secure margin in case of underperformance but primarily to stimulate margin development. This part of revenue management framework is about building a strong business relationship. Then, it requires transparency, tangible benefits, and profits for both sides in long-term horizon.

SUMMARY

The chapter delves into the strategic use of terms and conditions to safeguard margins and ensure customer adherence in B2B markets. It highlights how trade terms can be a potent tool for revenue management, particularly in long-term B2B relationships.

Key points include:

- **Revenue Management Pillars**: Different revenue management strategies are applied based on market type (B2C vs B2B). In B2B markets, trade terms and conditions play a critical role.

- **Customer Life Cycle**: Trade terms can influence every stage of the customer life cycle, from acquisition to advocacy, ensuring sustained business growth and margin protection.

- **Designing Trade Terms**: Effective trade terms address various aspects such as acquisition effectiveness, payment terms, profile compliance, business development, and brand positioning. Specific examples from the services and FMCG industries illustrate how tailored trade terms can drive business performance.

- **Acquisition Effectiveness**: Incentives like temporary rebates, stable variable conditions, and initial investments can enhance customer acquisition efforts.

- **Payment Terms**: Flexible billing periods and early payment discounts can improve cash flow and reduce financial risk.

- **Profile Compliance**: Predefined conditions based on customer profiles help maintain profitability and mitigate deviations from expected performance.

- **Business Development**: Offering rebates and bonuses for growth and improved service mix fosters stronger customer relationships and encourages long-term collaboration.

- **Brand Positioning**: Ensuring brand visibility and compliance with branding standards can enhance market presence and drive higher sales.

The chapter underscores the importance of dynamic and well-structured trade terms in fostering mutually beneficial B2B relationships, ultimately leading to enhanced margins and sustained business growth.

Part IV

Price enablement

14

Why pricing for consumer goods is different
The case of Asahi

Matthew Jipps

WHY IS PRICING IN A BUSINESS DIFFERENT TO SELL A HOUSE?

In theory, it is not. Where it starts to become harder is when then there are multiple objects to sell. What if you had to sell a hundred houses? A thousand? A million? At this point, you would be sharing the work with other people.

Consumer product goods manufacturers might easily sell several billions of products a year. How does this great pricing theory work in this environment when you are applying the thinking to a billion products?

ORGANIZING YOUR BUSINESS TO DRIVE GREAT PRICING CAPABILITY

A good place to start is working out who is responsible for pricing in an organization with such scale. The following is based on my experience of the last 25 years doing pricing or revenue management and being located in marketing, sales, finance, and strategic teams, at one stage or another.

SO WHO SHOULD BE RESPONSIBLE FOR PRICING IN AN ORGANIZATION?

Marketing team?

As Mr. Kotler once pioneered, marketing teams are focused on the 4Ps (Product, Price, Place, Promotion) of the marketing mix, maybe 7Ps as they are marketing a service (People, Process, and Physical Environment).

Marketing teams, rightly, very often focus on the consumer and getting the product and communication right. To use the house example, making sure the house is attractive for future purchases.

This clearly is critical and has a vital role to play when we are positioning our product.

Pricing is the only truly benchmarkable measurable element of our 4/7Ps for consumers. Think about it, can you measure features or quality or communication easily?

DOI: 10.4324/9781003535966-19

Their quality, their delivery to consumer? These things can be subjective. Price is just numbers, and consequently therefore easily measurable.

A good example of a category where price plays a key role is wine. How many of us are true experts on wine and make really well-informed decisions based on region, year, quality of vineyard, grape, and how many of us are led by color and price as our key guide?

Pricing is also a key driver of revenue and profit for the brand and product, and yet, despite this, in my experience, pricing is not given huge thought by marketing teams.

And how the product and price get to the market, they leave to the sales team.

Sales team?

When there is one house to sell, it is easy. The goal is clear. When it's gone it's gone. Normally within a business with a sales team, the ask of a sales team is to sell more. More, more, more.

We want to grow market share; we want to win in the market.

What is "more"? For some businesses, it may still be to grow more volume. Others focus on share. More sophisticated businesses will focus on revenue – a function of price, volume, and mix. More sophisticated sales team, still, will focus on profit.

Some businesses sell directly to consumer; many in CPG do not. They sell through wholesales, distributors, retailers, e-retailers. Effectively the estate agent who can help us access buyers for our house.

(Diagram here of product flow to consumer)

There could be multiple layers in the flow of the product to the consumer. Manufacturer to distributor/wholesaler, distributor/wholesaler to retailer, and retailer to consumer.

Our sales teams listen to the needs of these trade partners and what is important for them. They need to because these partners can help us grow, or not.

Crucially it is the final seller who decides the price that they will sell our products to consumers for. If we sell direct to consumer, then the price to consumer is our choice otherwise it is a trade partner. Whoever it is, the final retail price to consumer is the start of the value chain.

What is critical, often sales teams have short-term targets. And as with the house, if we have time pressure, sometimes this compromises our thoughts on maximizing the price – the price that a consumer is willing and able to pay for our product.

Finance team?

Finance team's help ensure that our business make money. When we sell our house, does it bring the amount of money we need to cover our costs? Our investments in decorating, the kitchen refurbishment?

Again, simple for one product, more challenging for thousands, millions, or billions of products.

What are our fixed costs? The costs that do not change no matter how much we sell. What are our variable costs? The costs that change in relation to how much we sell. What is our revenue per unit (our price)? How many did we sell? Which customers or sales channels did we sell to?

Ensuring we know the money we are making is obviously critical and a time-consuming job, and this is where our finance team spend a lot of their time.

All these teams have a role to play in pricing.

THE CHALLENGE IS PRICING SITS EVERYWHERE, BUT HAS A HIGH RISK OF BEING NOWHERE

Pricing considers the full value chain – using our house example:

1. The cost of our house – marketing team
2. The price that we give to agents – sales team
3. The property tax we must consider – finance team
4. Will the house price be attractive enough to a buyer to sell it, rather than a competitor house? – sales and marketing teams

If one or more of these elements of the value chain are not considered, or not working, we have a potentially broken value chain.

We have a house price that covers our costs, delivers the price we wanted, but is too expensive, and it will not sell.

We have a price that is good for the buyer, good for us, but does not give any value to trade partners to motivate them to want to sell it.

Figure 14.1
Simple example of a value chain for a CPG product.

Price to consumer

< Sales Tax

< Trade Margin

Price to Trade

< Variable Costs

Fixed Costs >

Our Profit >

We have a house price that is set to help it sell, but that does not cover our costs to sell.

It is necessary to consider all parts of the value chain when creating optimal pricing, and there is a strong risk that putting the pricing considerations into any one function will inevitably lead to some kind of bias and influence coming from that function and that no one is ensuring that pricing works for all the levels of the value chain.

It will also lead to suspicion from different functions that any pricing decisions are biased toward that function's objectives.

The following all reflect comments I have heard over the years:

Pricing in market, view from sales – "Our product is too expensive, it is not as good as you (marketing) think it is, it will never sell enough".

Pricing in sales, view from marketing – "Our product is great, why do you (sales) constantly sell it cheaply and destroy our value".

Pricing in finance, view from finance – "You (marketing) are adding too much cost into the product, and you (sales) are giving too many incentives to our trade partners".

I remember when my pricing function moved from a marketing function to finance. A year later someone said, "I didn't think the pricing team were involved in consumer anymore!"

THE OPPORTUNITY – A DEDICATED PRICING FUNCTION

Setting optimal prices require us to think about all levels of the value chain, like we did with the house, across many, many more products.

Given price works all the way through the value chain and has a significant impact on the P+L, is it not worth to give some dedicated resources to it? Objective from the other functions to ensure fair and balanced approach?

This team's responsibility would be to look across the full value chain and ensure that the tools and approaches described in this book are in place and used across all the functions. The resource should then ensure to drive consistency of approach.

Typical areas the team should support on:

- Category/portfolio price position
- Innovation pricing
- Brand product price position
- Promotional strategy
- Trade terms strategy

- Product execution strategy

- Market data collection

- Ensuring capability building within functions of the role of pricing in their decision-making

WHERE SHOULD IT SIT IN A PERFECT WORLD – AN INDEPENDENT STRATEGIC FUNCTION

A perfect price structure would see a pricing structure sitting independently to marketing, finance, and sales. Either a separate strategy function or reporting directing to the CEO, MD, GM, whichever is the title you use.

It gives independence, full value chain thinking, and a balanced voice for the business leader.

An ex-CFO of mine once said, "There are two people in the business that look at the full value chain. One is the MD, one is the pricing manager".

Ideally, the responsibility should be held by someone with the same weighting as the sales, finance, and marketing voice and full support from CEO, MD, GM.

NON-PERFECT WORLD – PRICING SITS IN MARKETING, FINANCE, OR SALES, BUT INDEPENDENCE SHOULD BE CRITICAL

Often, for reasons of scale of business and headcount restrictions, businesses do not have the financial resources to have a strategy team, and so a pricing function has to sit somewhere.

As mentioned earlier, I have had the pleasure of sitting in most functions at one stage or another, and it is possible to do it. There are however a couple of elements I believe are critical:

1. **The pricing leader knows they need to be independent** – even if you sit in finance, you need to spend most of the time with sales and marketing. Silos cannot exist for a good pricing leader.
2. **The pricing leader is empowered; the function leader knows that pricing should be independent** – if the pricing structure is not, and acts like a representative of a function, questions about bias will come into play. When placed in marketing, I once had a marketing director who asked me, "Do you work for marketing or for sales? You are always with the sales team". My reply, "If you want me to help execute your price position, I need to be with the sales team".

A pricing leader who becomes fully part of the home function will suffer from the same challenges as not having a dedicated pricing team.

One watch-out to consider with a dedicated pricing function is that other functions might believe they have permission to say, "Pricing is not my job". This is a real risk and can be mitigated though goals and incentive programs that are focused on revenue or profit or value market share. You cannot achieve your targets in these metrics without being aware and interested of what is going on with pricing. If targets remain volume focused, it is a bigger problem, but only increases the need for a dedicated pricing team!

Summary of pricing in each function – the pros and cons of each

Function	Pros	Cons
Marketing	1. Portfolio can support overall company price position. 2. Price can be aligned to the overall product offer (4Ps). 3. Should be thinking long term.	1. Focused on consumer price, not the needs of the trade partners who get the product to shopper. 2. In my experience less interested in the price as it is not perceived as part of consumer experience. 3. Does not consider short-term sales goals.
Sales	1. Close to trade partners. 2. Have considerable influence on how price is set to our trade partners. 3. Focused on what the competition is doing.	1. Often focused on volume, the easiest thing to measure. 2. Typically short-term-focused sales targets. 3. Short-term growth more important than long-term value. 4. Focused on what the competition is doing.
Finance	1. Good understanding of price impact on the value chain. 2. Helps relationship between cost and price.	1. Internally focused – not thinking about consumer or trade partners. 2. % margin focus rather than scale focused.
Strategy	1. Full view of value chain. 2. Puts pricing at heart of business strategy, rather than tactically at the end of the process. 3. Perceived as objective to all other functions. 4. Has longer-term view.	1. May be too distant from execution thinking. 2. Functions give away ownership of pricing – "no longer my job".

Where pricing sits, it needs the business lead to be a sponsor. It is that critical to the P+L.

SELLING A HOUSE

Many of us are lucky enough to have our own home. Many have a deep emotional attachment to our home. It is our castle; it is our safe place. We have often shaped it to exactly how we like it.

For many, we are often not thinking practically about how we are adding value to our homes when investing in them, we do things to make them more homely, for us.

Then, there often comes a point when we decide to move house. Suddenly our big emotional investment switches to what it usually is – the biggest single commercial asset in our lives.

At the point of selling, what is the most important factor when selling a house? I have no data points to confirm my theory, but I have some confidence that a key factor for most people when selling their home is, what is the maximum amount of money that I can receive for it?

At this moment we probably spend a lot of time seriously thinking about pricing.

The second biggest factor when selling a house is time. How quickly do we want to sell it? Do we need to release the asset's value quickly? Often, the next house can't be bought until the current one is sold. Sometimes, the best value is driven by someone's need to sell quickly due to personal circumstance.

Our pricing and our value of our house is driven by both rational and emotional decision factors.

So what is the process that we go through when thinking about the price of our house?

WE START WITH SOME RESEARCH

We check out the competition. We look at what other houses or apartments are selling for in our neighborhood to see what the market price for our home is. We will look at what features other homes have compared to ours. Number of bedrooms, how many toilets, a place to park the car, etc. Your list will be different to mine. More conscientious researchers may even find ways to visit other homes to look at the interior. All with the intention to benchmark our home against alternative offers on the market.

For sure, most of us will invite some "experts" to our home in the form of real estate agents to give us their opinion on what our home might be worth.

WE THINK ABOUT HOW TO MAXIMIZE THE VALUE

Were all the emotional investments that we made in our home, to make it ours, changes that someone else would value so highly? Was the flamingo pink bathroom with gold taps a good idea to maximize the selling price? Will others love it as much as us?

The more we tailor the home to our tastes, probably the less likely it will appeal to someone else. Unless you had maximizing the selling price in mind from the beginning of any work and went beige.

Once we are armed with our research, and our benchmarks, we decide on whether there is anything we could do to our home to increase its appeal.

Some of the work we do may be structural. Could we convert the attic to an extra bedroom? Extend the kitchen? Add an office space in the garden for home working?

Some of it maybe more cosmetic. We paint the walls, we landscape the garden, we lay new carpets.

We will consider whether the cost, in both time and money, of making these improvements will add sufficient value to the property. It is unlikely that we will consider adding an extension to the kitchen that would cost 20,000 Euros, if the additional value that it might generate in sales value is 10,000. We just wouldn't do it.

House developers consider these questions instinctively. Work out what a concept can sell for, calculate the cost of building it, and then decide whether it is worth it.

Hopefully, most of us don't have too big regrets that we didn't think about the attractiveness of a feature we added to our home and its impact to a selling price.

WE THINK ABOUT PRICE POSITIONING

Based on our need to maximize price, compared to speed we need to sell at. Based on our research of the competition. Based on our ability to get the house ready for sale. Based on feedback from the experts. We decide on a price.

We will also decide, in conjunction with our "expert", our negotiation strategy.

We might go high. A potential consequence is a risk of being uncompetitive on the market but allows us to give a motivational discount to the purchaser.

We might go low. To gain lots of interest and either sell quickly or create some competition demand.

We might match others' price on the market and hope our cosmetic features bring us a sale.

We almost certainly have a minimum price that we want to sell for in our head that we will not sell below.

WE ARE READY TO SELL – THE PRESENTATION AND SELLING STORY

Finally, the day comes when people come to see your home. We look to make the product as appealing as possible.

We bake a cake for the first time in years to create a homely aroma. We ensure that there is some fresh coffee brewing. For sure, the majority will tidy – make sure at the very least that all the laundry is in the laundry bin and the takeaway food is in the waste bin.

We have a story prepared about what we like about the neighborhood. Great schools, friendly neighbors (who are quiet after 10 p.m.), a bustling community that is both full of energy *AND* that you never be disturbed by from inside the house.

We create a world where our home is presented in the best light possible.

So summarizing that process of pricing a house to sell:

1. We start with research on the housing market and prices.
2. We consider how we want to develop our offer to better meet buyer needs and whether we want to maximize value or speed of sale.
3. We consider whether extra investment will allow us to charge a higher price.
4. We think about our starting price position – our first sales price on the market.
5. We plan how we might negotiate and our walk-away point.
6. We think about how the house will be presented to the potential buyers, thinking about all the other features the house has and ensure we communicate it.

At this moment in our lives, when thinking about our most important asset, not only do we think about price deeply, but we also follow a robust process that is not dissimilar to many chapters in this book. (it can possible to reference other chapters and link back to these points).

If it is so easy, why is it harder to do in business?

MAKING PRICING LIVE THROUGH YOUR BUSINESS – MAKING IT PART OF YOUR PROCESSES

The number of times in my CPG career that competitive insight on pricing is gained through a leaflet, or more recently, digital leaflets: "Have you seen what the competition are doing? They are trying to steal our share! We need to react!" or "We are not delivering on the numbers because the competition is doing THIS (one to three pictures of competitor price promotions are shown), and we need to react!"

If you have worked in CPG for any length of time, you are likely to have witnessed this experience or, indeed, be the person doing it. I confess, I have a couple of times!

We do this because we generally work in high pressure environments, particularly in sales teams, and people are asking us why performance is what it is, why we are not hitting our targets. More commonly the questions are about what our performance isn't. In sales, marketing, and finance roles, pricing is not ever the core focus, and so with the limited time available, we look for the most transparent information that is available – the leaflets that retailers shout about. That they put through our door, that they put online.

When pricing our house, we wouldn't look at one house price in the area. We would spend some time looking in a few real estate windows. We would look online at specialist property websites. We might, if available, look at land registry records. We would talk to our real estate agents about market trends. We may even ask family, friends, colleagues about the price of their house.

Let's suppose that your category is worth $2 billion. A big weekly promotion might be worth $13 million. I am thinking about the biggest one I can remember. Even that promotion is 0.1% of the category value. And yet the risk is that this activity that represents 0.1% of value is the information that people use to set the benchmark for the other 99.9% of value in the category.

Remember the process of selling a house? The moment when we are all close to be pricing experts. A reminder:

1. We start with research on the housing market and prices.
2. We consider how we want to develop our offer to better meet buyer needs, and whether we want to maximize value or speed of sale.
3. We consider whether extra investment will allow us to charge a higher price.
4. We think about our starting price position – our first sales price on the market.
5. We plan how we might negotiate and our walk-away point.
6. We think about how the house will be presented to the potential buyers, thinking about all the other features the house has and ensure we communicate it.

Selling a house/pricing	Where it sits in a business process
1. We start with research on the housing market and prices.	1. Market assessment
2. We consider how we want to develop our offer to better meet buyer needs, and whether we want to maximize value or speed of sale.	2. Assessing strategic options we could do to improve in the market
3. We consider whether extra investment will allow us to charge a higher price.	3. Strategic choices and plan
4. We think about our starting price position – our first sales price on the market.	4. Strategic numbers
5. We plan how we might negotiate and our walk-away point.	5. Budgeting
6. We think about how the house will be presented to the potential buyers, thinking about all the other features the house has and ensure we communicate it.	6. Activity plan and selling stories

1. We start with research on the housing market and prices/**Market assessment**
    Do you have broad knowledge on market prices? If not, get some! Chances are that price is one of the most impactful levers on your P+L. Deciding on the price that you want has significant implications. How much time do you spend understanding the market?
    Sometimes I am told that "we do not have any data sources for our market/ channel". My advice is, as an absolute minimum, is to get someone, anyone, to start looking at prices. Go into outlets and look at a basket of goods in a consistent way and record it. Like when we sell a house.
    What is important is that you start to have a sense of what is the reality of price movement over time.
    We then must share this knowledge. Market pricing should not be a secret in the sole possession of a few people in the business. It impacts work of all functions, and so transparency is critical.

2. We consider how we want to develop our offer to better meet buyer needs, and whether we want to maximize value or speed of sale/**Strategic options we could do to improve in the market**
    These are strategic questions that you won't be asking all the time. Typically, it will be a core task of people responsible for marketing and innovation teams who are thinking about the end users, the consumers, but also need to give some thought to how the product will be sold.
    It is likely that in your business that you will already have a meeting when you are thinking about strategy and information about market pricing, competitive position, and impact on the value chain should be key here.
    (Value chain v market price)
    Here we need pricing to be transparent to all as well as being able to model what is the impact on a value chain of different pricing positions.

3. We consider whether extra investment will allow us to charge a higher price/**Strategic choices and plan**
    Brand/product development teams will always be thinking about how to improve their products. As noted in the previous chapter, often their core focus is how to make it more interesting a product for consumers. In my experience, seldom do I hear, "This is the price that we want to achieve and so we have focused on what attributes we need to add to justify the price to consumers".
    Too often, I have sat in meetings where the intention is to make the product as great as possible, with extra cost AND keep the product at the same price. This does little for the value chain. If it were our own house, we would not add a new feature if it did not add value. We would not put a swimming pool in the backyard and keep the price the same. We would not invest in features to our house that we were not able to shout about. Would you change the color of your bedroom walls from camel hair beige to natural cotton beige? Not unless your walls REALLY needed painting.
    Yet I have seen countless examples of label changes over the years that are intended to increase customer appeal. Reality is that only a very few of our consumers are into our brands as much as we are, and as with camel hair beige

and natural cotton beige, very few people could tell the difference between new and old labels unless both are shown in front of them at the same time. Consumers are quicker to spot a change in price though. They also notice swimming pools. So when we do something, it should be obvious. Otherwise it will not have impact. Pricing is critical here because integrated and well-thought-through pricing should be part of the business cases written at this stage.

4. We think about our starting price position – our first sales price on the market/**Strategic choices and numbers**

    We have our portfolio of products; we want it to be in the market, and we are now getting to target setting. What we want and need our people to do.

    How would you feel if you put your house on the market and it sells to the first buyer within a week? If you were going for a quick sale, you might be pleased, but I am sure that there will be a nagging doubt. "Could I have asked for more?" In the world of CPG where we have potentially billions of products that we want to sell, fast-moving goods is what we are about, so an attractive price is good.

    Before launch, with brand teams, marketing and finance, we need to set the price position that will allow us to achieve our business aims. Our price strategy should be in line with our marketing, sales, and finance strategy.

    (go into different price strategy in more detail?)

    There are different price strategies that could be chosen. Low price for consumer trial and then take price up when they are liking the product. Price high to create a premium and then skim the price as more consumers want to engage with the brand or product as it moves through the life cycle. There are many options warranting a chapter on its own, but the important part is that all functions are engaged, otherwise the risk is the broken value chain or a price strategy disconnected from the other 3 Ps 3Ps plus P rather than 4Ps.

    Here the strategic options need to build up to a portfolio strategy for pricing and help inform the business numbers. We cannot build a P+L without robust pricing.

5. We plan how we might negotiate and our walk-away point/**Budgeting**

    This is where the sales team take a lead when it comes to pricing, but we need to give them guidance of where they can play.

    When we sell our house, the real estate agent will likely talk about parameters with us. What price do we want to start at? What is the price that we would be likely to accept? A set of guardrails. The agent will then keep you up to date with offers, buyers' circumstances, and so on.

    The guidelines are created to align with our strategy, and again it is important that all key functions are engaged in this to ensure consistency in approach.

    There will then be a need for review and maybe course correction as the reality of the house, the product, hits the market.

    Getting pricing to a more granular level is key to setting budget and informing goals and targets.

6. We think about how the house will be presented to the potential buyers, thinking about all the other features the house has and ensure we communicate it/**Activity plan and selling stories**

   Our commercial teams should have put together a plan of how we take our overall offer to the market – our value proposition.

   The story will talk about all the added value our product gives. The product features and benefits and the value that they will create. Depending on where you sit in the value chain compared to the final consumer, you may need to think about the benefits to multiple trade partners.

   With the house, we mostly focus on the end buyer. With our products we need to think about why a wholesale may wish to sell our products, as well as the retail outlet. Unlike our house, often we are selling business-to-business, not business-to-consumer.

   Because the intermediary is not interested in the benefit of the products to them, they are often over indexing the conversation on the price. When the business-to-business customer is a big one, most salespeople in my experience will say that the customer is "ONLY interested in price".

   Having worked in big retail and manufacturing, I know that no one is ONLY interested in price, and in the same way we need to demonstrate benefits to the consumer other than price, we need to do the same to business-to-business customers.

   Selling our brands or products should not be the sole role of our sales teams but again requires lined-up thinking cross-functionally.

MAKING IT HAPPEN

The temptation is to create a dedicated process in your business. This may make sense if pricing is VERY new to your business and the intention is to deliberately showcase that your business is now committed to taking pricing seriously.

I would however recommend that the pricing process is aligned to your existing process. It is likely that you already do some of the previously cited process in some way, shape, or form.

As described, good pricing decisions need the support and engagement cross-functionally, and so your market/business lead, marketing lead, sales lead, and finance lead should all be engaged. These people are always incredibly busy, and it is very challenging to find the time to create a whole new set of pricing meeting for these people.

Make sure a senior business lead is the sponsor. Have someone who is dedicated to pricing in all your business process meeting. Make time on the agenda of your current business process meetings for pricing. Start the journey.

SUMMARY

The chapter explores the unique challenges of pricing in the consumer packaged goods (CPG) industry, using the analogy of selling a house to illustrate the complexities of managing pricing across millions of products. Key points include the following:

- **Pricing Complexity in CPG**: Unlike selling a single item, pricing in CPG involves managing multiple products across various markets and channels, making it essential to have a dedicated pricing strategy.

- **Roles and Responsibilities**: Effective pricing requires collaboration between different teams – marketing, sales, and finance. Each team has distinct roles but must work together to ensure pricing strategies align with overall business goals.

- **Value Chain Considerations**: Pricing impacts the entire value chain, from production costs to the final retail price. A holistic approach ensures that all aspects of the value chain are considered to avoid broken links and ensure profitability.

- **Dedicated Pricing Function**: Establishing a dedicated pricing function within the organization can provide a balanced and objective approach, ensuring that pricing decisions are fair and support long-term business strategy.

- **Strategic Pricing Process**: A robust pricing process includes market research, strategic planning, price positioning, budgeting, and presenting the product effectively. Each step requires careful consideration to optimize pricing and drive business success.

The chapter emphasizes that pricing in the CPG industry is a complex, multifaceted process that requires strategic thinking, cross-functional collaboration, and a dedicated approach to manage effectively.

15

Pricing transformation at Schneider Electric
Success factors and key takeaways

Paola Andrea Valencia

Intro: *Hosted by pricing expert Maciej Kraus, Paola Andrea Valencia shares the history and powerful results of awakening interest in pricing for global giant, Schneider Electric, a company that moved from four to now more than 100 personnel devoted to pricing globally. Paola shares the company's past, present, and future pricing journey and global pricing framework. Packed with latest valuable tips and advice for anyone interested in taking advantage of pricing for profitability in 2024 and beyond!*

Thanks for joining me, Paola. Perhaps we could just kick things off by you letting us know how you got into pricing, and what is it about pricing that interests you most?

Yes, for sure. I got into pricing around 11 years ago by a total coincidence. I was a student doing my second master's degree when I joined Schneider. I was part of an elective program in France called Altena. Basically you would be one week in the office and three weeks in the school.

After my first year of this program, I was called to do pricing. I knew that pricing is part of the four keys of marketing, but I had no idea there was a full function that could be done through this and the importance within a company of pricing in order to get to the margin and the overall efficiency goal.

We are quite mature today in that respect, but at that time we were really starting from the basics. We didn't have tools, processes, teams, we were really only four people within a company of 170,000 employees that were trying to build what we thought was pricing.

Wow!

That was the start of us having some pricing books from the US and some literacy and some recommendations from some pricing consultants, but I don't think that the overall environment was super prepared or mature, so we were kind of learning by doing to be honest.

Also we experienced a very big raw material crisis, which was the reason I was put in this role of pricing. In 2018 we went through a very tough situation with RMI (raw material impact) and we didn't have any other choice other than really building some rapid impact pricing techniques.

DOI: 10.4324/9781003535966-20

Basically industrial companies like ours are very much affected not only through inflation and macroeconomics, like any other company, but we are also very much affected by RMI. For example, if the price of silver or copper is going up because our products are mainly affected through these prices, we are closely following many raw material prices worldwide. During this crisis we really needed to make sure that we were able to compensate in a way to not be in a tough situation and to keep our sustainability as a company.

The situation was not so much to even gain money but to stop losing as much as we were at that time. This is how I got into pricing and the reason I've been there since is because *pricing is at the core of many functions. We are in between marketing, sales, finances, strategy, and sustainability, and we are now adding more and more layers to the overall scope that we manage.*

The different experiences I have had with pricing has included changing teams, changing countries, changing scope. At the same time the challenges are becoming much different from the cycle that we had a few years ago when we were more or less operating by the "usual" or "normal" way of doing business.

We know that this is never going to come back, so it is extremely exciting. At the same time I'm very much resource oriented. In pricing you have the chance to work on your long-term goals, yet you are able to achieve some short-term results. So for me it's a very complete and, in a way, rich function, which is the reason I've been in pricing for such a long time, and it's still my number one passion.

Perfect, that's very interesting. As I understand it, you went through building the pricing function at a global, multinational company from scratch, from basically nothing to where you are today. If you could explain the pivotal moments or the entire journey of how it happened I think that would be super interesting for sure. Of course I'm not asking you to disclose any confidential information but more of how your journey evolved. I think the important element would be how this pricing function became integrated into other functions and processes within the company.

Of course. Let me start by explaining and describing how the pricing function is today and then I can go back a little bit to explain what was the momentum at that time that brought so much light into pricing all the way up to the Global Direction Committee at Schneider where we got some sponsors that help us.

Today we have four layers within the pricing functions at Schneider. We are a multinational B2B company with more than 160,000 employees operating in more than 120 countries to give you an idea of the extent of the company.

So we have these four layers.

The first layer is the global pricing team. Their goal and role is to build everything that is transversal regardless of the business unit or the geography where we have global tools that we use for building our pricing strategy.

Then we also have quotations tools that are very much linked to pricing. We have training programs, the methodologies, the golden rules, the dos and don'ts, so all the topics that need to be aligned, centralized, harmonized are defined in this first layer.

Then we have a second layer within the four that is the business units. The BU (business unit) pricing leaders also have a worldwide scope.

Could you give us examples of what are the business units at Schneider for the people who only know Schneider makes different electrical components.

An example of a business unit would be the residential business for home and distribution. That would be all the electrical components you put in your home for lighting, temperature and so forth. They have a smart way of managing the different electrical and digital mechanisms. So everything that is home and distribution oriented is one of the business units.

We have other business units for industry, for infrastructure, for hospitals, and so forth. Along with each business unit there will be a specialized team whose expertise is in those specific kind of products for the customers that are mainly buying those type of products worldwide. So when you want to be much more specific, when you want to go a bit more technical and you want to understand on a deeper level the added value that your products bring to an electrician onto a panel builder or an OEM, then you will go with the business unit, and they are complementary to the global team.

Then we have a third layer, which is one that I'm currently managing. I manage all the pricing quotation and commercial policy in Europe. So I have a regional role, and I have a counterpart who is managing East Asia and Africa and another that is managing the rest of the world, which is Australia and South America, and then other regions in China and the US are a bit separate from the central model.

The fourth layer is the people who are in each team. We usually have one pricing director and then one to three or more analysts depending on the size of the country.

So all of these teams have a specific role within the pricing function, and this is how we operate today. *We now have more than 100 people working in pricing while, as I mentioned, ten years ago we were only four in the entire company.*

One of the elements that created this momentum that brought us to where we are today was a sense of urgency. From one side, the fluctuation in the raw materials made the company fully understand that we really need to take pricing seriously if we wanted to protect our margin. The second fact was that we were becoming much more global and much more open to the world. It became clear for us that the trends were going to lead us toward a more digital world and e-commerce and our distributors having a shopping cart.

When you are becoming more global, you have much stronger exposure in terms of prices. We knew that all the discrepancies and price differences we could have in a region like Europe or in a region like AAG were going to become very critical for our brand and for our way of positioning ourselves.

We wanted to tackle the problem from the very beginning before it was too late, so we started adding more people around global pricing that started setting some of the pillars of this team.

So what was the igniting factor? Did it come from the CEO, or how did Schneider realize that hello, we are missing this one key element in our strategy. If you could expand on this a bit please.

Whether fortunately or unfortunately, it came from some external consultants that helped us create a sense of urgency in the Global Direction Committee of Schneider. When we were evaluating all of these trends we realized that a company like ours, which is highly complex in that we have multiple businesses, multiple channels, tons of countries and people, we needed to really structure much more with this function in mind.

When we started looking at the potential of having a pricing function and optimizing and bringing strong efficiencies in our way of managing the business is how the momentum was created. We started receiving a sufficient budget to build the team and to build the processes. Of course there was a very strong influence coming from the leaders at that time that created strong awareness of why pricing was so important.

When I started ten years ago the organization was more immature in our understanding of what is pricing, which is not only about setting the price of a product as there's many more things involved than that.

So there was a very strong push of influencing and sensibilizing and educating our leaders so they could understand why it was important to invest much more in pricing besides the work that this consultancy did together with us, and this is how the team started enlarging and having much more stronger influence in the organization.

Just to give you an example, in the past three years we again had a strong raw material crisis caused by COVID and many other factors. One of the top priorities of our CEO has consistently been pricing during this time. This was a very strong message for all of the organization, especially for the leaders in each country to understand pricing and the need to focus on that. So this is how we got strong sponsorship but at the same time ownership influencing the organization, so we are not only a support function we actually have clear objectives and a clear impact that we drive within the different countries.

That's super interesting. As you were describing this pivotal moment with the raw materials increasing and how you managed that in terms of pricing, can you describe it a little bit more in detail how you managed this particularly challenging pricing pressure, and what were the key elements that made you successful as well as things you tried that didn't work.

Absolutely. The main element that helped us gain momentum was the fact that we discovered value-based pricing. In industrial companies at that time, or the part that I have knowledge of, we were very much cost-plus oriented mixed with a little bit of competition pricing but not that much.

When you have a raw material crisis you start asking the question of up to what level should I really pass to the market, and how much should I absorb from my internal efficiencies, productivities, and different initiatives that I need to drive internally.

So we really started looking at value-based pricing, and this was one of the main elements that helped us compensate and reach a more differentiated approach in the way we were doing pricing.

We started looking at our commercial policy building the pillars of how we set list prices, how we build standard discounts, and when we can give additional discounts based on some big projects. For example, if you want to build a hospital in Poland for seven million euros, I might give you an added discount because of the volume I'm doing with you.

All of these criteria and policies started to become extremely evident for us that we needed to better manage the end-to-end process from defining the price up to getting to our margin, and this we were not able to do for more than 500,000 references in the same way only using cost-plus.

Okay, so this is interesting, so you have 500,000 items that you need to price.

Correct, and at that time we were using cost-plus, and when you are having a big crisis in raw material, your prices or cost could go from €1 to €100 ss, because we had such extreme cases happen. We also experienced this three years ago with some electronic components that were having extreme shortages. We were competing against Apple and Samsung, and as we were not buying large quantities as they were, our prices were 10 times to 100 times the cost they were receiving them for at that time.

If the offer and the demand is on an economic basis, how do you manage that, how do you make sure that you are still competitive and that you are not punishing your customer for some macro-economic situation that is happening.

Gaining our pricing power was a very strong concern that we were having in the company. This is the number one element that created this momentum after the RMI. So we started taking our first steps into value-based pricing into building a clear commercial policy. How can I ensure that even if I have only two customers of the same category that they are getting an equal price or price that is fair to both of them. This was also our point of concern because of the scale of the company we needed to have many more processes and tools so that we were able to monitor that with value-based pricing.

We were also working hand in hand with our teams for launches and innovation. So we were not only doing value-based pricing when the products were already finished and on the market, but from the very early stage when they were still in the innovation phase.

So this is the second step of really building the processes, creating a value-based pricing mindset and willingness to go in this direction.

A third element that really helped us a lot was that we had a very strong sponsor in the Global Direction Committee, who was very sensible about pricing. This was pivotal for the pricing evolution at Schneider. He fully understood that if we were not managing the topic seriously our value as a company for shareholders was going to be lost or at least not to the level that we were expecting.

Without strong sponsorship, you can have a great idea, a great process, a great tool, but it's going to be three times harder without it if you want to reach the level of maturity and investment that the company needs.

We are in this program for at least six or seven years now. We are no longer in a phase of building but more in a phase of stabilizing, scaling, and really making sure that the changes and the learnings we have achieved stay within the company even when people move to other roles.

You also asked what didn't work well. One thing that didn't work that well for us was the fact that because we have different business units we are not only selling products, we also sell software and services. When you go from the tangible to the less tangible offers you sell on the market, you cannot just copy paste and replicate the same pricing model.

That is one of the things we should have started earlier, also looking at the non-transactional scope, because this is the one that today is really bringing this strategical access where we want to develop ourselves, we want to become more a technological company.

Why this didn't work well is because today if we look at the different buckets of efficiency, the fact that we didn't look at all at the service or solution part is today creating a very large divergence in the level of maturity in the organization, the level of understanding, and the level of profitability, at the same time this was one of the elements and the second one of value-based pricing.

At one point we went into the trap of having value-based pricing everywhere, and we actually realized that some of our products are commodities. For example we have some cable trunking, which is simply a piece of plastic to protect your cable. And even though you are very smart and creative, it is a very simple product, so bringing in some value-based pricing, you over intellectualize, over complexify a pricing process that is not worth it.

So we needed to gain some maturity to realize that, yes, value-based pricing is great yet very demanding and time-consuming. It can have a strong reward, but you cannot apply it everywhere, and this was something we needed to make some mistakes in order to realize we went through some . . .

May I mention, I don't consider such things as mistakes. You tried, or it's what you are learning. You can't be world champions everywhere. I don't consider it a failure, perhaps it's more about finding the things that didn't work as planned, maybe this would be a better description.

Yes, exactly.

So you touch upon technology and how you now want to do pricing not only as a commodity or physical product supplier but also selling software and services.

So let's discuss about technology and pricing because this is super important. You mentioned you have your own tech stock that you build. So if you could speak a little about the technology that you use and how you see the technology impacting your prices as a person responsible for pricing.

Great, a very good question. Actually technology in pricing today is our number one point of focus we want digitalized. To give you an idea, three to four years ago we were still very much Excel based. We were doing our processes and building our tools very much in Excel.

Let me just comment that this is super interesting, that you can have a company that's a global leader with hundreds plus people, and they still do pricing in Excel. From my perspective a lot of people think that technology is the reason we cannot do pricing. Usually it's not the case. Of course, if you're world champion, Excel is not the limiting factor quite often for pricing.

Yes, I agree with you. It's not because you have Excel you cannot do good pricing, but it's also true that when you have a good tool you can scale, you can be more efficient and at the same time you are able to make much more sustainable processes. Excel is great, and I don't think that without Excel we wouldn't have, I mean, I don't think that Excel is good or bad or will decide the level of pricing or profitability that you are going to get.

You need tools when you want to make it scalable, when you really have the mindset to harmonize the policies, to centralize some management, to secure your global accounts are managed in the same way in every single country, that the price updates are in the right format and connected with the right methodologies, and sometimes going through the right validation processes, you need tools for this when you are so big. But I fully agree it's not because you have Excel that you cannot do the job.

We are seeing that this journey of getting the right tool is not that easy. We have extremely high expectations, but when you start building the tools you start to realize many of the complexities you have, because you have as many processes and ways of doing the things as you have countries.

Even though you have rules, you still do it differently as people are used to the legacy tools, they are used to the local way of doing things. Change for management when introducing a new tool is extremely tough, and I think that even though we knew it, we always underestimated it, and we are still going into a journey.

For me, looking at the technology, the most challenging part is that you cannot only look at what you are doing today, you need to look and think about what you need tomorrow and the day after. A new tool created for today is literally going to be obsolete tomorrow – things are moving that fast. The challenging part is to have the right people who are thinking about the tool with the right mindset where it brings value today, but it's future ready, it's scalable and is not people dependent.

Also, for those people that were doing a lot of manual work with very low added value, we need to adapt and reinvent their jobs in a way they can really have the light they deserve by performing much more interesting tasks that are needed where the machine is not able to do the work of a human. This is how we are now integrating more and more with AI.

AI is nothing fancy. ChatGPT really created a breaking point in the way that we do business and we think about business and in pricing was the same for us. So we have our own ChatGPT within the company, and we are introducing artificial intelligence more and more within the processes and mechanisms that we do in our company.

This is part of the journey that is needed. I don't think that if we would have done it one or two years later, it would have been a big change, yet my number one priority in Europe today is really securing that we are digitally connected.

To give you an example of our complexity, we had different ELPs, we have different processes. We were very much Excel-based, so if you asked me, what is the price of a product in Poland and in Spain, to secure that they are more or less within a price corridor, it was impossible for me to answer you within two weeks because I needed to manually extract each and every country and consolidate and secure that the data was clean, that I was comparing apples with apples.

This is the kind of elements I need to obtain with real-time data. To make real-time decisions that not only look at the past but is more predictive, more future ready, so that I can start anticipating and bringing more value to the business.

We work for the business, and the business helps us succeed. So the more we get into this trend, the more valuable collaboration with business will become.

Obviously, AI and machine learning, etc., are high on the agenda for many pricing experts today. Please tell me your perspective on how AI is going to change how you do pricing. How is it changing today, and how do you think it's going to change in the next year or two?

I believe it's going to be a radical change because we came from an industry where every single sales person had the power to set a customer's price, and it was not always optimized, it was not always following the best of conditions we would have expected.

So for me AI is going to bring a radical change because the more we are able to connect the data, the more we get to know our customers, and the more we are able to better adapt our price.

Today we have isolated tools that work separately. We have our CRM with the ELP, with the customer care center tool, so we are not able to tell if a customer has complained five or ten times or if they are slowly stopping to buy from us and switching to competitors. We don't know the scope outside Schneider.

For us to see the extent of the potential and be able to integrate all these different datasets within our pricing model is great, and I believe that it's going to continue to become richer. At the same time we always expect to give a more fair price for our customers, not only in an individual country, but wherever they go to secure a purchase.

We have great respect for our policies, so there's never a misalignment within the different zones and countries.

We know that pricing being people dependent and oriented is huge, because pricing is also a function that is very linked to the heart of the sales personnel and to the business relations they have with their customers.

The more we are able to make it rational in a way that they always have the last say but we secure right coherence, the more we will have a more efficient role.

So this is how the data is going to change the function itself. I think we will always need a pricing function, that's clear. And I think it's going to become even more exciting tomorrow because the very boring things that we do today such as crunching data in Excel or doing some basic analytics, we know that tomorrow there's going to be a machine that will be able to do it for us, and ten times more complex, with ten times more data, and ten times more criteria to analyze.

I believe our role as pricing experts will become much more pertinent in terms of business. The role of a pricing analyst will be less on the technical side and much closer to the way we do business with our customers.

The machine will give us some data, and we need to differentiate what is pertinent and what is not for the best business. This will play a key role in pricing, on top of creating the right level of awareness, sensibility, and understanding of market trends.

I think many tasks that we do today and many objectives of pricing will evolve and become much stronger, and we will then be able to dedicate more time to the human, thinking process rather than primarily doing the process from a really technical or operational perspective.

As you now have roughly 100 people in pricing globally, do you think in, say, three years from now, you're going to have more or fewer personnel involved in pricing?

I believe we will remain stabilized because the people who have been in the transactional business building this journey for the last ten years now have the knowledge to be able to build many new automations in the process we have today.

These people will need to move to more services, solutions, software, and other kinds of businesses, and we will still need to have the same number of people, so I don't think that there's going to be a move towards any replacement taking place.

Today some of our very bright and intelligent pricing analysts spend time just doing very basic analytics and tables because it needs to be done. Tomorrow I'm pretty certain the capabilities of these people will be used much differently, so I don't think that we will reduce, at least this is not the plan for us in the coming years. Rather we continue to automize we can use these resources to look ahead and discover new possibilities and again revamp the level of maturity in other areas of the company.

That's very interesting. I wonder if we can shift gears now into this strategic perspective. For me pricing is a tool that helps you to achieve your strategic objectives

and usually pricing is this certain dilemma. We want to have more volume, more market share, more profit margin, more percentage margin, so how do you manage such a vast complexity, how do you integrate those 120 countries worldwide with 500,000 items, and then balance the strategic objectives? How do you use pricing to optimize such volume, for market share for growth and profitability?

We rely very much on the local teams as they are the ones who know their markets better than anyone else. The reason is we are market leaders in some countries and last on the list in others. In some countries we face more challenges. In some cases our products are the most recognized in the market, while in some other regions we have much stronger local competitors.

So how do we manage this competitiveness, because clearly pricing is there to be sure that we achieve our strategic intention, yet we need to be competitive. Having a great price but not selling anything equals zero, so we need to really balance things out. The best way for us with such an extensive geographical outreach is to be sure that the local teams are empowered, and they are the ones really making the best decisions for the business they drive.

While sitting here in France I cannot decide what is the best policy in Czech Republic, Germany, and Spain, for example, when I have no idea what the local competitors are doing, how the market is behaving, and how much we can absorb in these various individual markets. So the best way is to have really good roles and responsibility setup within the organization and strongly empower the local teams.

At the end of the day what we know and what we do is benchmark some zones. We create some clear indicators where we can identify if we are going in the right direction or not without knowing the market. When you are not doing pricing and your market, your margin is going down for whatever reason you are doing something wrong.

So we do have some indicators that help us to support and make some point alerts when we see that the trend is not going in the right direction. At the same time we are not the ones making the final decision. It is really up to the country or the more operational level regardless of how it is set up in the different organizations that need to take a strong ownership on the final goal.

That's highly interesting, may we go a bit more in depth on this . . . If I understand correctly, this lets you have the central function, and having all those tools, what people might assume is there's not going to be any responsibility for the sales person to decide on the pricing, as you said it used to be not only with you but also in different businesses selling, let's say, specialized B2B products. It was the sales person who had the power to basically do much of the pricing. Whereas many people might think that those people will have no say, but what you're saying is it is still necessary to involve the expertise and understanding of the local market for competitive positioning into the pricing decision. So how do you see it evolving on who's finally making a decision on the price?

What I mean by wanting to keep the last mile within the sales function is just that. In the past it was very much people based, and it was more artisanal. It was dependent on your knowledge of your customer and the knowledge of your sales person. However, if you were a new person coming into the organization with little idea about anything, you could easily make wrong decisions because you were just learning.

What we are doing now is supporting the sales person so they can make the best decisions regarding pricing with all the dataset we have. We have a tool called Deal Guidance which basically gives a price recommendation for every single deal for every single customer.

The sales person has guidance. He's no longer alone in an ocean of possibilities but now is much more guided through a decision by tools that can help him to be in line with our policies, in line with our objectives, in line with our strategy. At the same time he can decide to go differently because he has a very good reason, and then he secures the right delegation of authority and validation from his manager to assure that their decision is in line.

So there's still strong empowerment of the local teams, yet we are doing it through the tools, and we are doing it in a way where we also give them much more security in the decisions they are making, and it's not like testing the wind each time to see which direction things are flowing.

Okay, if I understand then, your support and technology and the data is more to support the last mile person with the best pricing decision because they can still have the experience and gut feeling and perhaps have known the client for 20 years. But maybe they would need this healthy check saying, hey, you want to quote, say, €10 but based on this statistic the customer is willing to pay €12, so before you quote 10 at least think whether actually 12 would not be a better price or vice versa. You want to quote 10, but we should go for eight, because of those kind of things.

Correct, you have described it very well. Imagine you have 100 customers for ten years, you know the top runners, right? You know the key core products that each one of them buy, but as soon as you get a product that is less common, that has been bought less, you have no idea what is the price and right positioning you should take. So there is additional value when you are going into less visible zones to ensure that you optimize your price and you do it at the right level, but most importantly, you are not alone and receive strong guidance – so this is from a sales perspective.

Also looking at the pricing leaders in the countries who are also empowered to secure targets that we define as challenging yet achievable and in line with what they are seeing in the market. If we see very declining volumes in Market A and very strong growth in Market B, we are not going to stupidly say everyone needs to do 2% while we know that the opportunities and the trends are completely different. We don't want to replace ourselves by the local teams, yet we want to empower them by giving them the right tools and the right support to enable them to make the best decisions.

Super interesting. I have two final questions. One is after this pricing journey you have experienced going from four pricing personnel people to more than a hundred today, what advice would you have for companies that are a bit earlier in this process. Or for those who are just realizing the importance of pricing or are just getting started but they don't know how to approach pricing, how to scale it, how to grow this pricing function. So what would be your advice to them?

I have two pieces of advice. Number one is to bring a success story. You need to build a success story to show the company what is possible, to gain strong sponsorship, to build momentum for the company to hear you. Depending on which industry you are in, pricing can be misunderstood as being a part of finance, a part of marketing, a part of we don't know what – and then you really need to put some meat on the bone.

My number one recommendation is building a great success story with a country, a business unit that is already very much willing to go in the direction you want to go. Show them, and work with them to see that it is possible.

First give proof that it can be done on a smaller scale before you boil the ocean. Start with a glass of water and show we can do it.

And most importantly, show the value and the strong efficiency and result that managing pricing well can bring. If you are able to build a success story where you can monetize and quantify the value that you bring, this will gain you attention in your organization, and you need that. Let's not lie to ourselves, in all organizations you need a budget, you need sponsorship, and you need people that are willing to spend time there.

But if you don't have it and no one knows how it is going to be translated in your return over the investment, and your financial caveats, why should they give you a 10 or 20 person budget if they don't know what it is going to be used for. So start there and this is the very basics, don't boil the ocean, start with something that you can manage and you can monetize.

My second recommendation is to really spend time building a program of the right roles and responsibilities, these golden rules processes and methodologies.

Then after you can scale, because from the moment you get the attention, everyone would like to start doing their own cooking.

The teams will start growing, and you need to have the right support and scalability of the actions you are doing. You really need to build a very good methodology that you can scale, that you can start setting in place from the very beginning so that once you get the attention, you spend time setting what are the golden rules.

How do you want a pricing function to look like in a country, in a BU, and what does it mean in terms of training, in terms of resources, in terms of competencies? This is setting the pillars of the house that you are going to build afterwards. And then you will more or less need to be reactive. This doesn't matter once you get the right pillars in place, even if there is an earthquake, your house will stand strong.

Okay, super, and my last question would be for people, for individuals who want to get into pricing, who might read our conversation and get inspired from your story and feel like pricing is a thing for them or they want to explore it further. So what would be your advice for people, say, ten years younger than yourself, who want to start on their pricing journey?

First of all, if you like challenges, go into pricing. There is constant change, and you never get bored as every year brings different challenges and experiences.

Do what I would tell myself ten years ago:

Dare to try, because the beauty of pricing is that you are able to test many things in different areas. You can really go with finance and test some models with marketing, as well as test ideas. You see the beauty of being interconnected and in the center of many different functions but more importantly is taking a set direction and trying to maintain it.

What I see among many professionals of different industries is that one day they start doing cost-plus, another day competition pricing, another day value-based pricing, and another day they work in strategy, and there's no guiding lines.

You really need to build your long-term ambition and stick to it. Build it, make it evolve, yes, but really go in the direction that you have defined, because pricing is changing quickly, it is evolving very fast now, you have a lot of documentations, you have a lot of people who are becoming more and more experts in the market, you have a lot of consultants.

So there's a wealth of information in the market. Unless you define your guiding line and your own strategy, you are going to get lost in the middle. So my number one recommendation is very much common sense, which I see as sometimes missing, in the way that we address the topic is that we change as the world changes. If you do that, you are never going to reach your objective. So that will be my number two.

And my number three tip would really be to invest in pricing, in tools, in technology. I think there's enormous, incalculable power in data. The more data you have, the stronger your pricing will be. So really invest at the scale that you are able. By having the right tools and processes in your company, you will see how this is going to bring strong value and strong profitability.

Super, Paula, thank you so much for your input and the valuable insights and experiences you've shared. It's been an honor and pleasure to speak with you.

Paola Andrea Valencia, CPP, is currently vice president pricing at Schneider Electric

16

Building internal revenue management function at Lotte

Jacek Wyrebkowski and Wojciech Gorzen

Wedel is a Polish confectionary company, producing a variety of chocolates and sweets since 1851, which was acquired in 2010 by Lotte Group – a South Korean-Japanese multinational holding company. Wedel is a well-recognized brand of candy in Poland that is considered to be the "Polish national chocolate brand" (one could say that Wedel is "Polish Lindt").

Next to chocolate bars, among the most popular products of Wedel we can also find: Ptasie mleczko – chocolate covered marshmallow, flagship product; Mieszanka Wedlowska – assorted chocolate covered candy with a variety of fillings; Torcik Wedlowski – a large, circular, chocolate-covered wafer with hand-made decorations; Pawełek – chocolate bar with a flavored filling that contains a small amount of alcohol; Delicje Szampańskie – circular cookies with sponge base, mound of jam, and covered with chocolate (also known as Jaffa cakes).

After its reprivatization in 1989 following the fall of communism in Poland the company was bought by PepsiCo Foods and Beverages in 1991. Then in 1999 Cadbury Schweppes bought Wedel from PepsiCo and invested in modernization of the production lines. In 2010 Kraft Foods Inc. acquired Cadbury plc. Combined Kraft/Cadbury-Wedel would have too large a share of the Polish confectionary market, which was contested by the European Commission. To satisfy EC demand Wedel was sold to Lotte. This was the first investment of Lotte in Europe.

Approaching the end of the 201X decade Lotte Wedel was facing challenges typical for other FMCG companies. The company was growing and was introducing new products and product lines on the market. It also had quite typical, standard ways for managing its product portfolio, pricing, and profitability. It wasn't bad. It wasn't perfect either. There were some standard methods for setting prices (mainly based on cost+ and comparison to competition), some tools for basic analyses (mainly based on Excel). Initial attempts were made to define and standardize processes and procedures.

The management was keen not only to grow, but also to grow profitability. With the increasing complexity of the product portfolio, saturation of the market, and increasing competition, the company recognized the need for more structured and professionalized revenue management (RM). The first step on the way towards improved revenue management was the appointment of a revenue manager. This step made it

DOI: 10.4324/9781003535966-21

clear that there would be a dedicated revenue management in the company, and it would have importance and priority on the agenda of the CEO and the board.

What proved to be very helpful later was that the revenue manager was selected from the internal resources. As he had worked many years in the company in various units, he knew the company in and out and also had a good combination of skills to coordinate such an important and strategic area as revenue management.

Next to the appointment of the revenue manager, the key question then was how to set up the whole revenue management in a way that would be both effective and efficient.

The goal was quite transparent – improve the set of company's KPIs:

1. Total company's profitability, measured as **EBIT/NSV (%)**
2. Sales margin, measured as **GCBM/NSV (%)**
3. Cost level, measured as **COGS/NSV (%)**
4. Sales growth, measured as **NSV (PLN)**
5. Market share growth, measured as **Market share (%)**

And this requirement raised further, more specific questions:

1. Where should the RM be placed in the organizational structure?
   (Who should the RM report to?)
2. How wide and deep should the RM structure be?
   (How centralized vs decentralized should the RM be?
   What should be included in the RM structure, and what should be left in other units?)
3. How many (additional) resources should be dedicated to the RM?
   (How many people are needed directly in the RM unit?)

WHY WAS IT IMPORTANT TO GET IT RIGHT THE FIRST TIME?

Upon closer examination, the seemingly simple set of three questions required more thoughtful consideration. The company soon realized the high stakes involved. As with any significant initiative within a company, particularly one that necessitates substantial change, the implementation of new revenue management required a well-prepared and proper solution. The CEO and the board were in agreement and aimed to avoid the four most common pitfalls:

- *Alienation of the management*
  - when the top management might have some direction and ideas themselves, but the rest of the organization is not following
- *Pure chaos*
  - when everyone in the organization does what they think makes the most sense, but in an uncoordinated way

- *"Pulling" in different directions – torn organization*
  - when different units of the organization pull in different not aligned directions (like e.g. sales towards higher volume (even if at the expense of profit), finance towards simply higher margins (at the expense of volume if needed), and marketing somewhere between or towards e.g. revenue)
- *Blocking changes (consciously or unconsciously)*
  - because people in the organization don't fully understand them and prefer to keep the status quo as it might seem for them a safer option

Figure 16.1

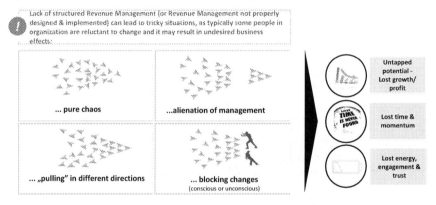

That deserved a proper project to design and set up properly revenue management in Wedel.

The goals of the project were clear:

A.   Development of a coherent and effective Revenue Management process:
  - Repeatable process
  - Consistent rules, formats, checkpoints
  - Data and support tools

B.   Designing the position and organizational structure of Revenue Management:
  - Role, tasks, skills required
  - Org. structure and interaction within the organization
  - Decision and recommendation responsibility

C.   **Preparation and support of effective implementation:**

  o   Implementation road map

  o   Training and knowledge transfer

  o   Systematic "check points" + coaching support plan

All of that after successful design and implementation should lead to three key outcomes:

1.   **Sustainable and profitable business growth**
2.   **Limitation of loss of income**
      + alignment of the organization towards the common goal
3.   **Efficiency increase and continuous improvement**

Figure 16.2

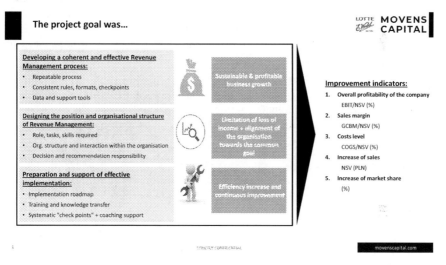

With that in mind and additionally to avoid trial-and-error approach the management together with the revenue manager decided to leverage external experience in the field. They simply looked around who could help them on that journey and selected an advisor for that. Long story short, they chose **Movens Advisory**.

APPROACH – HOW WAS IT DONE?

With joined forces of Wedel's revenue manager and experts of Movens Advisory, a project was launched to design and set up revenue management at Wedel. This was only the first step in what would be a RM journey.

The project itself consisted of four steps:

1. Status quo
2. "Blueprint"
3. Structure
4. Preparation of implementation

Status quo

The first step towards understanding the current situation was to establish the status quo. This involved using three main sources of information and insights:

1) Available data and reports review, including analysis of basic volume, revenue, and profit streams + an overview of the price and margin metrics used in the company
2) Internal interviews with representatives of various company units like marketing, sales, planning, forecasting, market research, finance, controlling, operations (ca. 20 internal interviews were held altogether)
3) Review of applied practices, including procedures, calculation methods, formats and templates, algorithms used

That was key to understand on the one hand all positive elements already existing or being implemented in the company that would support revenue management. On the other side, it helped to identify and structure key problems and challenges impacting profitable growth of the business.

Under positives one could certainly include the following:

- clear strategy and mid-term goals
- overall performance management system being properly set up in place
- profitability mindset
- good analytical base
- well-designed new product development process
- and a few more

However, there were also quite a few challenges like the following:

- two not aligned ways of thinking (brand view of marketing and channel view of sales)
- insufficient "cleansing" of the product portfolio to make room for new products
- limited scenario analysis
- lacking post evaluation of, let's say, promotions

- at times too simplified KPIs
- and some more

This review of status quo was also very helpful in addressing the pivotal question: What should good look like? What should be the recipe and approach for the feature to limit/eliminate the problems? Listing these problems and challenges in a structured way was also very useful as a reference to ensure that the new revenue management solution would effectively address and solve them.

Then, what needed to be done was to design the RM solution and describe in a very clear way understood in the organization. And that became a requirement for what was called revenue management blueprint – shortly the "Blueprint".

"Blueprint"

In the "Blueprint" step the actual design of the revenue management solution took place. In a series of common meetings with appointed revenue manger Movens Advisory experts developed a model solution which covered two main aspects:

- RM processes
- RM dimensions and granularity

RM processes

For the RM processes the Movens' framework of Set-the-Line -> Hold-the-Line-> Review-the-Line was used.

Figure 16.3

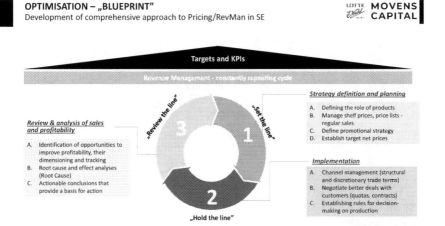

OPTIMISATION – „BLUEPRINT"
Development of comprehensive approach to Pricing/RevMan in SE

LOTTE   **MOVENS CAPITAL**

Based on this framework all revenue and pricing related processes were identified and listed in all three brackets od Set-/Hold-/Review-the-Line. In total 27 processes (11 + 6 + 10 in the three bucket respectively). Some selected examples of the processes you can see here:

Figure 16.4

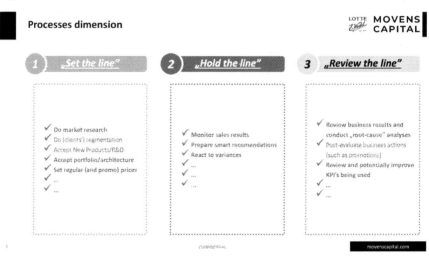

Then each process was defined and described in a pragmatic yet informative way on a one-pager using the template here:

Figure 16.5

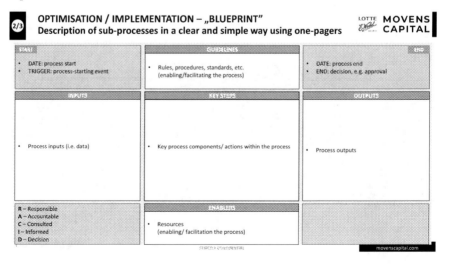

This structured template allowed to break down quite complex area of revenue management into understandable and "digestible" pieces and describe them in compact and informative manner, giving the answers to all key very practical questions:

1. WHAT?

   a. WHAT is it about? -> expressed explicitly in process name

   b. WHAT needs to be done? -> described in key steps

   c. WHAT is needed as an input? -> listed under inputs

   d. WHAT is the outcome of a particular process? -> defined under outputs

2. WHEN?

   a. WHEN does the process start? (date) or

      WHEN is the process triggered? (event) -> indicated in Start

   b. WHEN does the process end? (date) or

      WHEN is the process terminated? (event/decision) -> indicated in End

3. WHO?

   a. WHO is responsible for the execution of the process steps?

   b. WHO is accountable for the process – process owner?

   c. WHO is consulted during process realization?

   d. WHO should be informed about the steps and outcomes?

   e. WHO makes a final decision and approves the outcomes?

      – > all defined in RACID box

4. WHERE?

   a. WHERE to look for support? -> described under Enablers (indicating which are the resources, tools, and other elements that can/should facilitate the process)

   b. WHERE to look for guidance? -> described under Guidelines (indicating rules, directions, templates, controls, standards, etc., that the process needs to meet)

5. HOW?

   a. HOW is the process done? -> explained if/where needed under Key steps

To make sure that finally the processes lead to expected outcomes and are aligned with other company areas and processes (such as budgeting, demand planning, etc.), the sequencing was checked in both successive and reverse order. The latter check was particularly effective in identifying timing inconsistencies between dependent processes, allowing adjustments for optimal timing throughout the entire cycle. Such alignment proved to be very useful. It ensured proper definition of the process timings for which specific calendar dates could be set, making sure that they would neither start too late nor too early.

Again, to keep compact, such sequencing was outlined on a one-pager format like the one here:

Figure 16.6

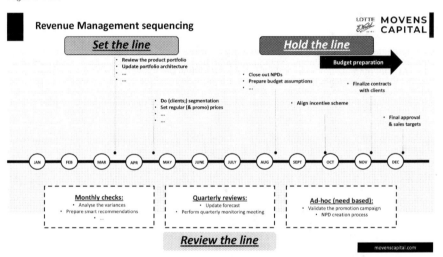

Once all the processes were defined and their sequencing aligned, the complete picture of the revenue management processes became complete. All units involved in these processes (such as marketing/brand managers, sales/KAMs, finance etc.) appreciated the material for its completeness and clarity when presented with it. Interestingly, everyone suggested that the material should be shared widely, believing that this would eliminate all "gray areas" of responsibility overlap or gaps and reduce misunderstandings and inconsistencies.

To further simplify matters, one-pagers highlighting processes specifically related to a particular unit or position were created, illustrated in the next section. This approach gave brand managers in marketing, trade marketing units, KAMs in sales, controllers in finance, and the revenue manager themself an overview of everything related to them. This initiative, too, proved to be helpful and was well received.

Figure 16.7

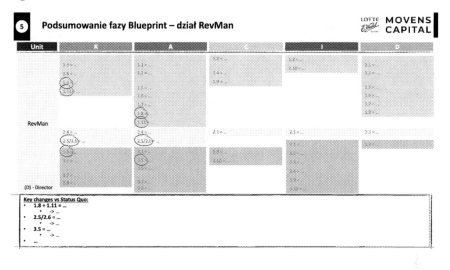

RM dimensions and granularity

Another important aspect of the "Blueprint" was granularity – that is, what level of details should be used to avoid two unwanted effects:

- on the one hand– too much aggregation -> leading to a picture that is good from a high-level overview perspective but too high level from an operational perspective (where, what, when to change?)

- on the other side – too many details -> leading to so many details that are difficult to digest, proceed with, and manage in practical terms

So looking for the "golden mean", including as many details as necessary but no more than needed – the granularity levels were defined across three key dimensions:

A. Product dimension
Here the total number of 150 different products were grouped into three buckets:

- o key products (3 products + key flavors)

- o additional important (6 products/product categories)

- o other – other focus/NPD/"long tail" (9 products/product categories)

This way the total number of product items to look at was reduced to just a handful of them.

Figure 16.8

 **Blueprint – Wymiary planowania/monitorowania/kontroli**

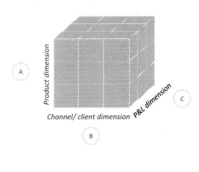

B. Channel/client dimension
Here all the clients were categorized into two main groups: wholesale and retail. Under these categories key partners were analyzed separately, while the remaining ones were grouped into "others" bucket. This approach effectively reduced the total number of clients to look at to ca. +/− ten items.

C. P&L dimension
Here simplified and yet insightful P&L structure was used containing only key entries allowing to clearly see what is happening between GSV (volume × price) and EBIT, going through CI -> NSV, COGS -> GCBM, Cost (3 main categories) -> EBIT.
This approach allowed to significantly reduce the level of details, making it practical while still providing enough information for decision-making.

Structure

Once the revenue management processes were clear, it was time to answer the three organizational structure questions:

1. Where should the RM be placed in organizational structure?
(Who should the RM report to?)
2. How wide and deep should the RM structure be?
(How centralized vs decentralized should the RM be?
What should be included in the RM structure, and what should be left in other units?)
3. How many (additional) resources should be dedicated to RM?
(How many people are needed directly in the RM unit?)

The first question was quite easy to answer, or rather to confirm. Since in Wedel from the very beginning – meaning from its appointment – the revenue manager was placed directly under the CEO. This choice was simply confirmed after reviewing existing solutions and alternative placements of the RM in other organizations and weighing their advantages and disadvantages.

Placing the RM in a defined place within the corporate structure (with clearly defined reporting line, budget, etc.) might initially appear as the key advantage of situating the RM in one of the company's departments (like sales, marketing, finance/controlling). However, the disadvantage is that the Revenue Manager being placed in any of those departments might be influenced too much by the agenda of those departments and lose his objectivity, for example:

- Sales department might press too much for lower prices to achieve higher sales

- Marketing department might be too much product centric and not enough client centric

- Finance department might be too much driven by financial plans with not enough understanding of what is achievable in given market conditions

So from the point of view of effectiveness and efficiency, the revenue manager fulfils his role most effectively by reporting directly to the CEO (or in very large corporations through the VP level) – this gives him independence in decision-making and enables a significant and swift impact on the organization.

For the second question regarding the width and depth of the Revenue Management organization, various options were analyzed. Among them more centralized options with a dedicated, separated RM structure as well as decentralized options that leveraged shared resources. All options were evaluated against a defined set of criteria like quality of decisions, agility, effectiveness, as well as additional cost for company, chances of success, long-term influence on mindset, and organizational culture.

Ultimately, the preferred option was the lean revenue management structure with revenue manager supported by revenue controller and RM analyst and other resources related to RevMan shared with their previous places and from there supporting RevMan processes and activities.

To address the third question and ensure that there were enough RM resources straightforward comparison of RM workload vs resource capacity was conducted like illustrated next. The workload was calculated based on estimated time needed to manage all defined RM processes and monthly capacity resulted from number of working days in a given month less holidays, etc. This quite simple but insightful verification confirmed the number of resources needed in the RM.

Figure 16.9

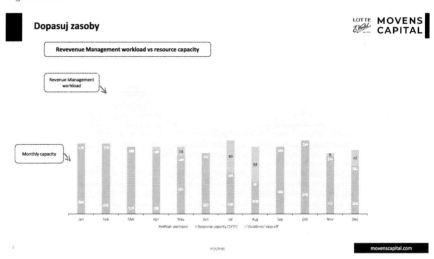

Preparation of implementation

Finally, when the RM Blueprint was finalized and the RM structure was defined, the only thing left was the implementation plan. Here the short-term and mid-term objectives and steps were outlined. Along the implementation timeline, a risk map was prepared, including mitigation actions with clearly defined responsibilities.

Based on this plan the actual implementation was initiated. Step by step, the elements of the RM Blueprint were being implemented. One could say "just in time", as it was the last season before COVID.

OUTCOMES/RESULTS

The question after such an initiative is almost always the same: what did it bring?

Looking back and comparing the current state to ways of working five years before, there is clear advancement in that area, meaning all four aspects of comprehensive revenue management (Strategy and approach + Processes + Organization + Tools) are linked and aligned, making it more "SPOT-on" solution.

Which in turn helps to harness any actual and potential "loose ends" into a robust revenue management cycle. And that translates into well-functioning "revenue machine". Such solution makes company more resistant to difficult situations on the market.

Actually, this strategy helped the company to get through COVID time. Especially the first period of COVID (2020–2021) had lesser negative impact on the company compared to its competitors (bear in mind, in times of crisis or uncertainty customers

Figure 16.10

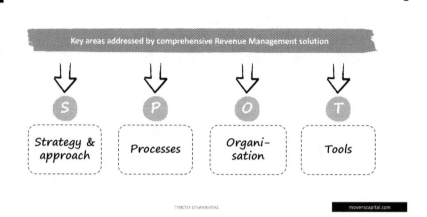

tend to spare "pleasure expenses" like premium confectionary – not making it easy to companies like Wedel). As the revenue manager put it, "God bless we designed and started implementation of the revenue management solution before COVID. Otherwise, we would have been hit by it much harder, like most, if not all of our competitors in the sector. With proper revenue management in place, we are much more immune to such adverse situations on the market".

While exact figures cannot be disclosed due to confidentiality reasons, a comparison of Wedel's results with its competition clearly demonstrates that Revenue Management has elevated the company to a new level and continues to support its profitable growth despite numerous market challenges, including COVID, significant increases in energy costs, and rising cacao prices.

Such results would not have been possible without the revenue management implemented and continuously improved since 2019.

SUMMARY

This success neither was nor is automatic. There are some important factors which allowed translation of well-designed solution into successful implementation. The key ones to mention are the following:

- Management sponsorship and stewardship – starting from CEO
- Independent position of revenue manager (reporting directly to CEO)
- Involvement of various departments in the creation of the solutions

- Openness in the organization (for new solutions)
- Open communication across the whole organization

Again, with the revenue management in place the company is now on a different level and keeps going up. And it is really nice to see how it is developing further.

Figure 16.11

17

How to evaluate economic indicator trends to maximize profit and minimize loss with effective pricing at Ahold Delhaize

Thaynara DuBois and Christien DuBois

In this chapter, we will review the fundamentals of economic indicator analysis and recommend pricing tactics, leveraging leading economic indicators, lagging economic indicators, and coincident economic indicators. We will utilize publicly available economic data to stay ahead of negative market trends, protect profit targets, producing greater profit results in a sustainable way across all market conditions.

To measure pricing effectiveness, we need to combine internal analysis with outside economic data available. Relying solely on internal data limits our ability to see the full business landscape evolving over time. Failing to consider these external factors blinds us to the relevant data in the global ecosystem, especially after our last recession in 2020.

Organizations should work towards being less reactive, not just simply responding to economic effects happening around them, and become more proactive, being able to anticipate them and translate these events into a competitive advantage in the marketplace. That is the goal for pricing maturity, moving from traditional pricing to a new pricing strategy.

To minimize the risk of being unprepared in the face of a future recession, we should not rely on projections made in a vacuum without having looked at the broader economic results and trends. Making pricing changes without proper analysis of economic data significantly increases the risk of failure. For example, Silicon Valley Banks post-COVID did not correctly hedge or prepare for significant changes in the crypto asset marketplace. Bitcoin, in early 2023, lost more than 65% of its value due in part to simply talk of interest rate increases by the Fed. Being unprepared in this manner has a ripple effect on the broader economic ecosystem.

Economic changes and events don't just impact our businesses; they also impact our customers' behavior, suppliers, investors, and everyone else we interact globally. Many organizations are aware of inflation and its impacts. Still, countless other equally relevant economic changes have as much of an impact on the bottom line as inflation, such as unemployment numbers, disposable income, and stock market performance. Organizations will ultimately go through the effects of these changes, and it is crucial for pricing professionals to help mitigate the downside and maximize their upside.

DOI: 10.4324/9781003535966-22

The previous examples clearly demonstrate the need for companies to increase pricing agility and adjust to the constant changes in cost, economic policies, and the global competitive landscape many of us are currently experiencing.

Economic indicator analyses are also essential for companies that don't have strong pricing power, with the ability to raise prices without a meaningful loss in customer base demand. It becomes extremely important to understand the full spectrum of economic analysis and, with this information, make wise pricing decisions for cost-conscious customers within the overall current ecosystem. Having the ability to properly plan pricing changes is crucial for organizational survival.

One simple exercise to start: if we could go back to March 2020, which marks the very beginning of the pandemic and the beginning of the most recent documented economic contraction. How and when would we calibrate our pricing strategy without reacting to a market with such a sudden adjustment? How could we have had more confidence in our pricing execution and operation excellence?

The answer I found while conducting analysis using 11 of the most relevant economic indicators to align with future market behavior. It was key to use these indicators to increase price, lead the market, and revenue manage products without raising elasticity. The result at the end of 2020 was that I helped the company increase its profit margin by 10 million dollars.

I want to make clear from this point forward that using economic values is not sufficient on its own. Still, when complemented with an overall mature pricing and analytical process, it can help maximize profit and minimize loss while ensuring your pricing remains proactive instead of reactive.

The analysis began by building a statistical model that utilizes one standard deviation and adjusts future changes according to the recession watch indicator, which I will go over in depth and explain how to use it effectively.

Before that, I would need to explain that all of this fits into the stages of the business cycle that is demonstrated in the graph on the next page. It's important to cover that as it's part of the larger picture. There are typically three stages to a business cycle. Each of these cycles corresponds to a period of time that can span either several months or potentially several years. The length of time each phase of the business cycle lasts varies based on normal market operations, geopolitical or environmental effects, or even government intervention.

The first of these phases begins with economic recovery and a period of rapid growth. During this phase, the economy recovers from the last recession or economic trough. The economy experiences significant increases in employment, income levels, and production. The economy might have yet to grow past the previous peak during the recovery phase. Eventually, the economy will transition into a general expansionary phase, where it will surpass the previous high. Growth levels tend to be slower than the recovery period, but the economy continues to trend upward. Eventually, this growth period will lead to recession or depression, followed by a new recovery cycle.

These cycles are continuous and never change order. The key for investors, traders, and pricers, and in the topic for this chapter, pricing professionals, is to know when these events are happening and how to maximize these events in their business and pricing decision-making process.

Figure 17.1

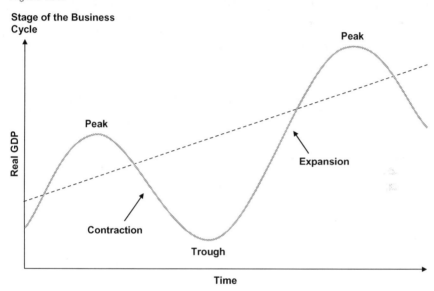

Figure 17.2

The Conference Board Leading Economic Index® and Component Contributions (Percent)

Figure 17.3

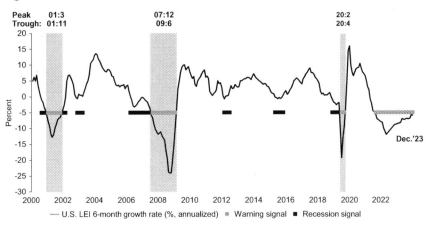

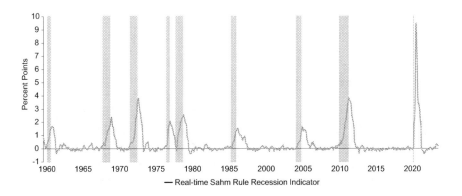

While appearing rather mundane and simplistic, identifying when a peak is forming and when a contraction is beginning can mean the difference between millions of dollars in profit growth or millions of dollars in missed opportunities for your company. While not intending to be an economics lesson, this provides a high-level overview for the businessperson to understand how these cycles are important to time changes correctly.

ECONOMIC INDICATORS

There are three different types of economic indicators. Each type of indicator helps establish where in the business cycle we are presently in, what came before, and what will happen next. The first variety of economic indicators are leading economic indicators. Leading economic indicators are used as a predictive tool for establishing where the business cycle and economy are heading rather than measuring where we are now or what has come before. Examples of leading economic indicators are specific stock market indices such as the S&P 500, building permits for new home constructions, and new unemployment claims. In addition to these singular indicators, there are also entire indexes of leading economic indicators that aggregate these leading indicators into a single, measurable metric. One of the most widespread indexes is the Conference Board's leading economic index (LEI).[1] As of December of 2023, the United States LEI[2] signaled for recession. The warning signal should be the start and anticipation of pricing strategies for 2024.

The second variety of economic indicators is coincident economic indicators. These indicators are a pulse on what state the economy is presently in. One of the most common use cases for them is that a current economic or business cycle pattern is in progress. These indicators point to economic events and changes happening in real time and provide insights into the current state of the economy. A few examples of common coincident economic indicators are the consumer price index (CPI), otherwise known as inflation, gross domestic product (GDP), and manufacturing production numbers.

The third type of economic indicator you will run into is lagging economic indicators. These are economic indicators that measure economic activity that previously occurred. Lagging economic indicators are essential because the indicators solidify our understanding of where we came from. They help policymakers assess the effectiveness of specific economic policies and help investors complete risk assessments. Additionally, lagging indicators allow for historical comparisons, which allow researchers to understand how economic conditions have evolved and changed over time. Common lagging economic indicators are the unemployment rate, corporate profit reports, and consumer spending.

The incredible value of economic indicators is that the data is free to use. All economic indicator data is published by government agencies or vetted and reputable non-governmental organizations (NGOs). This data is published regularly and is incredibly reliable in its accuracy. The challenge posed to you will be selecting which economic indicators are suitable for your analysis and ascertaining how far back you wish to examine the data.

A common question I get asked along with how far back the data I use should go is, "Should the economic data from COVID be considered an outlier or part of a larger trend?" Ultimately, the COVID pandemic and the recession that came with it are part of the larger business cycle. The recession would have come later than it did, or perhaps not as swiftly and as steeply as the recession was. One of my favorite tools to illustrate this is the Sahm Rule Recession Indicator,[3] published with Federal Reserve Economic Data published by the Federal Reserve Bank of St Louis. It shows that recessions have occurred periodically, but the one during the pandemic was notably steeper and sharper than previous ones. Additionally, the economy had not contracted since the 2008 recession, making the timing of this recession particularly significant. The previously discussed tool highlights these points effectively.

Furthermore, you need enough historical data to establish what happens to your business from a pricing standpoint during certain economic events. For example, does a price increase or decrease happen when a recession occurs? Do your sales increase or decrease? What happens when the economy recovers? Understanding these scenarios, along with pairing major business decisions your organization has made to point in time economic events, is essential. An industry like a grocery store or pharmaceutical company is not impacted nor responds the same way as the technology sector.

I found success using economic indicators by taking several practical steps utilizing this data and the company data you have access to. Pricing is a complete operations exercise. The goal is to deliver on your margin targets without being reactionary to market and economic events. We want to examine where we can calibrate pricing independent of market forces and ultimately have higher confidence in our projections.

This must be done by relying on something other than historical trends. Examining overall economic trends using a suite of economic indicators related to your industry and examining the broader ecosystem, we will be able to better forecast the profit and loss (P&L) with greater accuracy and confidence. For example, I am a pricing manager for a grocery store. In this instance, I will have a much easier time forecasting overall sales trends for my organization by examining the Food at Home vs Food Away economic indicator published by the US Department of Agriculture.[4] Accessing this data and a complete picture of the P&L helps make more informed pricing decisions. Ask yourself: if you could go back in time to March of 2020, right before the COVID recession took hold, would you have made any pricing-related decisions than you did? Would you have been more data-informed with this data than without it?

Before the pandemic, I could rely possibly upon between 70% and 80% confidence in internal historical trends to make pricing decisions. What I realized, though, is despite the absolute best forecast with existing internal data, economic events also impact my customers. Business cycles and economic events impact their buying behavior, therefore necessarily impacting our complete picture. There are countless individual topics prices often used to make decisions. I can talk about elasticity or the importance of value-based pricing, but those are not the entire landscape, nor do they account for deviations. There is no question of the individual importance of these topics, but value-based pricing with no regard to economic conditions is pricing with blinders on. The time dedicated to pricing analysis should be in tune with the regularly scheduled economic publications. This is a simple thing to do, dramatically enhancing the clarity of your data picture.

Understanding how certain economic conditions impact the global marketplace is important. For example, when economic releases consistently signal economic growth over a long period, it's essential to understand the implications of that. You may be in an industry where higher incomes and greater consumer spending power signal more sales and more significant sales. However, the long-term impact of that is eventually an inflationary event. Your costs will eventually rise, and being prepared to price in inflation ahead of time is crucial. Pairing this price increase with an offering of greater value or coinciding with a new product launch before inflation becomes apparent in the economy can preserve customer sentiment and condition them to the new prices before they feel the effects themselves. Inflation impacts your customers just as much as it impacts you. Waiting and becoming reactionary to inflation may leave you increasing your prices in response to an increase in your costs, just as your customers are experiencing cost increases. A secondary strategy a pricer can use to maximize the effects of inflation is to use this as an opportunity to maximize efficiencies within the cost structure of your products. The impact of price optimization in conjunction with cost optimization can have two positive effects on your company's P&L at a time when costs in most other areas of the business are rising.

We know that inflation causes an increase in costs across your organization, so it's vital to protect your business's cash flow. If your business either offers flexible payment terms or negotiates as a course of regular business, we must use this as an opportunity to either protect cash flow or extract additional value from your customers. During periods of inflation, your customers will also be looking to protect their cash flow, whether they are business-to-consumer (B2C) or business-to-business customers (B2B). If you are unable to deter your customers from flexible payment terms and they are frequently choosing to stretch payment terms for more extended periods, you are in a position to compensate for the loss of cash flow by simply increasing the price for your customers choosing to extend payment terms. You will mitigate, albeit marginally, your cash flow by each payment becoming more significant, and you will increase profit over the long term. Regardless of the economic situation, a pricer with an understanding of how to maximize the situation can turn the most unfortunate economic situation into an opportunity.

It's especially important to be mindful of economic indicators when engaging in cross-border transfers and tax transfer pricing. Inflation can be wildly different across international borders, and engaging in these transactions without the proper due diligence beforehand can lead to financially irresponsible deals, tax transfer pricing penalties, and fines. For example, the inflation rate of the United States looking one year back from December 2023 was approximately 6.5%,[5] whereas in Turkey, the inflation rate was over 61%.[6] Charging the same price under such conditions is almost impossible, but tax transfer pricing practices create obstacles that pricers must overcome. Being aware of economic indicators allows you to make more informed decisions.

RECOMMENDATIONS

I want to provide a road map you can use to leverage economic indicators for profit growth through a specific example of a brand of one of the largest food providers and grocers in the world, Ahold Delhaize, during the pandemic. We all can remember the early days of the pandemic when many of the items we were used to purchasing were consistently sold out. Many grocery stores missed enormous opportunities for profit growth and protecting their supply and stock of many products by not reading the indicators and signs early enough. What I saw working in this industry during the pandemic is that when unemployment rises, income is down, and recession sets in, people shop and spend more at "consumer staples" like grocery stores. I began collecting 11 economic indicators most relevant to this sector, and I decided to examine data dating back to 2020. The economic indicators I found most helpful for my industry were the following:

1. Sahm's recession watch, illustrated before
2. Leading economic indicators index vs last month
3. GDP real-time estimate vs last year
4. GDP real-time estimate vs last quarter
5. Real disposable income vs last month
6. Food at home ratio vs last month
7. Food at home ratio vs last year
8. Current economic activities
9. Initial unemployment claims
10. New housing permits
11. State recession watch (the area we serve)

These data points outlined previously will be updated as new data becomes available. The model would reflect and map where the state of the economy is segmented by leading, lagging, and coincident indicators. An excellent question I received on my model during a talk I gave on economic indicators analysis in Amsterdam during the Professional Pricing Society's 2023 European Summit was on the relevance of using coincident indicators rather than using large amounts of data, thereby making the model strictly a predictive tool. One of the most significant value drivers in taking the time to update and make this a comprehensive tool is it allows a complete historical mapping. You can better examine your pricing decisions and see how successful (or not) they are based on the changes in the business cycle. Furthermore, utilizing coincident indicators allows you to confirm the trends identified and projected in the leading economic indicators previously analyzed. Confirmation of trends allows for a more reliable dataset to make more confident pricing decisions.

The two primary leading indicators I would use to project future trends were Sahm's recession watch and the LEI. Furthermore, I had state-level recession watch data as well for the region my business was serving. Some states had a more significant seasonal impact on some products than others, and the recession impacted some areas. This was a significant data point for pricing highly seasonal and elastic goods.

Once I was confident in the data I had collected and analyzed, I first prepared a report of my findings. This summary highlighted the relevant takeaways and changes that had occurred since the last period. This would be shared throughout the business units and with C-Suite leadership. Once distributed for knowledge management and to allow other business units to leverage economic data, critical pricing decisions could be made. Profit and revenue growth can be best maximized with other relevant pricing levers, such as seasonality and understanding the competitive landscape. Let's take, for example, a more premium product, one you would buy something nice if you were staying in on the weekend. Let's say, for this example, we have historically been priced lower than our largest competitor. My coincident and leading economic indicators saying the economy and disposable income are steadily growing, I may decide, after looking at this data and understanding the seasonality, let's say the middle of the New England winter, to price this product in line with the competition rather than lower. People with more money at their disposal to spend are more likely to purchase premium products. Being lower than the competition on a premium product is simply leaving money on the table.

Conversely, during a recession, pricing in this sector becomes even more important. People tend to shop in grocery stores more during a recession and economic hardship. When economic indicators were signaling a recession, it became crucial to price products that drive business incredibly carefully. "Staple" products and highly competitive products like milk and canned goods could be, at times, priced incredibly competitively to competition to help drive volume. Driving customers into the business allowed the company to price other ancillary products, for example, beverage products, in a way to counteract the margin leakage.

Economic indicator analysis wasn't a golden key that unlocked massive profit on its own, but I found that using the analysis helped inform customer behavior often before it occurred. When implemented correctly, we began leading the competition rather than reacting to it. We also found efficiencies that had yet to exist previously. Product procurement and ordering could be better mapped and managed during certain economic conditions. Understanding customer behavior during the business cycle was crucial for this. Hiring decisions during predicted upswings in business and hiring slowdowns during predicted lulls also became possible. Countless different business units can find value in leveraging economic indicator analysis.

I found a reasonably seamless buy-in from leadership in taking on this initiative. One of the reasons for this was the data is free to acquire. This is an extremely low-cost exercise where one of the only roadblocks to its success is your willingness to commit the effort to the analysis. While my case study was in an industry that's considered a consumer staple and actually performs better during recession periods, as we experienced during the pandemic, many businesses experience the opposite. The pricing exercise, when the business cycle signals recession, is to help make your business as resilient to recession as possible. In industries that may not be as dynamic and fluctuating in their pricing as grocery products, preparing and shielding your business against cost increases will be essential. Businesses pass along their cost increases to their customers; this is a common and accepted reality. However, economic indicator analysis allows you to make that change more on your schedule than ever before. Being able to better determine when or where these price increases take place gives you greater control over your P&L to drive customer behavior in a far greater capacity than if you were pricing in a reactionary way.

Another critical area where pricers can drive revenue and profit growth for businesses that do better during periods of economic growth, or what economists call "cyclical businesses" is to calibrate pricing during new product launches. If your business does well during periods of economic growth, you may calibrate pricing when the economy is signaling growth. In addition, you may work with other teams within your business to plan new product releases and price those accordingly to maximize the new value created by the release.

Every business and industry is unique. While I certainly can't speak for all of them, I've highlighted what has worked for me. There are countless resources and support systems for pricers to find expertise and knowledge in, such as the Professional Pricing Society. I hope this economic indicator analysis has given you one more idea and opportunity to drive profit for your business in addition to the best practices already out there. When leveraged thoughtfully, economic indicator analysis has been an excellent tool to find new growth, new efficiencies, and most importantly, new profit.

SUMMARY

- **Economic Indicator Analysis**: Utilizing a range of economic indicators helps businesses anticipate market trends and make proactive pricing decisions. This includes leading indicators (e.g. stock market indices, new unemployment claims), coincident indicators (e.g. consumer price index, GDP), and lagging indicators (e.g. unemployment rate, corporate profits).

- **Business Cycle Awareness**: Understanding the phases of the business cycle – recovery, expansion, recession – is crucial. Knowing where the economy stands can guide strategic pricing adjustments to align with economic conditions.

- **Pricing Agility**: Businesses need to increase pricing agility to adapt to constant changes in costs, economic policies, and the global competitive landscape. This is particularly important for companies with limited pricing power.

- **Historical Data Utilization**: Incorporating historical economic data alongside internal data allows for better forecasting and pricing strategy development. This holistic view ensures pricing decisions are informed and less reactive.

- **Sector-Specific Indicators**: Different industries respond differently to economic events. For example, grocery stores and pharmaceutical companies may not react the same way as the technology sector. Tailoring economic indicator analysis to the specific industry enhances pricing accuracy.

- **Practical Implementation**: The chapter outlines practical steps for implementing economic indicator analysis, using a case study from Ahold Delhaize during the pandemic. By tracking 11 key economic indicators, the company successfully adjusted pricing strategies to maximize profit margins and improve operational efficiency.

- **Proactive vs Reactive Pricing**: The goal is to move from reactive to proactive pricing strategies, using economic indicators to anticipate market changes and optimize pricing before market forces necessitate it.

By leveraging economic indicators and integrating them into a mature pricing and analytical process, businesses can achieve greater profitability, minimize losses, and maintain a competitive edge in fluctuating market conditions.

NOTES

1   www.conference-board.org/topics/us-leading-indicators, 3 and 4 (do reference of graph)
2   www.conference-board.org/topics/us-leading-indicators
3   https://fred.stlouisfed.org/series/SAHMREALTIME#
4   www.ers.usda.gov/data-products/chart-gallery/gallery/chart-detail/?chartId= 58364#:~:text=Food%2Dat%2Dhome%20spending%20increased,total%20food%20 expenditures%20in%202022
5   www.bls.gov/cpi/
6   www.barrons.com/news/turkish-inflation-rate-holds-near-61-percent-c76c2f59

Acknowledgments

This book would not have been possible without the generous contributions of pricing practitioners who shared their knowledge, insights, and experiences. Their willingness to impart their expertise has enriched these pages and undoubtedly enhanced the value of this work.

We extend our heartfelt gratitude to each and every pricing practitioner who took the time to offer their perspectives, whether through interviews, discussions, or written contributions. Your dedication to the craft of pricing and your willingness to engage in meaningful dialogue have been instrumental in shaping the content of this book. Readers will find the names and a short profile of all contributors in the following chapters.

We would also like to express my appreciation to the organizations and institutions that supported this endeavor, providing resources, access, and encouragement along the way. Your commitment to advancing the field of pricing is commendable, and I am grateful for the opportunity to collaborate with you.

Finally, we are deeply thankful to our families, friends, and colleagues for their unwavering support and encouragement throughout this journey. Your patience, understanding, and belief in us have been invaluable, and we are truly grateful for your presence in our life.

Last but not least we would like to thank our editorial and publishing team for all your help and support. Taking any book from idea to publication is a team effort, and we really appreciate your input and help – thank you, Rebecca Marsh, for having supported with enthusiasm this editorial project right from the beginning and for the support in the previous editorial projects.

Printed in the United States
by Baker & Taylor Publisher Services